Oxford Shakespeare Topics

Shakespeare and Outsiders

OXFORD SHAKESPEARE TOPICS

Published and Forthcoming Titles Include:

David Bevington, *Shakespeare and Biography*
Lawrence Danson, *Shakespeare's Dramatic Genres*
Janette Dillon, *Shakespeare and the Staging of English History*
Paul Edmondson and Stanley Wells, *Shakespeare's Sonnets*
Gabriel Egan, *Shakespeare and Marx*
Andrew Gurr and Mariko Ichikawa, *Staging in Shakespeare's Theatres*
Jonathan Gil Harris, *Shakespeare and Literary Theory*
Douglas Lanier, *Shakespeare and Modern Popular Culture*
Ania Loomba, *Shakespeare, Race, and Colonialism*
Raphael Lyne, *Shakespeare's Late Work*
Russ McDonald, *Shakespeare and the Arts of Language*
Steven Marx, *Shakespeare and the Bible*
Robert S. Miola, *Shakespeare's Reading*
Marianne Novy, *Shakespeare and Outsiders*
Phyllis Rackin, *Shakespeare and Women*
Catherine Richardson, *Shakespeare and Material Culture*
Bruce R. Smith, *Shakespeare and Masculinity*
Zdeněk Stříbrný, *Shakespeare and Eastern Europe*
Michael Taylor, *Shakespeare Criticism in the Twentieth Century*
Alden T. Vaughan and Virginia Mason Vaughan, *Shakespeare in America*
Stanley Wells, ed., *Shakespeare in the Theatre: An Anthology of Criticism*
Martin Wiggins, *Shakespeare and the Drama of His Time*

Oxford Shakespeare Topics
GENERAL EDITORS: PETER HOLLAND AND STANLEY WELLS

Shakespeare and Outsiders

MARIANNE NOVY

OXFORD
UNIVERSITY PRESS

Great Clarendon Street, Oxford, OX2 6DP,
United Kingdom

Oxford University Press is a department of the University of Oxford.
It furthers the University's objective of excellence in research, scholarship,
and education by publishing worldwide. Oxford is a registered trade mark of
Oxford University Press in the UK and in certain other countries

© Marianne Novy 2013

The moral rights of the author have been asserted

First Edition published in 2013

All rights reserved. No part of this publication may be reproduced, stored in
a retrieval system, or transmitted, in any form or by any means, without the
prior permission in writing of Oxford University Press, or as expressly permitted
by law, by licence or under terms agreed with the appropriate reprographics
rights organization. Enquiries concerning reproduction outside the scope of the
above should be sent to the Rights Department, Oxford University Press, at the
address above

You must not circulate this work in any other form
and you must impose this same condition on any acquirer

Published in the United States of America by Oxford University Press
198 Madison Avenue, New York, NY 10016, United States of America

British Library Cataloguing in Publication Data

Data available

ISBN 978-0-19-964235-9

For all outsiders, including those who are also insiders

Acknowledgements

Julien Yoseloff of Associated University Presses has kindly agreed to grant permission to reprint, with revisions, material that appeared in *Shakespeare's World, World Shakespeares*, ed. Richard Fotheringham, Christa Jansohn, and R. S. White (Newark: University of Delaware Press, 2008), under the title 'The Merchant of Venice and Pressured Conversions in Shakespeare's World'.

I would like to thank the students who participated in classes that I taught on the theme of 'Shakespeare and Outsiders', as well as my two *Othello* seminars, and continued to reinforce my view of the fascination of this topic. My experiences during this time of writing also reinforced my sense that there really is an academic community: so many people were generous. Thanks to Peter Holland and Stanley Wells, editors of 'Oxford Shakespeare Topics', for their support, and also to Associate Dean James Knapp of the University of Pittsburgh for approving an early sabbatical to work on this book, and to the intellectual communities I found that year (2006–7) at Duke, where I was a visiting scholar, as well as at the nearby National Humanities Center and the University of North Carolina.

Earlier versions of the *Merchant of Venice* chapter were presented at Diarmaid MacCulloch's 2004 Seminar on English Reformations at the Folger Shakespeare Institute, the 2004 Shakespeare Association of America seminar on the morphology of conversion, run by Jonathan Burton and Kathleen Lynch, the 2005 Waterloo Conference on Religion and Theatre, run by Kenneth Graham and Philip Collington, the 2006 International Shakespeare Congress seminar on *The Merchant of Venice*, run by Charles Edelman and Dympna Callaghan, and at the Duke University Department of English. Thanks to these organizers for their suggestions, and also to Sarah Beckwith, Ilona Bell, Jane Degenhardt, Leigh DeNeef, Alan Dessen, Jennie Evenson, Simon Friedman, Daryl Gless, Hannah Johnson, Erin Kelly, Ryan McDermott, Joseph Porter, Marsha Robinson, and Jeffrey Shoulson, for comments on various versions of Chapter 1, and to Susannah

Monta, Sean Keilen, and Georgianna Ziegler for suggestions and John McDiarmaid for a transcription of a document in Elizabethan handwriting.

Versions of other chapters were presented at the 2011 World Shakespeare Congress in Prague and at many SAA seminars: on *King Lear* (2006), run by Richard Strier; on Race, run by Virginia Vaughan and Jean Feerick (2010); on England and the Islamic World, run by Linda McJannet and Bernadette d'Andrea (2009), on Revenge Drama, run by Sara Deats (2008); on Talking about Sex, run by Stephen Guy-Bray (2007), on Shakespeare and the New Feminisms, run by Deanne Williams (2011), and on *Merry Wives of Windsor*, run by Phyllis Rackin and Evelyn Gajowski (2012). I am grateful for suggestions from other participants during those events and from Susan Andrade, David Carrier, Sanford Freedman, James Hirsch, Peggy Knapp, Andrew Moran, Carol Thomas Neely, Meredith Skura, Bruce Smith, Ian Smith, Susan Harris Smith, Jennifer Waldron, and Linda Woodbridge.

For arranging talks where I outlined preliminary ideas for much of the book, I thank Ralph Savarese at Grinnell College, Darryl Gless at the University of North Carolina, Don McDermott at National Kaohsiung Normal University, Peter Hwang at Tamkang University, and Yuan-guey Chiou at National Chen Kung University (all in Taiwan), Sr. Ananda Amritmahl at Sophia College in Mumbai, Aparna Lanjewar at the Mohile Parikh Center in Mumbai, Revathy Venkataraman at the University of New Delhi, and the English Literary Society of St. Stephen's College at the University of New Delhi. Penny Gay, Kenneth Graham, Su Fang Ng, Meredith Skura, Margaret Tudeau-Clayton, and Rob Watson sent me copies of papers not yet published. Edouard Macherey gave me references on social psychology and prejudice, and Bruce Goldstein sent me electronic copies of a number of such articles. Lisa Brush helped with social theory, and Nancy Glazener (who gave me the Melville reference) and Lynne Bruckner with discussions over email and lunch. Tom Cartelli, Heather Dubrow, Phyllis Rackin, and Linda Woodbridge gave other assistance.

I would like to make special mention of exchanges with Susan Andrade, Peggy Knapp, Carol Thomas Neely, Meredith Skura, and Jennifer Waldron that challenged me to develop and clarify my thoughts further. Finally, my husband, David Carrier, frequent crosser of disciplinary and other boundaries, has been a constant reminder of the benefits of an outsider's fresh perspective.

Contents

Introduction	1
1. *The Merchant of Venice* and its Pressured Conversions	17
2. Outsiders and the Festive Community in *Twelfth Night*	47
3. Women as Outsiders and Insiders in Shakespeare	69
4. Othello and Other Outsiders	87
5. *King Lear*: Outsiders in the Family and in the Kingdom	121
Epilogue: *The Tempest*, Outsiders, and Border Crossings	147
Notes	156
Further Reading	189
Index	197

Introduction

Every playgoer remembers Shakespeare's outsiders. Shylock, Othello, and many others have occasioned attacks on Shakespeare for his biases, praises of Shakespeare for being really on their side, and rewritings by authors who use them to articulate post-Shakespearean ideas about minority, female, or colonial experience. But what has not been so much noted is that many of Shakespeare's characters move between inside and outside—begin with acceptance and end outside the play's community, reverse the trajectory, or move back and forth many times.[1] A group of characters mocking or expressing hatred for another character who is in some way different from them is a structure that frequently occurs in his plays, whether tragedies or comedies, but it is often a temporary structure. Characters who are outsiders may shift between human and monstrous, suffering and threatening, and some can be admirable and fascinating. Critics often refer to a range of Shakespearean characters as outsiders, but that condition is something more fluid and ambiguous than most previous critics have noted, because it is a position that can be moved into and out of, toward which other characters (and the audience) can have many different attitudes. It is a relative identity and not a fixed position. Often the plays are ambiguous about exactly what is the most important category of outsider into which a character fits, when he or she does, both in emotional and in sociological terms. Is Othello an outsider because he is African, because he is thought to believe in Islam, or because he doesn't understand Venetian culture? Does the Venetian senate (except for Brabanzio) admire him for a while? Does Malvolio become a hated outsider primarily because he is a steward giving orders to aristocrats, because he is a puritan, or because he is too self-loving, or because he is a spoilsport? These questions may not have just one right answer.

Such questions complicate a long-held debate about whether Shakespeare's plays exemplify ideologies of exclusion or protest against the treatment of outsiders. One of the oldest views of

Shakespeare—traceable from the seventeenth-century Margaret Cavendish through the eighteenth-century Elizabeth Montagu to Keats, Coleridge, and most recently Stephen Greenblatt—is that his works show wide-ranging sympathy.[2] The nineteenth century critic Hazlitt, for example, wrote of Shakespeare, 'His talent consisted in sympathy with human nature, in all its shapes, degrees, depressions, and elevations.'[3] However, since the late 1960s, many scholars and creative writers have emphasized Shakespeare's share in the prejudices of his own time and culture, or possibly his share in creating those of later times, and therefore the limitations of his sympathy.[4] Some have even dismissed the idea that a writer could or should attempt to use sympathetic imagination in representing people of such different groups. Near the beginning of these critical revisions, which were closely linked with international moves toward postcolonial, anti-racist, and feminist consciousness, Leslie Fiedler's *The Stranger in Shakespeare* analyzed the representation of the woman, the Jew, the Moor, and the 'New World Savage' as strangers, but his approach was mythic and psychoanalytic, considering these figures mainly as shadows of something in the dominant European psyche.[5]

Forty years later, this book takes a new and comparative look at the representations of difference and outsiders in Shakespeare's plays, with regard to the representations of prejudice and sympathy towards them and the implied call to the audience/reader to feel either attitude, using some insights of recent scholarship about historical evidence of prejudice, respect, tolerance, or sympathy in his society, and also about the complexity of the construction of race, religion, sexuality, and other categories. This book brings historical and theoretical learning to bear on the plays without assuming that they have a unified perspective of either prejudice or sympathy. As background to the plays it is worth noting that other ideas than dominant and traditional ones were circulating, as I will discuss later. England was a hierarchical society, but people did move up and down in the hierarchy.[6] London was a city with many newcomers, from elsewhere in England and also from other countries, and theatregoers had experiences of diversity and flux in their lives as well as in the plays.[7]

Some critics have claimed that in order to appreciate Shakespeare's plays readers need to imaginatively inhabit the dominant ideology of the early modern period, with all its biases; others, that in order to

Introduction 3

analyze them readers should understand how those biases structure the plays. The biases are relevant, and the plays evoke them at times, but the plays also often explore outsiders' viewpoints, and a spectator's sympathy with one of these characters should not necessarily be considered a misunderstanding of the play. Using the term outsider does not assume that rigid binaries make characters always either outsiders or insiders, or that the plays always present outsiders as evil and insiders as good or do the opposite. Being an outsider is more a position that can mean several different things than a firm identity. Some characters affirm their place as relative insiders by the way they treat others as more outsiders than they are.

The categories I will study are not just racial, religious and ethnic, but also social, psychological (which could include being sad from unrequited love, or more general melancholy), physical, moral, gendered, and (ambiguously, as I will discuss in a moment) sexual. I am interested in the differences in the presentation and social treatment of characters in each of these categories, but also in how the dynamics in the theatre may be parallel for characters who are outsiders in markedly contrasting ways. Malvolio is mostly treated as a social outsider among aristocrats and their other servants, moves into and out of the category of puritan, and briefly is treated as a madman, whereas Shylock's role as a religious and ethnic outsider occasionally merges with that of moral outsider, but there are many similar aspects in the way they function in their plays. Lear also moves into madness while his age becomes a mark of weakness rather than of authority, and he becomes an economic outsider in his homelessness. Recent scholarship argues about whether same-sex lovers were outsiders in Shakespeare's society.[8] I shall consider this question while adducing the association of the Antonios of *The Merchant of Venice* and *Twelfth Night* with other possible outsider categories: 'melancholy' and 'pirate'.

The representation of women especially shows how shifting the condition of being an outsider can be. Portia is an outsider in the Venetian court (though less so than Shylock), and Antonio is more of an insider, but they compete with regard to who is the insider in their relation with Bassanio, and in the last act Portia is the insider and Antonio is the outsider. In *The Taming of the Shrew*, Katherine begins as an outsider who receives verbal abuse and ends as an insider who gives it, though in a more dignified way: she calls her sister and another woman 'you froward and unable worms' (5.2.173).[9] A number of women speak of women as a group, sometimes to emphasize their weakness, sometimes to protest against restrictions on them. In the comedies some women function well, usually in disguise, in a man's world; in the tragedies both those who break out of restrictions and those who follow them are likely to be destroyed.

This book will focus on representations and treatments of outsiders that have both personal and political dimensions. I will not say much about characters who are only situational outsiders, new to the play's community, who fit in easily as part of its dominant group—for example, Sebastian, who arrives in Illyria in *Twelfth Night*, and ends up married to Olivia. I will note whether characters speak of outsider groups to which they belong, but I won't consider characters who appear with many other members of their class or ethnic or national group, such as the French in *Henry V* or the plebeians in *Julius Caesar*, with little attention to them as individuals. I will discuss old age, but not childhood, since Shakespeare's attention to characters in the latter category is much more limited than to those in the former.[10]

If 'outsider' means so many different things, why is it a useful concept in writing about plays? Inclusion, marked difference, and exclusion are highly visible on stage. We can vividly see a process in which one character is mocked or humiliated or badgered by a group, or, on the other hand, welcomed, or in which two characters compete for acceptance. Such dynamics are important in drama as well as in ordinary social life, and imagining a character moving between insider and outsider permits discussion of many kinds of social differences and how they are negotiated. It also relates to the issue of how and when the audience or reader can identify with various characters, and how unstable the audience point of view is in many plays. For example, when Othello thinks that Desdemona is a moral outsider he must kill, the audience sees him turning into a moral outsider, but that may change when he learns the truth and repents.

Furthermore, Shakespeare's stage often shows a household characters may enter, be barred from, or leave, or another kind of non-localized space with an area beyond it, from which various kinds of outsiders speak.[11] Shakespeare's Globe Theatre was located on the margins of London, the suburbs outside the walls, along with other suspect institutions like the bear-baiting ring and the brothels, and it has been argued that this liminal position is a key to the role of the plays. As Stephen Orgel writes, 'Elizabethan drama is often dependent on otherness.'[12] This included both male actors playing women and English actors playing Spaniards, Italians, Moors, and Danes. Furthermore, the professional situation of actors made them outsiders themselves: socially they could be both at the bottom of the class system and the object of adulation. They were often referred to as 'proud beggars', and Shakespeare shows them thus in several of the plays—as dependents in great men's houses. Meredith Skura has argued convincingly that Shakespeare's own experience as an actor shaped many aspects of his plays, including their frequent focus on outsiders who experience both power and humiliation.[13]

Two passages suggest the range of representations of outsiders in Shakespeare. In the play first performed under the title *Richard Duke of York* (but since the First Folio of 1623, referred to as *Henry VI, Part 3*), Richard emphasizes his physical deformity and resolves to play the role of villain to which he seems to be doomed:

> Then since the heavens have shaped my body so,
> Let hell make crooked my mind to answer it.
> I had no father, I am like no father,
> I have no brother, I am like no brother;
> And this word 'love', which greybeards call divine,
> Be resident in men like one another
> And not in me—I am myself alone.
>
> (5.6.78–84)

Richard here presents his 'crooked' mind as a mirroring response to his hunchback and other physical anomalies such as his birth with feet forward and already possessing teeth—he can find no mirroring of himself in his father (to whom he seemed attached while he was alive), his brothers (who are at this point living characters in the play) or anyone else. He sees himself as monstrous and presents himself to the audience that way. Certainly he has no sense of himself as part of a group of people with disabilities![14] Nevertheless, the play has given the audience a way to make him more humanly comprehensible in an earlier speech that frames his villainy as a response to further deprivation—'love forswore me in my mother's womb' (3.2.153). Richard has clearly become a moral outsider—yet for much of the play the audience is invited to more complicated feelings toward him than simple moral judgment. As we hear his soliloquies, we are invited to appreciate his skill at deception; theatregoers often see him as the consummate actor as he fulfills his promise to 'add colours to the chameleon, | Change shapes with Proteus for advantages, | And set the murderous Machiavel to school' (3.2.192–4). This anticipates the protean fascination of Iago. Richard, like many later outsiders in Shakespeare, shifts between a monstrous stereotype and a more three-dimensional character and back again.

However, Shakespeare's plays present many outsiders with emphasis on a common humanity with the audience rather than a rejection of it. The importance of being aware that you might some day be in an outsider's position is explicitly stressed in a passage from a little-known play, *Sir Thomas More*, on which expert scholars think Shakespeare was a collaborator in a revision. One of the passages usually attributed to him is a speech in which More calms an anti-immigrant riot. Immigrants, called 'aliens' or 'strangers', made up about 4 or 5 percent of London's population at the time, but many Londoners feared that they were more like half the population, taking their jobs and money and plotting against them. Many in the government tried to respond by having all foreigners register; some wanted to forbid merchants from other countries from selling their wares. Libellous fliers were posted, and in 1593 someone in the Privy Council proposed expelling all foreigners within three months. A few years later, probably around 1600, several playwrights submitted to the state censor a draft of a co-authored play that reenacted the bloody anti-alien riots of 1517.[15] The censor wanted it revised, and asked, among other things, for more on Thomas More calming the mutiny. Around 1603–4, the original playwrights called in some helpers. At this point Shakespeare wrote the scene in which More speaks. He asks the native workers who feel their jobs are being taken away to

> Imagine that you see the wretched strangers,
> Their babies at their backs, with their poor luggage
> Plodding to th' ports and coasts for transportation.
>
> (Add.II.D.81–3)

He argues that their bullying behaviour would eventually put themselves at risk, and if they travelled to other countries, natives there would 'Spurn you like dogs, and like as if that God | Owned not nor made not you' (147–8). He has an impact on the crowd, one of whom says, 'Let's do as we may be done by' (Add.II.D.154). More's argument here parallels many Shakespearean passages in which one character asks another to put himself or herself in another's place, or argues that his or her group should be treated equally with others. (Historically, hostility to immigrants continued after More's speech, and this play apparently was never performed, probably because the controversy was too sensitive.)[16] The passage also resonates with the number of times those who hate outsiders compare them to animals, very often dogs, in Shakespeare's plays.

In his plays outsiders may sometimes be admired, especially in the tragedies. But when they are scorned, they may be compared not only to animals but also to objects. Their rights are limited. They do not participate in the play's society in the ways others are allowed to do. Stories about their bad behaviour are easily believed, and to many people this justifies the limits set on them. And sometimes they do behave badly. But sometimes others protest against their treatment.

And they very often argue that they are similar to others and therefore should be treated as well, or that some of their own behaviour is mirroring that of others to them. 'Hath not a Jew eyes?' (3.1.49–50) asks Shylock. 'My dimensions are as well compact, | My mind as generous and my shape as true, | As honest madam's issue', (1.2.7–9) says Edmund. This rhetoric is sometimes accompanied by plot structures or verbal echoes which suggest similarity between the outsider and other characters and thus, perhaps, a process of projection—characters from a dominant group may be punishing or suspecting an outsider because of their own faults. Closely related to the issue of commonality across categories is the rhetoric of identity switching, engaged in both by those female characters (Rosalind, Portia) who argue that they can successfully play the roles of men or boys, and by others, such as Beatrice and Lady Macbeth, who express a wish to do so.

Suspicion of women is generally treated somewhat differently in the plays than suspicions of other kinds of outsiders. Several plays emphasize a central character's mistrust of women, but focus on women—Hero, Alice Ford, Desdemona, Imogen, Hermione—who go against that stereotype and are finally vindicated.[17] However, Shylock's behaviour never refutes Antonio's comparison of him to the devil (unless his forced conversion is counted), though his arguments give a more complicated perspective, suggesting that suspicion of him becomes a self-fulfilling prophecy. Brabanzio attributes to Othello 'practices of cunning hell' (1.3.103) in abusing Desdemona, and Othello's murder of her could appear to fulfill that suspicion, though what we see of his thought processes and their manipulation by Iago, as well as his attempt to atone by killing himself, points to a different interpretation.

Clearly an interest in outsiders, their inclusion or expulsion, their resourcefulness, defensiveness, and overreaching, is a central feature of Shakespeare's dramatic imagination. To complicate recent contextualization that has often emphasized the prejudices of Shakespeare's culture, we should be aware of the circulation in his time of writers such as Erasmus, Montaigne, and lesser known figures who, whether seriously or playfully, took positions close to what we might now identify as feminist, post-colonial, or relativist. (Further examples have been pointed out by Richard Strier and Thomas Cartelli.)[18] The playwright Robert Wilson, in his 1584 *Three Ladies of London*, showed a Jewish moneylender, Gerontus, morally superior to a Christian debtor.[19] Montaigne argued that the European torture of people over religion was worse than cannibalism. Cornelius Agrippa praised the superiority of women. Agrippa, and some other such figures, may have sometimes been, as Joel Altman argues, writing in the mode of rhetorical exercises stemming from Elizabethan school techniques of arguing on both sides; nevertheless such school exercises seem to have contributed to the range of perspectives found in the Elizabethan theatre.[20] A. J. Hoenselaars goes so far as to claim that 'The early modern period witnessed the development of a discourse on stereotyping, generalization, and projection not dissimilar in perspective to that which has prevailed for a number of decades now in the humanities and social sciences.'[21] Probably at least some members of the audience did sometimes sympathize with the outsiders who speak in the plays. I won't argue that each play began with a humanitarian purpose, but rather that the question of how a character marked as different relates to society repeatedly ignited

Shakespeare's imagination, producing drama that often includes or invites protest against prejudice. Extending the kinds and attitudes of characters represented—showing for the first time a Moor who loyally serves Venice, for example—and making the audience frequently shift their sympathies during a play contributes to exciting theatre, and that may well have been his main goal.

The relation between individual and community is important in both comedy and tragedy, and often the individual focused on is a potential or actual outsider. In both comedy and tragedy, outsiders overreach and suffer because of it. In both there may be moments—or more—in which we are invited to identify with some outsiders as feeling people. In comedy there are often some attempts near the end to bring the outsider into the main community; in tragedy the main outsider must die.[22] Perhaps a community forms among his mourners in death, or perhaps (or also) he joins a new, better community of those who die along with him. In both comedy and tragedy, the outsider is sometimes analyzed as a scapegoat whose punishment saves the society, and Jean-Pierre Guépin has generalized that the audience is expected to sympathize with the scapegoat in tragedy but not in comedy.[23] In Shakespeare's plays, there is often something like a structure of an attack on a scapegoat, but it seldom concludes with a satisfying expulsion or killing. Sympathy is a question of degree, though audience members and readers would differ among themselves in their reactions, with some sympathy invited in comedies but more criticism, and some criticism invited in tragedies but more sympathy, at least for the hero. This contrast, and a kind of progression (though not a progression that another choice of plays would necessarily parallel), appears in the plays discussed in this book at greatest length. In *The Merchant of Venice* the script gives no one words of sympathy for Shylock, though some of his speeches often evoke it.[24] In *Twelfth Night* Olivia says to Malvolio, 'Alas, poor fool, how have they baffled thee!' (5.1.358) and Orsino tries to bring him back into the community (though partly for self-interested reasons). Cassio calls Othello 'great of heart' (5.2.359) at the end, and many of the audience may concur, but no other character does openly. All the surviving characters are finally united in sympathy for Lear, though Kent is very critical of him in the first act.

All of Shakespeare's plays could be discussed in terms of their representation of outsiders and difference, but I have chosen to treat at greatest length these four in which outsiders are particularly marked, memorable, and self-conscious: two comedies and two tragedies, one of each including a famous ethnic/racial outsider and one in which other differences play a greater role. In my third chapter I also discuss other plays that show issues in the representation of women as outsiders and insiders, and in my epilogue the question of outsiders in *The Tempest* and how it relates to others of Shakespeare's concerns. Let me here contextualize these plays in relation to some more in the variety of Shakespeare's genres to show changes in his representation of outsiders throughout his career.

In comic tradition, the ending affirms the bonds of community, yet as Northrop Frye wrote in *A Natural Perspective* and C. L. Barber explored in more detail on individual plays in *Shakespeare's Festive Comedies*, there are often characters outside the community at the end.[25] The suffering of a character from a marked outsider group is not equally important in all of Shakespeare's comedies, but it increases after his first plays. Shakespeare's early *Comedy of Errors* focuses on a foreigner's arrival, confusion, apparent madness, and exorcism, but he is the identical twin of a citizen of the same city, and this contributes to showing the hostility between Ephesus and Syracuse as irrational and to integrating the newcomer and his servant into the community at the end. In *Taming of the Shrew* Petruccio's 'taming' of Katherine by tantalizing her with food and clothing and then withdrawing them is a different sort of trial than most outsiders receive, and her final speech involves a lecture to the other female characters which elicits approval from the men; she has found the language that will give her relative social acceptance. In *Love's Labour's Lost* and *Midsummer Night's Dream*, there is marked class contrast between aristocrats and less privileged characters and the humiliation of the latter is theatrical heckling directed at the whole group more than at one character—and in *Love's Labour's Lost* the national outsider Don Armado has the same penance the princes do. Sometime in the period 1596–8, however, Shakespeare wrote two comedies in which marked outsiders are dramatically punished—*Merry Wives of Windsor* and *Merchant of Venice*. In *Merry Wives* Falstaff is ritually pinched by a group of young people in a kind of festive exorcism onstage, after we have seen him hiding in a basket of dirty laundry and enduring a beating while in disguise. In *Merchant of Venice* Shylock is forced to give up at least half his money and agree to be baptized.

My first chapter will point out that Shakespeare added Shylock's forced conversion in a culture where many people had recently converted between different branches of Christianity because of state pressure, and that Shylock's situation in some ways paralleled that of Catholics in Shakespeare's England, while his words 'I am content' were used by one famous Protestant in his pressured conversion. *Merchant* adds explicitly anti-Semitic language to its sources, and also adds language humanizing Shylock. Thus this character, though one of the most explicit outsiders in Shakespeare's works, often so threatening, also appears at least occasionally as one with whom some in Shakespeare's audience might sympathize, especially because of the similarity of his situation to that of Christians who converted under pressure.

As Chapter 1 also discusses, *Merchant*'s Antonio is presented as different from the other characters because he is melancholy and because his strongest love is for someone of the same sex, but the play raises the question whether he is therefore an outsider. Graziano and Solanio tease him about his melancholy, but the other characters do not, and the temperament could be seen positively. Is his relationship with Bassanio an admirable male friendship? This is the view of the characters in the play who discuss it. But why does Antonio describe himself as a 'tainted wether' (4.1.113)? The play keeps ambiguous the question of whether Antonio is an outsider or just different. Similarly it is unclear whether Jessica is accepted as a Christian or is still an outsider at the end because of her Jewish ethnicity.

The next two comedies call attention to an outsider near the conclusion but in less troubling ways. It is announced that Don John, the trouble-making bastard of *Much Ado*, has been captured, and Benedick promises to devise punishments for him. In *As You Like It*, Jaques, the self-consciously melancholy character who has been criticizing life in the forest all the way through, announces that he won't return to the court with the others.

As Chapter 2 will show, *Twelfth Night* returns to the vivid portrayal of an outsider's punishment, but includes more explicit suggestions that the punishment is excessive. Malvolio makes the choice to leave Olivia's court after his humiliation, but Olivia and Orsino are eager for him to return. The nature of Malvolio's outsider status is ambiguous: we see antipuritanism in Sir Andrew and in much of the mockery of Malvolio, yet Maria denies that he is a puritan after she has introduced the term. Most obviously he is an outsider because, on the comic stage, he objects to clowns and jokes.

In all these plays, the comic spirit has to confront sadness. The outsider status of Don John and Jaques is explicitly associated with their melancholy temperament. Near the beginning of *Merchant of Venice*, *As You Like It*, and *Twelfth Night* other characters also announce their sadness. Portia is sad because her father's will doesn't seem to give her a choice in her marriage, Orlando because his brother treats him like a servant, Rosalind because her father is banished, Olivia because her brother has died. The comic plot solves these characters' mood problems, but it can't help Jaques (though he may actually enjoy his melancholy), it can't help Malvolio, who in mocking Feste shows that he is basically against the spirit of comedy, and it can't help *Merchant*'s Antonio, who says he doesn't know why he is sad.

Antonio's sadness and his unwillingness to explain it is a long-standing problem in *Merchant* criticism. My first chapter relates it to the ambiguity of his position as a man who loves men in a society in which 'gay' or 'homosexual' is not yet a widely recognized identity category and in a literary genre which typically ends in heterosexual marriage for most of its characters. However, in *Twelfth Night*, the other Antonio, who is also in love with a man, is not identified as sad, but is an outsider in another way, as a suspected pirate who has been on the other side of a bloody sea-battle with Orsino. Recent scholarship shows evidence of socially accepted male-male homoerotic love in England at the time, yet if the relationship crossed class or national boundaries or involved someone suspected for religious or political reasons it might be seen as sodomy, and perhaps the situation of the two Antonios registers this ambiguity as well as the difficulty of fitting same-sex love into a traditional comic plot.[26]

A man who loves another man may be rejected in a history play also, though again not clearly for that reason. In *Henry IV, Part 1*, the companionship of Hal and Falstaff first leads to a relativization of inside and outside, as Hal is an outsider in the tavern scenes and Falstaff is an outsider in the court scenes. Political rebels are punished at the end but Falstaff survives after playing dead. But this doesn't last. The punishment of Falstaff as an outsider in *Merry Wives of Windsor* has a close parallel at the end of *Henry IV, Part 2*, probably written about the same time, where his former friend Prince Hal upon his coronation denies knowing Falstaff. While Falstaff is given the promise of a reconciliatory dinner in the comedy *Merry Wives*, in the succeeding history play, *Henry V*, we learn that demoralization from this rejection has led to his death—'The King has killed his heart' (5.2.79). On the other hand, that play also shows the possibility of the inclusion of other kinds of outsiders: representatives of various ethnic groups fight together under Henry V (though the Irish soldier's anger suggests a continuing problem), and the king's marriage to Katherine of France suggests a reconciliation with the country which at the beginning of Shakespeare's history plays provided some of the most threatening women.

Shakespeare's two problem comedies, mostly likely written after *Twelfth Night*, also show the humiliation of outsiders. In *All's Well that Ends Well*, Paroles is exposed as a coward and a traitor, and loses the respect of the central male character, Bertram, for whom he might be considered a scapegoat.[27] *Measure for Measure* reveals that the apparently puritanical Angelo, a more threatening and serious version of Malvolio, is corrupt and guilty of sexual coercion, and catches Lucio, in a sense Angelo's more flippant double, in more lies as well as an attempt to escape child support and marriage.

Chapter 3 bridges the comedies and the tragedies as it discusses the ambiguous semi-outsider status of Shakespeare's women. In *Taming of the Shrew*, the woman who protests against the marriage system is treated as an outsider in her society, and shown as threateningly angry, for much of the play. In *Much Ado*, Beatrice can criticize marriage and still be accepted as a friend by the other characters. However, Hero is treated as an outsider when her fiancé and her father readily believe slanders of her, as happens with several of Shakespeare's women. Other female characters highlight their outsider status and protest against it by their frequent ability to function in male disguise, lines such as 'O that I were a man' (*Much Ado* 4.1.300–1), or, in Emilia's case, attacking the double standard on the ground of the similarity of men and women, an argument that has parallels in a few other writers of the time.

Tragedies involve a conflict between one or two characters and their society, and at the end the central figure or figures have usually left their society in death. Although all tragic heroes might be considered as outsiders in some respect, this book will focus on those who are part of a resented or subordinated group in some way; it will not, for example, discuss Macbeth, who begins as a powerful general and becomes a moral outsider because his ambition leads him to kill his king. The early *Titus Andronicus*, with its elderly titular hero and its Moor, Aaron, could be said to foreshadow the plays I will discuss, but in *Romeo and Juliet*, *Julius Caesar*, and *Hamlet*, the heroes are outsiders mainly because of their more intense and more imaginative consciousness, which is closely related to the sadness of some comic outsiders but has more power and eloquence.[28] Some recent critics give good reasons why the outsider condition is important in tragedy. Paul Hammond, in *The Strangeness of Tragedy*, writes that tragedy involves 'an estrangement of the protagonist from his home territory, or from what had seemed to be home ground.'[29] Writers such as René Girard, John Holloway, Linda Woodbridge, and Naomi Conn Liebler have discussed the tragic hero's complicated relationship to scapegoat ritual in great detail.[30] Shakespeare's and Marlowe's tragedies, Thomas Cartelli argues, are built around the conflict between the audience's identification with transgressors (a term that could apply to most outsiders in drama) and distantiation from them.

Chapter 4 will discuss the doubleness of Othello's position at the beginning: honoured by the Venetian Senate but hated by Iago, a parallel to the ambivalence towards Africans and Moors in previous traditions. It also parallels the marked polarization of women in the play's discourse: at first Desdemona's idealization contrasts with the contempt for women in Iago's language, later Othello shows both attitudes toward her. The play juxtaposes the situations of a white woman and a male Moor by showing the impact of Iago's hostility to both. By inventing a character who uses two different kinds of stereotypes to influence others, the play encourages us to think about prejudice in general as well as about Iago's particular power. To contribute to an explanation of that power, as well as the discrepancy between earlier critical admiration of Othello the character and some current critics' views that the play's portrayal of him is racist, the chapter draws in part on recent research in social psychology.

Chapter 5 will show how *King Lear* deals with outsiders in the family (especially the bastard and the difficult elderly parent) as well as in the kingdom. In a time when poverty was marked by the increased visibility of bastards, elderly poor, and beggars, the play dramatizes these outsider issues in Edmund, Lear, and Edgar (in his disguise as Poor Tom), as well as reflecting them in Kent, Gloucester, and the Fool, other homeless men on the heath. By contrast to the many plays in which outsiders compete to be insiders, here most of the social outsiders come together in a community to help Lear. This includes Cordelia, but excludes her sisters Goneril and Regan, who have revealed themselves as moral outsiders.

Shakespeare's last two tragedies show great variations in the treatment of outsiders. In *Antony and Cleopatra*, the changing of places emphasizes that Antony is an outsider in Egypt and Cleopatra in Rome. Although Cleopatra receives her share of scorn, she is also described in more admiring words than are most of the other ethnic or national outsiders. The lovers construct and reconstruct their own space, and Cleopatra dies with glory in Roman as well as Egyptian terms. On the other hand, Coriolanus fails in an attempt to reconstruct his national identity. Though Coriolanus is a Roman and exemplifies many professed Roman values, his scorn for its people earns him expulsion from Rome; after he returns to Rome to take revenge at the head of the Volscian army and backs down after his mother's plea, he suffers hatred from the Volscians and is killed by his own Volscian soldiers. Though for a while generally admired for his military honor, he eventually becomes a hated outsider in both places.

In Shakespeare's late romances, various characters are sometimes treated like suspect outsiders and/or expelled early in the play. In *Cymbeline*, Shakespeare's first comic butt with royal blood, Cloten, is killed at the same time as Imogen's suspicious husband is reforming, making Cloten a scapegoat-like substitute, but the plays mostly have endings in which apparent outsiders are recognized, vindicated, and/ or forgiven, and take part in family reunions and reconciliations. However, the most memorable outsider in Shakespeare's romances is Caliban, who will be treated briefly in the coda. The coda discusses how through Caliban and Prospero Shakespeare relativizes the meaning of outsider in *The Tempest*, and relates this to the concern with seeing resemblance between self and others frequent in his plays.

Each of this book's chapters shows ambiguity and ambivalence in Shakespeare's treatment of outsiders. The book shows how often Shakespeare's plays break down oppositions and categorizations— they are structured by a juxtaposition of several kinds of outsiders or potential outsiders who may contrast in obvious ways but also have points of similarity.[31] While, in varying degrees, the outsiders may resonate with stereotypes, they also break out of them. Many plays deny the simplicity of scapegoating an outsider, whether because the punishment goes too far, because some characters want the outsiders in the community, because a less obvious outsider is really to blame, because the outsider repents, or because he apparently can't be killed or exiled. Showing the complexity of Shakespeare's outsiders, this book suggests why many of them have been so memorable that evoking or rewriting them has often been a way that recent members of subordinated or minority groups have negotiated their relationship with a dominant culture. The African-American Paul Robeson considered his playing of Othello a milestone for civil rights. The postcolonial Caribbean writer Aimé Césaire made Caliban the hero of his rewriting, *A Tempest*. *Shrew* was the name of a feminist paper in 1960s England. The Jewish playwright Arnold Wesker reimagined Shylock in his play *The Merchant*. Paula Vogel and Anne-Marie MacDonald both wrote plays in which a central figure is an adventurous Desdemona. Jane Smiley's novel *A Thousand Acres* gives a modern version of Goneril, set in 1970s America, a chance to tell her family's story from her own point of view. Though all these recent appropriations except Robeson's contest Shakespeare's plays in some ways, all of them build on aspects of Shakespeare's outsider characters that speak across time to a world where some members of their group still feel excluded. This book aims to contribute to showing why those characters and their plays originally had resonance as well as why they have it today.

1

The Merchant of Venice
and its Pressured Conversions

The Merchant of Venice contains the character whose outsider status might be considered the clearest in Shakespeare. As Shylock says, 'What's his reason? I am a Jew' (3.1.49). But the play frames him so that the attitude audience members can take toward him may vary widely at different moments. And the play sets him in opposition to a title character who from one standpoint may seem the total insider— 'The good Antonio, the honest Antonio—O that I had a title good enough to keep him company' (3.1.10–12)—but nevertheless refers to himself as 'a tainted wether of the flock, | Meetest for death' (4.1.113–14) and in many productions seems uncomfortable as the odd man out in a final act of couples. If we look at the verbal/theatrical details in relation to other texts and to historical context, even *The Merchant of Venice* shows how fluid Shakespeare's presentation of outsiders can be.

Shylock, Anti-Semitism, and Other Persecutions in England

Shylock as an outsider is sometimes threatening and sometimes threatened himself. At some points he protests on behalf of the common humanity of Jews, or shows human feelings; at others his unrestrained anger makes him not just a social outsider but a moral one, without a necessary sense of right and wrong. Many critics have argued that one or the other of these views is the dominant one in the play, or perhaps like René Girard that there are two different ways to read the play, one which scapegoats Shylock and one which is about the process of scapegoating him.[1] But what is theatrically most powerful about this play is the way in which it moves back and forth between these two versions of Shylock. Part of the context that enabled this shifting for its original audience was England's recent history of persecution of religious outsiders, and the shift back and forth under various monarchs about who the religious outsiders were. In this chapter I shall emphasize the possibility of seeing Shylock's humanity under persecution in this chapter because it has been underplayed by recent critics, but I shall note occasions where seeing him as a monstrous threat is unavoidable.

Religious persecution was a vivid memory or a current reality for many in Shakespeare's audience. Mary's persecutions of Protestants, which killed nearly 300 people in four years, have been emphasized in dominant English history—but Elizabeth executed 131 priests and 60 Catholic laypeople between 1581 and 1603, and it was hard to distinguish religion from suspicion of treason as causes.[2] Popular opinion about *The Merchant of Venice* today, I hypothesize, too readily assumes that the play's original spectators never identified with Shylock as a victim of persecution.[3] Lindsay Kaplan has emphasized the connections between Shylock's situation and that of Catholics in Shakespeare's time. 'As a Jew and an alien in Venice, Shylock is susceptible to laws that apply only to a religious minority and carry both financial and penal threats. How would Catholics who lived under analogous circumstances respond to the trial scene in Act 4 of *The Merchant of Venice*?'[4] But Protestants knew that their churches too had been persecuted in England and were still being persecuted in other countries.

Shakespeare's father withdrew from the town council and started having business difficulties at the same time that recusant Catholics began to be punished more severely, and left behind a 'Spiritual Testament', a profession of Catholic faith based on a model written by St. Charles Borromeo.[5] My argument does not, however, depend on the view that his father was Catholic, much less that Shakespeare was, but that he and much of his audience were aware of the cost of religious persecution to Catholics in his own time and Protestants in the generation before, and that when invited they could cross boundaries to make a connection with Shylock to the extent that he was also pressured to convert.[6]

Would Jews always have been considered so alien that the analogy between the pressure on them to convert and similar pressures on both Catholics and Protestants in England would have been entirely unnoticed? The play's most famous speech describes a Jew as being 'hurt with the same weapons, subject to the same diseases, healed by the same means...as a Christian is' (3.1.51–9). And contrary to a frequently-held belief that there were no Jews in England at the time, some Londoners did have a chance to meet flesh-and-blood Jews, not just to think of them as bogeys. Jews had officially been expelled from England in 1290, unless they converted; Shakespeare's England included a few Jews who practiced their faith in secret, and others who had converted sincerely but were always suspect.[7] One community was located near the London neighborhood of Houndsditch, where Shakespeare lived until 1596, close to the time he wrote *Merchant*. It included mostly pawnbrokers and sellers of old clothes.[8] But there were also Jews in London, some of them practicing, who were doctors and merchants. When Shakespeare lived in Houndsditch, he may have observed not only prejudice but also what Alexandra Walsham calls 'the considerable reserves of tolerance embedded in early modern society'.[9]

Adding to the effects of a historically documented tendency toward practical everyday tolerance, Paula Blank has shown that the idea that all human beings by nature had much in common and could be considered as equal was available in the words of writings from Cicero in classical tradition and Augustine in Christian tradition. Writers who agree on little agree on this: Anglican apologist Hooker writes that men are all 'of one and the same nature', and of the 'relation of equality between ourselves and them that are as ourselves.' The skeptical political theorist Machiavelli declares, 'All men, having had the same beginning, are equally ancient and have been made in one mode.'[10] The founders of the United States did not follow the most universal implications of 'all men are created equal', which they affirmed in the Declaration of Independence, but the idea was there to be developed. Similarly, the idea of human equality was available for development in Shakespeare's time.

Furthermore, partly in reaction to England's bloody history of persecution, the language of religious toleration was circulating in the Elizabethan period. John Donne in his 'Satire 3' advocated freedom of the individual conscience.[11] Both Protestants, e.g. John Foxe, in his influential multi-volume *Acts and Monuments*, also called Foxe's *Book of Martyrs*, and Catholics, William Allen and Robert Parsons, in shorter discourses, wrote of its importance.[12] In 1599–1600, not long after *Merchant*'s probable first performance, the evangelical preacher Matthew Hutton objected to Sir Thomas Cecil's forcing Catholic recusants to listen to puritan sermons. In other words, he was protesting against an abuse of the religious freedom of people from whom he himself was religiously different. Similarly, Foxe, who criticized the persecution of both Jews and Protestants by the Spanish Inquisition, pleaded for mercy from the English government for the Catholic Edmund Campion and declared that Christ 'forced no one against his will'.[13]

There were other influential advocates of tolerance both before and after Elizabethan times. Boccaccio's *Decameron* included the pro-diversity fable of the father who leaves identical rings to Christian, Jewish, and Muslim sons, without telling them which one is the true ring. Sebastian Castellio, the Swiss reformer, had protested against Calvin's execution of Servetus.[14] Ficino and Nicholas of Cusa had both suggested that variety of religion might be a good thing, probably influencing some aspects of Thomas More's Utopia. The great humanist reformer Erasmus, some of whose writings were used as texts in 16th century schools, denounced the burning of heretics.[15] Montaigne, whose essays Shakespeare alludes to in *Hamlet* and *The Tempest*, specifically decried the repeated change of English religious laws in his lifetime in arguing for freedom of conscience.[16] Much evidence thus contradicts the claim of such mid-twentieth-century critics as Nevill Coghill that only moderns think that 'a religion imposed is a tyranny'.[17] Most of the voices for tolerance were minority voices, and often they were pleading for their own party, but respect for conscience as a principle was possible. A little later, in 1609, King James himself said, 'God never loves to plant his Church by violence and bloodshed.' In 1612 the radical Baptist Thomas Helwys wrote, when those being persecuted were Catholics, 'Men's religion is between God and themselves; the king shall not answer it; neither may the king be judge between God and man. Let them be heretics, Turks, Jews, or whatsoever. It appertains not to the earthly power to punish them in the least measure.'[18] James' behaviour did not respect freedom of conscience as much as his words previously quoted suggested; Helwys paid with his life for his statement, so it is likely that others, not so brave, might have thought similarly without saying so.

Helwys clearly includes Jews among those who should have freedom of conscience. John Coffey has found a number of other English writers of the time, such as Bishop Bilson in 1585, who argued against forced conversions of Jews, Muslims, and pagans, while noting that they had occurred elsewhere.[19] They could be considered less blameworthy than heretics because they never had been Christian and were ignorant of the truth, and the influential theologian Tertullian's statement that belief could not be forced could apply without the qualification it was given in other cases.[20] William Covell, discussing how far Jews ought to be tolerated, wrote in 1604, 'Charity ought to make us careful to instruct them in the way of truth, but unwillingly we dare not compel either them, or their children, to be Baptised.'

Some of Erasmus' works were textbooks in Elizabethan schools. Foxe's *Acts and Monuments*, reprinted many times, was the most popular book in Protestant homes after the Bible. From his education and their prominence, Shakespeare and some of his audience would probably have known the support for freedom of conscience of at least Erasmus and Foxe, among those above, and if he had family and educational ties to recusants, more of these writings might have struck close to his heart.[21] Furthermore, he and some of his audience probably were aware of the virtuous Jews used to criticize Christian behaviour in Boccaccio's *Decameron* and Wilson's play *Three Ladies of London*, not just the vicious one in Marlowe's *Jew of Malta*.[22]

Against this background, consider some of the changes that Shakespeare makes to his main source, *Il Pecorone*—the basic story of the Jewish usurer's loan with a pound of flesh as surety. This plot has an anti-Semitic structure. *The Merchant of Venice* has more anti-Semitic language and anti-Semitic characters, but these additions call attention to anti-Semitism rather than justifying it. In *Il Pecorone*, Antonio's original, Ansaldo, is the richest Christian merchant in Venice, but is described neither as competing with usurers by lending money gratis, nor as habitually spitting on the Jewish usurer whose bond he takes. In giving a source character identified mainly by his wealth and his generous love of his godson such a habit, the play presents a conundrum about the coexistence of love and hate, unusual in literature but not so uncommon in history. Some critics have ignored Antonio's complexity because of their assumption that there were no objections to anti-Semitism within the Christianity of the time. In spite of what Perez Zagorin calls 'the Christian theory of persecution', there are recorded conflicts even between religious authorities about how Christians should behave to Jews.[23] Some Popes, for example, ordered that Jews be treated humanely; in the mid-sixteenth century, Pope Paul III 'banned performances of a wildly popular Passion play in the Colosseum because it incited attacks on Rome's Jews'.[24]

Antonio's hostility to Shylock is underlined by Shakespeare and should not be simply taken for granted. The very way that Antonio asks Shylock for money is rude and condescending, as Linda Woodbridge has shown, and quite different from the way Bassanio speaks to Shylock.[25] Shylock is given several speeches that describe Antonio's previous provocative behaviour toward him:

> You, that did void your rheum upon my beard
> And foot me as you spurn a stranger cur
> Over your threshold. Moneys is your suit.
> What should I say to you? Should I not say,
> 'Hath a dog monies'?
>
> (1.3.113–17)

And when Antonio's ships fail, Shylock presents his own response as a fulfillment of Antonio's implicit expectations:

> Thou calledst me dog before thou hadst a cause,
> But since I am a dog, beware my fangs.
>
> (3.3.6–7)

The first reason Shylock has given for hating Antonio is his Christianity; these descriptions of Antonio suggest that to Shylock, Christianity means anti-Semitic behaviour.

Graziano, the character who mocks Shylock the most in the trial scene, is not in *Il Pecorone* at all. He is, in a sense, spun off from one aspect of Antonio's original that does not fit at all with Antonio— Ansaldo marries one of the Lady's maids at the end. Graziano's anti-Semitism in the trial scene is a double of the anti-Semitism that

Antonio showed earlier in unrepentantly spitting at Shylock, before his life was ever threatened. Graziano's open bigotry makes the other characters look restrained by contrast. But his link with the earlier Antonio suggests the fraudulence of the claim that the baptism—suggested by Antonio, not the ostensibly impartial Duke—occurs because of concern for Shylock's spiritual welfare.

Shakespeare adds to his sources not only anti-Semitism in Antonio and Graziano, but also three other characters who speak anti-Semitic language: Lancelot, the servant who is the play's fool, who calls Shylock a devil, and the virtually twin characters Salerio and Solanio, who are sufficiently uncharacterized that they may represent the dominant biases of the play's Venice. In the scenes directly following Shylock's famous claim of common humanity, their language denies it to him. Solanio repeats the dog image of Shylock, 'It [notice the pronoun] is the most impenetrable cur | That ever kept with men' (3.3.18–19). This imagery will culminate in Graziano's courtroom speech, 'O, be thou damned, inexorable dog, ... Thy currish spirit | Governed a wolf ... hanged for human slaughter' (4.1.127, 132–3).

The wolf image may have reminded the audience of the 1594 execution of Rodrigo Lopez, Queen Elizabeth's ethnically Jewish physician, who bore a name similar to the Latin word for wolf and was accused of treason for poisoning her. But the imagery recalls Shylock's own words about how Antonio's treatment of him as a dog has summoned corresponding behaviour. Furthermore, Shylock's immediate response to Graziano refutes the animal image from another perspective. Shylock makes a calm and civilized response to Graziano:

> Till thou canst rail the seal from off my bond
> Thou but offend'st thy lungs to speak so loud.
> Repair thy wit, good youth, or it will fall
> To cureless ruin. I stand here for law.
>
> (4.1.138–41)

This is almost the self-control of Othello's 'Keep up your bright swords, for the dew will rust them.' (1.2.59). Shylock may be planning Antonio's death, but clearly he is not behaving in a dog-like way. Common as the association of Jews with dogs was, Shylock easily shakes it off.

Just after Shylock has made his 'Hath not a Jew eyes?' speech (3.1.49ff) in front of the mocking Salerio and Solanio, the play reminds us of his humanity in two other ways emphasized nowhere else. He has been talking about Jews as 'us', and a Jewish friend outside his family appears, Tubal. And with this friend, he recalls his wife Leah and the turquoise ring she gave him before their marriage. 'I would not have given it for a wilderness of monkeys' (3.1.102) can draw more sympathy for Shylock than anything that Salerio and Solanio say draws for themselves. But it is in the very next speech that Shylock says, of Antonio, 'I will have the heart of him if he forfeit' (3.1.105–06), suggesting cannibalism, which he had also hinted at much earlier when saying to Antonio, 'Your worship was the last man in our mouths' (1.3.55). Such switching between a critical perspective on Shylock and a critical perspective on his attackers is a key technique of the play. James Shapiro has documented the persistence of myths of Jewish cannibalism as well as many other hostile myths about Jews in Shakespeare's day.[26] While these myths must have affected many early spectators' reactions to Shylock at some points (and some at all points), there are many details in the play that can put this mythic version of Shylock in doubt.

Perhaps most importantly, Shakespeare added Shylock's forced conversion to his source. *Il Pecorone* has a Jewish usurer who lends money asking for a pound of flesh for security and is defeated in court, like Shylock, because flesh cannot be cut without shedding blood—but after his defeat he tears his bond and no more is heard from him. Bullough's sources and analogues include no other conversion stories.[27] James Shapiro says 'coerced conversions were virtually unheard of in the various narratives circulating about Jews in sixteenth-century England'. Marlowe's Barabas, in *The Jew of Malta*, briefly pretends that he will convert, and his daughter converts once as part of his scheme and then a second time sincerely.[28] The only extant earlier English play with the conversion of a Jew to Christianity is the *Croxton Play of the Sacrament* (surviving text from the mid-sixteenth century—the full title is *The Play of the Conversyon of Ser Jonathas the Jewe by Myracle of the Blyssed Sacrament*).[29] In this play Jonathas buys a host from a merchant, claiming that he might convert. He and his servants stab the host and it bleeds; they put it in a cauldron and it turns the oil into boiling blood; then they put it in an oven and Jesus appears to them and reproaches them. Jonathas immediately professes his faith and asks mercy. He goes to the bishop to report the miracle, asks for a general absolution and is baptized.[30]

The critics who write of *The Merchant of Venice* as a theological allegory and assume that all the audience would have felt that Shylock's baptism should be seen as saving his soul are writing as if his conversion were presented as in this play.[31] Instead, *The Merchant of Venice* presents Shylock's conversion as required by Antonio if he is to keep some of his money, and then required by the Duke to save his life, because as an alien he has earned a death sentence by plotting Antonio's death.

Shylock makes no clear comment on the requirement that he convert. He does, however, speak two key (and apparently contradictory) lines after the conditions decreed by Antonio, the Duke, and Portia: 'I am content' (4.1.389) and 'I am not well' (4.1.392). What did these lines mean at the time? Do they express feelings about agreeing to a forced conversion which the audience might have been able to liken to feelings of a Christian similarly pressured?

Each of these sentences is uttered by another early modern figure in the context of what we might call externally pressured conversions. 'I am not well' appears in Robert Daborne's 1612 play *A Christian Turned Turk*, one of the few other plays of the time to deal with such conversions.[32] It is spoken by the Christian pirate Ward, after the protest of his page against his plan to convert for romantic and socioeconomic reasons. The page, a disguised woman, argues that afterwards 'guilt each hour | Would strike your conscious soul with terrors' (7. 210–15). 'This boy's words trouble me', says Ward after this speech, and a few lines later comes 'I am not well' (7.216, 226).

At several places this play suggests analogies between Ward and Shylock. When Ward does become Muslim, it is clear that the Turks are always suspicious of him as a convert. His vulnerability to the charge of attempted murder by the Turks who don't accept him as one of them could be compared to Shylock's vulnerability as an alien to the charge of planning the death of a citizen. Furthermore, the first time he is tempted to convert, the reasons that he gives against conversion might be applicable to Shylock as well. He adduces 'nature... | Which doth in beasts force them to keep their kind,' (7.190), notes that his sincerity might be doubted, and is reluctant to abjure 'My name—and the belief my ancestors | Left to my being' (7.74–6). While the play is in many ways a polemic against conversion to Islam, it does, like *The Merchant of Venice*, touch on issues in other forms of conversion. Obviously Daborne, who wrote later, could not have influenced Shakespeare, but Shakespeare might have influenced Daborne. *A Christian Turned Turk* suggests that 'I am not well' could be taken to indicate that a pressured conversion might evoke serious qualms with which Christians might identify.

Some readers may assume that Shylock's phrase 'I am content' expresses the positive side of an ambivalence about converting. Examining the use of the word at the time suggests that this is not true. The phrase is an echo of words signed in the process of one of the most famous pressured conversions between branches of Christianity in sixteenth-century Europe.

Under Queen Mary, Thomas Cranmer, who had been Archbishop of Canterbury under Henry VIII and Edward VI, author of the Book of Common Prayer and supervisor of reforms in the Church under those monarchs, was jailed for heresy and put under pressure to recant. While in prison, he signed six different statements of submission to the queen. The first one begins, 'Forasmuch as the King and Queen's Majesties, by consent of their Parliament, have received the Pope's authority within this realm, *I am content* to submit myself to their laws herein, and to take the Pope for chief head of this Church of England, so far as God's laws and the laws and customs of this realm will permit' (emphasis mine).[33] The third one begins, '*I am content* to submit myself to the king and queen's majesties, and to all their laws and ordinances; as well concerning the pope's supremacy as others,' and concludes, 'And for my book which I have written, *I am contented* to submit me to the judgment of the catholic church, and of the next general council' (emphasis mine). In spite of his recantation of Protestantism, Queen Mary would not relent, and Cranmer was burnt at the stake for heresy. In the public ritual before his execution, where another confession of heresy was expected, instead he recanted his recantation. When he went to the stake, he put his hand in the fire first, saying that he did this because it 'offended, writing contrary to [his] heart.'[34] Cranmer's death and his statements of submission were supposed to be propaganda for Queen Mary's Catholic government; his written statements were published by the government under the title 'All the submissions, and recantations of Thomas Cranmer, late Archbishop of Canterbury'. Ironically, the probable Catholicism of Shakespeare's father makes it more likely that his son might have known this pamphlet, since it was 'conscientiously circulated by pious Catholics'.[35] But his final recantation made the whole story an embarrassment to the queen, and the story was retold by John Foxe in *Acts and Monuments*.

Whether or not Shakespeare knew exactly what Cranmer had written, 'content' is a perfect word to use in a case of forced conversion or submission, because of its range of meanings. As a noun it can suggest happiness or even ecstasy, as when Othello rejoices at his reunion with Desdemona by saying, 'It gives me wonder great as my content | To see you here before me' (2.1.178). As a verb it can also mean 'please', or something stronger, as when Prospero promises to show Alonso 'a wonder to content ye | As much as me my dukedom'—the wonder is Alonso's apparently lost son playing chess with Miranda (5.1.172–3). But when Shakespeare's characters use 'content' as an adjective, they are usually enjoining someone to, or acknowledging, resignation or patience. The first Oxford English Dictionary definition is 'having one's hopes bounded by what one has, though that may be less than one could have wished.' For example, in *As You Like It*, Touchstone, after complaining about the Forest of Arden, says, 'When I was at home I was in a better place; but travellers must be content' (2.4.12–14). Angelo says to Isabella, 'Be content, fair maid. | It is the law, not I, condemn your brother' (2.2.81–2). The term is often used when conflicting wills are negotiating, and in a case of forced conversion it leaves some desirable ambiguity about the degree of enthusiasm with which an assent is made. Clearly 'I am content' was a formula that could be used by a Christian in a pressured conversion.

The likelihood of Shakespeare's knowing Cranmer's words may be increased because he seems to have been particularly interested in Cranmer, who, like him, wrote speeches for public performance (in Cranmer's case, in the liturgy), took language from everywhere, and arguably was similar in often trying to mediate opposing views. Tom Bishop has recently shown many similarities and parallels between Shakespeare's ritual deposition of Richard II and Foxe's narration of the ritual degradation of Cranmer.[36] And Cranmer, as Jeffrey Knapp says, 'Shakespeare's one peace-loving bishop', is one of the heroes of Shakespeare's much later co-authored play *Henry VIII*. He is put on trial before Bishop Gardiner, his truth and integrity are vindicated by the king, and near the end of the play he baptizes Princess Elizabeth and prophesies the glories of her reign and that of her successor King James. In this play, says Walter Cohen, the one where Shakespeare comes closest to treating religious persecution in England directly, 'The notion of conscience...is deployed by the playwright to judge Catholics and Protestants alike.'[37]

One other detail of the language around the conversion might have made some of Shakespeare's audience might think of Cranmer, or at least of the many forced conversions between Protestant and Catholic in England's recent history. The Duke who presides over the trial, upon hearing of Antonio's conditions for mitigating Shylock's penalties, says, 'He shall do this, or else I do *recant* | The pardon that I late pronounced here' (4.1.386; emphasis mine). 'Recant' is an unusual word for withdrawing a pardon.[38] The word on its own would not necessarily have recalled Cranmer specifically, but it does juxtapose the Christian/Jewish issues of the play more immediately with heresy trials within Christendom. The famous story of Cranmer's final reversal might well have contributed to the likelihood that the word 'recant' would call him to mind, even more than the word 'content', and especially to the likelihood that he would be suggested by the two words in conjunction. In some editions of Foxe from Shakespeare's time, one of the headings of Cranmer's story is 'The Archbishop Content to Recant'.[39]

Thus Protestants as well as Catholics in Shakespeare's audience might have in their literal or spiritual ancestry members who had converted under pressure—if not so dramatically as Cranmer or Shylock—and might have been sympathetic to Shylock in the final section of the trial scene.[40] Analogously, showing sympathy across a religious boundary, in an account of Cranmer's death, a Catholic bystander, J.A., writes, 'I think there was none that pitied not his case, & bewailed not his fortune.'[41]

Shakespeare added the forced conversion of Shylock to the story in his source for *The Merchant of Venice* because freedom of conscience was literally a burning issue in his own time, and because it would give a highly theatrical change of sympathies to the end of the traditional story of the Jewish moneylender. Even the love story portion of this play includes imagery to recall the threats to such freedom. Portia says to her suitor Bassanio, 'I fear you speak upon the rack, | Where men enforced do speak anything' (3.2.32–3), and earlier Antonio promises that his credit will be 'racked' (1.1.189–1) to lend Bassanio money. In the last two speeches of the play, Portia and Graziano jokingly refer to the men's imminent questions to the women as 'inter'gatories' (5.1.297, 299)—a word used of the questioning in heresy trials. Sixteen interrogatories were part of Cranmer's trial.[42] A pressured conversion also appears metaphorically in the lovers' plot, when Bassanio asks Graziano to baptize himself before they go to Belmont—'allay with some cold drops of modesty | Thy skipping spirit' (2.2.167–8). Graziano promises to 'wear prayer books in my pocket... while grace is saying hood mine eyes | Thus with my hat, and sigh and say "amen".' (2.2.173, 154–5). But Graziano himself underlines the punitive elements in Shylock's forced conversion:

> In christ'ning shalt thou have two godfathers.
> Had I been judge, thou shouldst have had ten more,
> To bring thee to the gallows, not the font.
>
> (4.1.394–6).

True, Shylock is not being executed, but Graziano suggests how closely the forced conversion is linked with the wish for Shylock's death, and underlines what Sigurd Burckhardt calls 'the violence and merciless secularity of this act of grace.'[43] It is a bitter irony that grace is the word from which Graziano's name is derived.

Il Pecorone never gives its moneylender either a family or a name; he is simply 'the Jew'. Shylock has both, but in the trial scene, after he denies Portia's request that he provide Antonio with a surgeon, she never uses his name again. After she produces the anti-alien law that would condemn him to death, she addresses him simply as 'Jew', in the same hostile way Graziano does. The first quarto, the base text of all modern editions, underlines this identification by its frequent use of 'Jew' rather than 'Shylock' as a speech heading, particularly in the trial scene. Nevertheless, once Portia suggests that he might die if he takes more or less than an exact pound, he becomes Shylock again, starting with the speech 'Give me my principal and let me go.'

(4.1.330).[44] This speech shift marks the end of the threat he has posed to Antonio, and his role as a representative of the power of the law, allegorically associated with Judaism by the Christianity of Shakespeare's time.[45]

As has been many times observed, Shylock's nominal conversion, which theoretically recognizes his salvageable soul and brings him into the Christian community, on stage has the effect of exiling him from the play, and he is hardly mentioned in the last act. Ironically, at the very end, in presenting Lorenzo and Jessica their enforced 'deed of gift', Nerissa, now Graziano's wife, refers to Shylock as 'the rich Jew' (5.1.291) as if the conversion had never taken place. She might simply be referring to his ethnicity, or recognizing that this conversion could not be sincere. Or her lines might exemplify the contemporary doubt that Jewish conversion ever could be sincere. Note that Graziano refers to the freely converted Jessica as an 'infidel'—surely not thinking of the way that word would now describe her from the Jewish point of view.[46] The phenomenon of secretly believing differently from one's public profession was frequent enough in Shakespeare's time to be given the name Nicodemism, so it would not only be in Shylock's case that the audience might see coerced conversions as ineffective.[47]

The Shakespeare I imagine, who adds a forced conversion with the expectation that some spectators will feel that hostility to Shylock goes too far, fits well with Jeffrey Knapp's view, developed in *Shakespeare's Tribe*, of the Shakespeare concerned for religious toleration. Knapp shows that the plays tend to give negative views of divisive Catholic bishops and cardinals and also of divisive puritans, but often equivocate about whether the satirized puritanical characters, such as Angelo and Malvolio, are really puritans at all. He argues that Shakespeare is so much against divisiveness in religion that he does not want to be divisive in his own satire.[48] Furthermore, recent biographical research on Shakespeare is tantalizing with its implications with regard to the possible relevance to his own life of *The Merchant of Venice*. Less known than his father's possible recusancy is the fact that Shakespeare and his father both had sidelines in moneylending—his father, at least, at the illegal rate of 20 per cent, which certainly counted as usury.[49]

Was it because of his submerged identification with Shylock as a moneylender that Shakespeare, in writing about forced conversion, focused on a Jew rather than on a Catholic or a Protestant? Perhaps it was more immediately that, because of state censorship of the theatre, directly treating current or recent persecution in England within Christianity would have been much more dangerous. I know of only one Elizabethan play dealing directly with recent English religious persecution, *The Conflict of Conscience*, written in 1581, under the Protestant Queen Elizabeth by Nathaniel Woodes, a minister in Northern England. In this case, the characters who force conversion, Tyranny and Cardinal, are clearly identified as Catholic.[50] It is not clear whether this play was ever performed.

However, I am not arguing that *The Merchant of Venice* is only about forced conversion. The play is not a unified attack on anti-Semitism or religious intolerance. Shylock is not a hero. But we don't have to find Gloucester a hero to recoil at his blinding, and I think some audience members would have reacted similarly to Shylock's forced conversion.[51] Thomas Nashe in *The Unfortunate Traveller* describes an analogous sudden sympathy touching observers of Anabaptists being tormented for heresy: they 'now thought them, suffering, to be sheep brought innocent to the shambles, whenas before they deemed them as a number of wolves up in arms against the shepherds.'[52]

Is there any direct evidence of such sympathy for Shylock? Comments on this point in the play would have been extremely dangerous to make in Shakespeare's time—and extant criticism on such plot points before the late eighteenth century is rare indeed. The play's stage and reception history shows that it can be treated both as an anti-Semitic play and also as a play about, and critical of, anti-Semitism. But the likelihood of some contemporary unease at Shylock's conversion may well be heightened when we recall that his words of submission echo Cranmer's, and that Daborne's Ward expresses regret about a pressured decision to convert that is clearly presented as wrong with the same phrase that Shylock uses. Shakespeare's world was different from ours in many ways. Still, Shylock's conversion is one of the many points where the discomfort most modern audiences feel is not simply a matter of our historical distance, but a possibility in the text from the start.

Note that I say a possibility. I do not claim that everybody in Shakespeare's original audience had sympathy for Shylock, even at his most vulnerable points. People do and did respond to the same play, even in the same theatre, differently. René Girard's claim that *Merchant* is written for a double audience, some of whom scapegoat Shylock, others of whom look critically at his scapegoating, is quite plausible.[53] Though a director can, probably, today, limit the number of people in the audience who would see Shylock through Graziano's eyes, it is hard to exclude this possibility. But we should not assume, either, that all the original audience were Grazianos and Antonios all the time. Many of them might have changed the way they felt about Shylock as the play proceeded.

Antonio—'Good' or 'Tainted Wether'?

Is Antonio an outsider or not? And if so, what kind of outsider is he? At the beginning, Salerio and Solanio try to get him out of his sadness and Gratiano mocks him for the silence that accompanies it; though Antonio does not get a chapter in *The Stranger in Shakespeare*, Fiedler puts him in the category of 'odd man out' since he is notoriously uncoupled in the last act's revelry of teasing about sex.[54] Yet Salerio and Solanio praise him later; Portia rewards him with the return of his ships. The ambiguity of Antonio's position in *Merchant* is connected with the ambiguity of same-sex love in early modern England—it could be glorified as male friendship, but it could also be suspect as sodomy, and the ambiguity was maintained further because the culture did not believe in a distinct homosexual minority, for whom alone such desire was possible.[55] But even if we assume that Antonio is too respected to be accused of sodomy, does his melancholy make him an outsider? It was a temperament that could be idealized in the Renaissance—but that's not the language with which Antonio's temperament is discussed. Furthermore, Antonio, as a merchant, is of a less prestigious class than Bassanio and his friends, even if he has more money than they do. This is why he can be arrested for debt, as Bassanio, a lord, cannot.[56] Does this make him an outsider? In Shakespeare's source he is of an older generation than Bassanio, and he is usually still cast as older—does this make him an outsider? There are many different ways groups can divide themselves, many different kinds and degrees of exclusion, some very minor and temporary, and this play puts its main emphasis on Shylock's exclusion; nevertheless there are differences among the Venetian Christian men, and very early on in the play Antonio's difference is marked.

Antonio's melancholy is announced in his first words—'In sooth, I know not why I am so sad' (1.1.1)—and, unlike the weariness Portia claims in her first lines, arguably follows him to the end. It is not simply proclaimed in one line, but discussed by the other characters for almost all of the first 112 lines. 'Why then, you are in love' (1.1.46), is one of the explanations of his sadness offered by Solanio. Lover's melancholy is one of the categories on which Burton will spend many pages in his *Anatomy*, as well as one that, in Shakespeare's next play, Rosalind, Orlando, and Jaques will play with. Burton includes sodomites among his examples of unhappy lovers, and like other Englishmen of his time, he sees Italians as particularly prone to sodomy.[57] However, this thought might hover in the background of Antonio's characterization rather than appear established beyond doubt. As Paul Hammond observes, 'Shakespeare carefully [leaves the relationship between Antonio and Bassanio] undefined.' Other explanations of his melancholy are offered—his preoccupation with his merchandise (he denies this explicitly) and his wish to be thought wise. It is, however, beyond doubt that he is melancholy (in a way unusual in his circle), loves Bassanio, and gives more to Bassanio than Bassanio gives him in return, except insofar as what Bassanio gives him in return is the enjoyment (to whatever degree) of his youth, beauty, and charm. Shakespeare could have placed their friendship in a quasifamilial/ religious context, as did his source in making Antonio's original, Ansaldo, godfather to Bassanio's original and best friend of his recently deceased father.[58] All that recalls this is that Solanio initially speaks to Antonio of 'Bassanio, your most noble kinsman' (1.1.57). Instead there is an emphasis on Antonio's melancholy and a relationship in which the apparent age, class, and temperamental difference easily casts it as more specifically homoerotic.[59] (Never having met Antonio, Portia says later that since they are friends the two must be similar; this shows the problems of depending on neoplatonic friendship theory to judge people.) When Antonio rejects the view that he must be in love, he exclaims 'Fie, fie!' (1.1.46), a word sometimes used in Elizabethan drama when an unacceptable sexual allusion has been made (as when the Duchess of Malfi responds to her brother Ferdinand's innuendo about women's enjoyment of sex).

The men of Venice use the word 'love' fairly freely of their relationships—Graziano, giving advice to Antonio to talk more, says, 'I love thee, and 'tis my love that speaks' (1.1.87). When Bassanio acknowledges that to Antonio he owes 'the most, in money and in love' (1.1.131), in asking for more money, he may sound as if he is putting all the friends on a continuum, but when Antonio says that Bassanio wrongs him in trying to 'wind about my love with circumstance' (1.1.154) when he is willing to do anything to help, the suggestion continues that their relationship is special, at least from Antonio's point of view. There is no suggestion of disapproval of this love in the choral language of Solanio and Salerio: he is 'good Antonio' (2.8.25) and 'a kinder gentleman treads not the earth' (2.8.35). Salerio notes deep emotion at his parting with Antonio—the 'tears' (46) and 'affection wondrous sensible' (48) with which he wrings Bassanio's hand at parting. It is not surprising that Solanio notes Antonio's 'heaviness' (52) and makes a comment very close to his earlier suggestion of love-sickness: 'I think he only loves the world for him' (50)—words recalling concluding lines in Shakespeare's sonnets such as 'if the while I think on thee, dear friend | All losses are restored, and sorrows end' (Sonnet 30). But 'the public language of male friendship contains within it the possibility of a more private and sexual relation'.[60]

As Alan Sinfield points out, in this period a man could be married and also love men without a necessary sense of conflict.[61] King James was an obvious example. Nevertheless, the dramatization of the relationships of Antonio, Bassanio, and Portia in *Merchant* provide an outstanding evidence for Bruce Smith's statement that an early modern man might well be faced with the question of whether his emotional loyalties were devoted more to male friendship or to marriage. Antonio's language frequently sets these bonds explicitly in competition. The farewell speech as recounted by the Venetian choral figure of Salerio memorably introduces the theme of Antonio's disparagement of Bassanio's marriage by contrast to their relationship. He urges Bassanio to spend as much time on the courtship as he needs by saying 'Slubber not business for my sake'

(2.8.38). After referring to Bassanio's 'mind of love' (42) he encourages him to 'courtship and such fair ostents of love | As shall conveniently become you there' (44–5). This emphasis on what is appropriate and external contrasts with the emotion he himself is showing at their separation.

When we finally see Antonio making a request of Bassanio instead of simply giving to him, that hint of disparagement continues. Antonio is desperate since his ships are wrecked and Shylock is going to pursue the pound of flesh, and he asks to see Bassanio before he dies. The letter finishes, 'Notwithstanding, use your pleasure. If your love do not persuade you to come, let not my letter' (3.2.318–19). In other words, he is here setting not Bassanio's business with Portia—the engagement has been made—but his pleasure with Portia against his love of Antonio. (Portia's response, 'O love! Dispatch all business, and be gone' (319) invokes *her* claim to call Bassanio love.) Elsewhere in Shakespeare the words 'use' and 'pleasure' frequently have sexual double meanings, intended, as in Sonnet 20's 'thy love's use' (1.1.197–8) or unintended, as when Isabella in *Measure for Measure* says to Angelo 'I am come to know your pleasure' (2.4.31), and it is suggestive to put these connotations together with Antonio's scorn for 'use' in the sense of 'interest' as taken by Shylock. Antonio likes to see himself as above 'use' in either economic or sexual senses. The audience, especially the modern audience, may well feel that this is self-deception. But there could also be audience members who take his bond with Bassanio more seriously than Bassanio's bond with Portia. And regardless of which an audience member would like Bassanio to prefer, the question remains: is Antonio an insider because Venice is a world of male bonding, which in many literary and social traditions has been valued above marriage? Or is he an outsider because it is a world organized around heterosexual marriage? Or is he both?

Antonio's strangest line, uttered in the trial scene just before Portia enters, is 'I am a tainted wether of the flock | Meetest for death' (4.1.113–14). It links his position in the play and his melancholy with both castration and disease, and, in the immediately following lines—'The weakest kind of fruit | Drops earliest to the ground, and so let me'—with weakness. It may seem that Antonio sees himself as a scapegoat, a sacrificial animal with a semi-biblical doom, the structural prototype of the outsider at his/its most vulnerable. However, a 'tainted wether' is not the sort of sacrificial animal expected in the Bible. Leviticus 6.6, for example, prescribes a *ram without taint* as an offering to be made to atone for sin. The best kind of animal of a breed should be sacrificed, not one that is castrated and tainted. In a time when more audiences knew the Bible, perhaps this hinted that either Antonio's self-hatred or another taint flaws his attempt at self-sacrifice. Ironically, the name of Shakespeare's closest source, *Il Pecorone*, means, literally, 'big sheep', though figuratively 'dunce' or 'blockhead', referring to characters who behave extravagantly in love; did Shakespeare write Antonio's words with a glance at these associations?[62] Or, linking Antonio with the theme of persecution for religion explored elsewhere in the play, would the phrase have recalled 'mangy sheep', an image borrowed from St. Jerome to refer to heretics by some early modern preachers?

His farewell in the trial scene makes it explicit that Antonio imagines his death as victory in a rivalry between himself and Portia over who loves Bassanio more, or whose attitude deserves to be called love.

> Say how I loved you, speak me fair in death,
> And, when the tale is told, bid her be judge
> Whether Bassanio had not once a love.
>
> (4.1.270-2)

This rivalry is further pointed by Bassanio's reciprocating farewell, in which he offers to sacrifice 'life itself, my wife, and all the world' (279) to Shylock in order to deliver Antonio, and Portia, in her disguise, notes how unattractive a wife would find this offer.

After Portia saves Antonio with her quibble and anti-alien law, she sets a test for Bassanio which further reinforces the theme of rivalry. Having heard Antonio declare that they are 'indebted...in love and service...evermore' (408-9) to her/him as Balthasar, she asks from Bassanio 'for your love' (423) the ring that she, as Portia, gave him: 'you in love shall not deny me this' (425). Bassanio refuses this, citing his vow to her, but Antonio persuades him in the following terms: 'Let his deservings and my love withal | Be valued 'gainst your wife's commandëment' (446-7). Once more marriage is seen as a matter of duty, not of love, even as the term 'love' can be applied to a service done by an apparent stranger. This picture of marriage does, of course, have some basis in the fact that marriages in the time period often were made for dynastic or economic reasons, but Portia's vision of her marriage is clearly more emotional.

Much of the last act of the play consists in the game in which Portia teases Bassanio about what happened to the ring, while Antonio stands by uncomfortably. 'I am th' unhappy subject of these quarrels' (5.1.237), he acknowledges, repeating the reference to his unhappiness with which the play began. Portia does not stop teasing Bassanio about his duplicity until Antonio finally pledges by his soul (a complement, as he notes, to his earlier pledge by his body) that Bassanio will not break faith with her again. She now has enforced his profession of belief in the importance of marital love, in a gesture perhaps parallel to Shylock's enforced agreement to convert to Christianity.[63] Next she brings forth letters to assure marital fidelity to Bassanio and Graziano and prosperity to all present. The taciturnity criticized by Graziano appears again, though transmuted to suggest the silence of amazement, when Antonio's response to this news of his ships' rich reappearance is 'I am dumb' (277).

Alan Sinfield notes the ambiguity of the ending of *Merchant*. In 1905 the play was performed with Antonio and Bassanio entering the house together.[64] I have seen it played against text to emphasize a continuation of male bonding between Antonio, Bassanio, and Graziano while Portia speaks her lines from offstage. But both those choices are unusual. In the Radford film of 2004 and the 2010 Broadway production directed by Daniel Sullivan, Antonio is one of several characters whose isolation at the end is stressed. If the text is examined carefully, the key question about Antonio at the ending is how to take Antonio's last lines,

> Sweet lady, you have given me life and living;
> For here I read for certain that my ships
> Are safely come to road.
>
> (285–7)

Portia has given him life when she saved him during the trial, now she gives him living. Antonio has already said in the trial scene that he is reconciled to death rather than living on without wealth 'To view with hollow eye and wrinkled brow | An age of poverty' (4.1.265–6).

Shylock, when at his most vulnerable, says, 'You take my life | When you do take the means whereby I live' (371–2), words recalled by Antonio's at the end. But at the beginning of the play Antonio stated that the risks to his ships were not enough to make him sad. Is their return enough to make him happy? Is the wealth that he professed himself glad not to outlive really material wealth, or is it his companionship with Bassanio, his belief in Bassanio's love? Antonio's earlier explanation why dying is better than experiencing the misery of poverty is a kind of analogue of the melancholy bravado of Shakespeare's Sonnet 90 about why losing his love sooner is better than losing him later: 'other strains of woe, which now seem woe, | Compared with loss of thee will not seem so.' Perhaps Antonio's last speech is another profession of conversion, this time of being satisfied with material goods instead of love. Sinfield says, 'Shylock, for the social cohesion of Venice, has to be killed, beggared, expelled, converted, or any combination of those penalties. Same-sex passion doesn't matter nearly so much; Antonio has only to be relegated to a subordinate position.'[65]

Little that is distinctive about Antonio appears in Shakespeare's major source. Ansaldo has none of Antonio's melancholy temperament, though he is understandably upset when he thinks his son, as he refers to him, has died, and each time he finds out about the loss of the money he has lent. He is not sad at Giannetto leaving him to woo the lady, he does not refer to himself as anything like 'the tainted wether of the flock', he does not disparage the love of the lady of Belmont or boast of his own, he does not beg Giannetto to give away her ring to the lawyer, he is not uncomfortable in the last scene during the lovers' quarrel, and he marries a lady's maid who was helpful to Giannetto. The suggestions of homoeroticism in Antonio's relationship to Bassanio all are Shakespeare's additions, although *Il Pecorone* does say of Bassanio's prototype that 'All the ladies and gentlemen appeared in love with him.'[66]

Does Antonio say anything to suggest a sense of a minority sexual identity, or membership in a dissident group? He has no verbal parallel to the clear way that Shylock claims equal rights as a Jew or Edmund rights as a bastard. When Antonio sounds melancholy, when he calls himself 'a tainted wether' and 'the weakest kind of fruit', there is no sense of any consolation or romantic glory in being part of a group of melancholy people. It has been argued that Antonio's language suggests internalized homophobia, but he is never explicit about why he feels tainted. On the other hand, as he thinks he is about to die, Antonio is proud of his love for Bassanio: 'When the tale is told, bid [Portia] be judge, | Whether Bassanio had not once a love' (4.1.272). That attitude, however, does not explicitly continue in the last scene.

Among nobles in fifteenth century Venice, Stanley Chojnacki has shown, 42.3 per cent apparently never married, a strikingly large number. Though Chojnacki speculates that some died too young to marry, and some were bachelors because of the lack of money for inheritance for all sons in large families, he also speculates that some had 'a disinclination to marry for sexual reasons'.[67] Venice punished active sodomy by death, but according to Guido Ruggiero the passive partner, usually much younger, 'was normally let off with a light penalty or no penalty at all', though suspects were routinely tortured and there are records of a sixteen-year-old whose genitals and left arm were mutilated by torture before being sentenced to two years of prison and three of exile.[68] Michael Rocke finds that in Florence—in the later fifteenth century—'the majority of local males at least once during their lifetimes were officially incriminated for engaging in homosexual relations', though for most it appears to have been part of their adolescence or twenties,[69] and Nicholas Davidson says that across Italy, the prosecution of sodomy diminished in the fifteenth and sixteenth centuries. Though most of this research refers to time a century or more before *Merchant* was written, it suggests that, on the one hand, England's suspicion that sodomy was frequent in Italy may have had some basis, and on the other hand, it also reinforces the sense that categories of sexuality were still somewhat fluid. However, the evidence about Antonio remains ambiguous. And it is not clear that historical evidence about Italian sexuality at the approximate time would be more relevant to the play than evidence about English sexuality at the approximate time, since we don't know what Shakespeare or his audience really knew about Italy, and since his plays very often refer to his own society even when ostensibly set elsewhere.

At any rate, in England there was much less prosecution for sodomy, which had only been made a crime punished by the state, as opposed to the church, in in 1533–4. 'During the forty-five years of

Queen Elizabeth's reign and the twenty-three years of King James I's reign only six men are recorded as having been indicted for sodomy in the Home County assizes, for example, with only one conviction.'[70] Those few prosecutions mainly involved rape of a minor. Alan Bray argues that this shows an English refusal to see that ordinary men, as opposed to foreigners or traitors, could commit anything as bad as sodomy.[71] However, Kenneth Borris maintains that the reason prosecutions were few was the English legal system, which demanded witnesses who would testify that anal penetration had occurred, and, unlike the continental system, did not use torture to get confessions.

Are the Women Converted? For Whom is the Ending Happy?

Jessica's conversation with her new husband Lorenzo in the fifth act is the occasion for Lorenzo's speech about the harmony of the stars and of immortal souls, and this is sometimes taken to suggest that their marriage contributes to an overall emphasis on harmony at the end of the play. According to some critics, this shows that the hostility to Shylock in the play's world is not based on biology and therefore is really anti-Judaism rather than anti-Semitism. Other critics explain it by a general sense that Jewish women could be more easily accepted as Christian than Jewish men. Recent productions, respecting Jewish identity, have often suggested Jessica's regret about her marriage and/or conversion at the end; some have shown Jessica and Lorenzo visibly alienated from each other. Trevor Nunn's film version (2004) ends with Jessica, clearly unhappy, singing the Hebrew song which Shylock had earlier sung to her.[72] Is Jessica an insider who becomes an outsider, or not? Does she unsuccessfully want to become an insider? If she succeeds, should this be considered a good thing or a betrayal?

As is surprisingly often true with Shakespeare's text, the answer is indeterminate. In 3.2, when Jessica first appears in Belmont, Graziano doesn't accept her as a Christian: he refers to 'Lorenzo and his infidel' (217). Bassanio doesn't even mention her in his greeting to Lorenzo and Salerio. While the others are concerned about Antonio's letter, it's left to a perhaps repentant Graziano to say, 'Nerissa, cheer yon stranger. Bid her welcome' (3.2.236) Jessica wants to join her husband's friends and dissociate herself from Shylock and other

Jews—by comparison to them, she thinks she *can* be an insider in this community. After hearing about Antonio's business failures and indebtedness to Shylock, she recalls his preference for the pound of flesh over money in speech to 'Tubal and to Cush, *his* countrymen' (3.2.284; emphasis added). Not *our* countrymen. Jessica is, accordingly, accepted well enough that Portia trusts her and Lorenzo to keep Belmont in her absence, sharing with them a secret she does not tell Bassanio.

The opening of the last act, beginning 'The moon shines bright' (5.1.1), was cited by C. L. Barber as an example of 'full expression of harmony' unparalleled in Shakespeare until the late romances.[73] But all the love stories Lorenzo and Jessica recall end unhappily. Perhaps Jessica is trying to relieve postmarital anxiety by joking when she accuses Lorenzo of 'Stealing her soul with many vows of faith, | And ne'er a true one' (5.1.19–20). However, the sequence shows that they both know classical mythology (unlike, for example, the ill-matched Touchstone and Audrey), and if she is going too far, Lorenzo forgives her. The ambiguity continues when Jessica responds to Lorenzo's description of the music of the spheres and of immortal souls, and his call for the musicians to play, by saying 'I am never merry when I hear sweet music' (5.1.68), her last words. Lorenzo responds, 'The reason is your spirits are attentive', proceeding to discuss how music calms colts and moves trees. But is she really saying that she pays attention to the music, or is this an acknowledgment of sadness (a frequent opposite to merriment in Shakespeare), like those heard from Antonio and Portia near the beginning? Should we imagine Jessica as having the regrets parallel to those Daborne would, a few years later, imagine that Ward would have if he converted to Islam and 'abjured the name and belief [his] ancestors left to [his] being'? Is Lorenzo simply not understanding Jessica because he does not want to, thinking she has been turned into an insider when she, having entered the world she thought she wanted, still feels like she is outside? This interpretation makes the most sense of her last line, unless 'merry' has suggestions of unruliness (it could, but the Oxford English Dictionary examples of this all associate this usage with drinking too much) and Lorenzo is glad to have her under control. These multiple possibilities for Jessica's mood at the end are close to the multiple possibilities about Antonio's.

Portia too, after Bassanio chooses the right casket, says that she is undergoing a conversion in marriage, with words partly suggestive of economics, partly of deference: 'Myself and what is mine to you and yours | Are now converted' (3.2.166–7). Some recent productions have suggested that Portia is also alienated from her husband at the end, making this another unhappy conversion. On the other hand, after this pledge Portia never acts or speaks as if she has really given up her power, her money, or her house, except insofar as she is pretending in the courtroom to be a boy legal prodigy.

Before considering the end, it must be noted that Portia is from the beginning both an outsider and an insider. As Nerissa says, her good fortune is abundant; she has wealth, beauty, class privilege, and intelligence. On the other hand, her father's will sets up a test for her suitors rather than allowing her to make her own choice, and although this is an idiosyncratic limitation it is suggestive of the official subordination of women in her culture; indeed, upper-class women were more likely to be under pressure from parents about whom they would marry. When Portia caricatures her suitors, she is the insider dismissing men who fit into national stereotypes (including the Englishman, whose problem it is that he doesn't know any other languages, a metatheatrical joke on English ethnocentricity), but also she is the potentially subordinated wife contemplating what it would be like to be married, for example, to a man who 'doth nothing but talk of his horse' (1.2.35–6).

The theme of Portia as a justified disdainer of ethnic outsiders continues as the Princes of Morocco and Aragon choose the wrong caskets. She is tactful enough while they are present, as she will later be with Shylock, but after they leave, shows her distaste for Morocco—'Let all of his "complexion" choose me so' (2.7.79)—and the folly of both suitors. She is no Desdemona. On the other hand, their speeches discourage the audience from having sympathy with them. As they speak on, they show their egotism and their obliviousness to the clues the caskets offer them and even to Portia's words. When Portia says to Aragon, 'To these injunctions everyone must swear | That comes to hazard for my worthless self' (2.9.16–17), he responds, 'And so have I addressed me', seeming to agree that she is worthless. Aragon has the pride Elizabethans expected to find in Spaniards. Yet he is duly humbled by the message from the fool's head inside the casket, and could receive some audience sympathy as he leaves saying, 'With one fool's head I came to woo, | But I go away with two' (2.9.74–5).

When Bassanio takes the same test, Portia is no longer in danger of being the pawn of her father's will. Knowing the secret of the caskets, she also knows how to give Bassanio hints about it—the deceitfulness of appearances, the song in which every line rhymes with 'lead'. Bassanio even unwittingly anticipates this outcome—accepting the role of the accused traitor, he observes that she, his 'torturer [,] Doth teach [him] answers for deliverance' (3.2. 37–8). Neither Morocco nor Aragon knows, as Bassanio does, how to use or respond to the language of modesty at the right time, or, as Katherine Maus has pointed out, to a language of metaphor associated with a Christian cultural background.[74] But Bassanio can read the clues. Portia, having apparently submitted to the casket test while orchestrating it for her purposes, has the husband she wants, and when he receives the letter from Antonio about his danger, seems to have the insider's monetary power that can solve all difficulties: 'Pay him six thousand and deface the bond' (3.2.298).

However, in order to resolve Antonio's problems she has to become more truly an outsider in going to Venice dressed as a boy. The trial scene shows that Shakespeare can imagine an outsider—a nonVenetian woman in an all-male courtroom—who will be admired for her intelligence as she, posing as a boy, deals with the more threatening outsider Shylock on behalf of Antonio. Antonio's melancholy now seems less incongruous than earlier as he prepares to sacrifice himself for Bassanio and, in a sense, as he says, for the continuation of Venetian international trade (3.3.26–31). As she earlier respected her father's law and pretended to respect Morocco and Aragon, Portia, dressed as Balthasar, admits, more clearly than any Venetian, that Shylock has a claim in justice. As she seems to orchestrate preparations for flesh-cutting, she shows that Shylock's desire for vengeance has become the disregard for human life of a moral outsider. Immediately, Antonio and Bassanio make their emotional farewells to each other, ending in Bassanio's wish to sacrifice his wife (as well as his life and all the world) to save Antonio. Portia/Balthasar responds, 'Your wife would give you little thanks for that | If she were by to hear you make the offer' (4.1.283–4). Portia and the audience are reminded that she is not just, in her disguise, an outsider in Venice, or in a law court, but that she is also an outsider to the friendship of Bassanio and Antonio. Even Shylock notices this, saying, 'These be the Christian husbands' (4.1.290), and regretting that his daughter is married to one of them.

Through Antonio's language in much of the play and Portia's trickery with her ring, the play frequently positions heterosexual marital love and the love of male friends as in opposition to each other, although in her words about the friendship before she meets Antonio, Portia portrays them as in harmony. Is Portia the outsider because her society is built on male bonds, or is Antonio the outsider because it is built on marriage? Whose defence of relationship (whether as an outsider or an insider) should we applaud as justified, and who should we consider an interloper? Were marital bonds generally weaker at the time the play was written than now, because among the nobility marriage was often more a financial than an emotional tie, and so was Shakespeare more innovative in giving the victory to Portia? Or is this an irrelevant question, because of the long tradition making courtship and marriage the expected plot of comedy? The answers we give to these questions depend not only on our ideas of social and literary history, and our theatrical experience, but also on our investments in same-sex and/or cross-sex bonding, and the multiple possibilities of understanding the play in these terms are part of why it is so fascinating.

However we feel about it, the words of the text present Portia as winning a power struggle over Bassanio and Antonio at the end. As Karen Newman has shown, she has won partly by the grand gestures of liberality she is able to make, but also partly by the her ability to disguise herself as a boy and trick both Shylock and Bassanio, one into showing explicitly his desire for Antonio's death, one into giving away the ring he has promised to keep.[75] In the earlier scene, Shylock is punished by Antonio and the state; here Bassanio has only to be grilled by Portia and repent in embarrassment—'I never more will break an oath with thee' (5.1.247)—and briefly endure the fantasy of being cuckolded by the young doctor who was actually Portia in disguise. When Bassanio says, 'Were you the doctor and I knew you not?' (5.1.279) he recognizes Portia's power, and reconciles himself to it with a joke, his last line in the play: 'Sweet doctor, you shall be my bedfellow. | When I am absent, then lie with my wife' (5.1.283–4). The joke may suggest that she can win his loyalty from Antonio partly because she can, imaginatively, be a boy to Bassanio as well as a wife. But Antonio either is genuinely glad at the news of his ships' safety that she gives him, or decides to put a good face on it, for his dignity and the general harmony: 'Sweet lady, you have given me life and living' (5.1.285).

We don't really know whether to believe Bassanio's promise to Portia, if we imagine what comes after the fifth act: nevertheless, she is the one who presides over the further distribution of gifts after both Bassanio and Antonio have spoken their last in the play, until the final speech of Graziano. And when she jokes about being charged on 'inter'gatories', she reminds us of the interrogation in trials for heresy and treason, as well as the interrogation she has been giving Bassanio and could give him again in a less playful way. Graziano may promise a sexual possessiveness of Nerissa at the end, but as often in Shakespeare's comedies the central female character has more power than the others do. Belmont is still, as she has just said, Portia's house (5.1.272).[76]

I have earlier pointed to some parallels in the outcomes for Antonio and Shylock. Let me return to this point, and this time include Portia in the comparison. Like Portia, Shylock believes that rings should stay within marriage, and the way she repeatedly demands her ring from Bassanio, as Sigurd Burckhardt pointed out, echoes the way Shylock repeats his demand for his bond.[77] Both sometimes treated as suspect, they seize on whatever advantage a contract or promise can give them to exert power. Antonio, by contrast, has no contract or promise to use in his relationship with Bassanio, but appeals to their love. As Shylock's survival partly depends on his agreeing to a religion in which he does not believe, and passing on his property to a son-in-law he does not want, Antonio's survival as Bassanio's friend, at the end, apparently depends on his swearing to Bassanio's fidelity in his marriage to Portia. This is a marriage which previously Antonio has spoken deprecatingly of as a matter of business and duty, not of love. It is as if Antonio must change his faith in same-sex love to faith in marriage. So Shylock's persistence in asking for what he thinks are his rights is parallel to

Portia's, and his final compromise is parallel to Antonio's—are these two kinds of behaviour the main alternatives for outsiders? Shylock's dependence on money, his own or another's, to gratify his emotional needs is a quality shared by virtually all the major characters. Antonio, Portia, and Shylock are similar from the beginning in their involvement with money, though Antonio presents his as simply generous rather than self-seeking. Spiritual usury was a term used in early Christian theological writing to refer to 'hoping for gratitude, or some other kind of binding obligation, in return for giving a loan'.[78] Perhaps this is as unavoidable in the emotional realm as literal usury has turned out to be in the modern economic realm. But we might consider Kiernan Ryan's critique, '*The Merchant of Venice* unmasks a supposedly civilized society as in fact based on barbarism, on the ruthless priority of economic values over human values.'[79]

However, Ryan misses the extent to which at least some spectators/readers may be less detached from the play than his critique suggests. René Girard's claim that *Merchant* is written for a double audience, some of whom scapegoat Shylock, others of whom look critically at his scapegoating, is quite plausible.[80] But Girard too easily overlooks how thrilling it is for spectators to find their reaction to a character frequently changing, as the character who has been the threatening outsider becomes the threatened one. There is similar fascination in seeing the way Antonio and Portia navigate the play—spectators might, for example, begin feeling sympathy for Antonio because of the way he is badgered by Salerio, Solanio, and Graziano about his sadness, and also for Portia because of the conditions of her father's will, but their feelings might change for one or both of them as the play progresses, and one question that might keep their attention in the final act might be who is going to be the emotional insider with Bassanio. And they might also wonder whether Jessica will ever be an insider—although that is a question about which the text of the play gives many fewer clues.

The religious changes in Shakespeare's England may have contributed to a sense in his audience that keeping up with 'who's in, who's out' could be dizzying in real life. Besides, there were many other shifts happening in their social worlds. Shakespeare's ability to manipulate changes of sympathy in his plays may well have been part of the reason so many of them found, and many of us still find, his plays compelling.

2

Outsiders and the Festive Community in Twelfth Night

In *Twelfth Night*, as in *Merchant of Venice*, one character is most clearly an outsider in the sense of one who evokes hostility from a community, and that character has often been the greatest source of interest in the play. A 1640 edition of Shakespeare's poems, listing his achievements as a playwright, builds up to this: 'The Cockpit Galleries, Boxes, all are full | To hear Malvoglio, that cross-gartered Gull.'[1] There is a fascinating similarity between the dynamics of shifting sympathy in these two comedies. Olivia needs Malvolio to handle her household accounts, as Bassanio and Antonio need Shylock to provide money, and so these characters have power resented by others, whom they resent in turn. Malvolio suffers the penalty (lesser than Shylock's) of being tricked into thinking his lady Olivia loves him, wooing her so aggressively that she believes he is mad, and then being imprisoned in a dark house, supposedly to cure his madness. When Malvolio thinks that Olivia loves him and thus is vulnerable to him, as when Shylock thinks Antonio is vulnerable to him because his ships are lost, he goes too far. Then the humiliation of Malvolio, culminating in his confinement for madness, like the forced conversion of Shylock, also goes too far, with shifts in sympathy working somewhat like the 'whirligig of Time' (5.1.364) Feste invokes at the end. And also like *Merchant of Venice*, *Twelfth Night* includes another kind of social outsider, another Antonio who like the earlier one loves another man too much to be included in the heterosexual couples of a traditional comic ending.

But for the two most obvious outsiders of *Twelfth Night*, the chief social reason they are outsiders is more ambiguous than that in *Merchant*. This Antonio, instead of also being marked as an outsider to a comic world by sadness, may have a different outsider role, that of pirate—but he denies it, and productions generally show him released from custody. And while there may be ambiguity about whether most hostility to Shylock focuses on his race, his religion, or his behaviour, it is clear that Shylock is a Jew. With Malvolio, the ambiguity about why he is an outsider is greater. Hostility against him is not clearly based on his religion or class, and it is not even clear what his religion or his class is. And finally, at the end of the play, it seems the court community still needs him for the wedding between Orsino and Viola to take place, so there is ambiguity about whether some continued interaction with him should be imagined.

Malvolio

At the end of the play Malvolio is clearly an outsider, but at the beginning he may seem an insider because he has authority in Olivia's household. But even in that position he is an outsider in the comic theatre because he doesn't like comedy. His first lines in the play are attacks on the play's fool. 'I marvel your ladyship takes delight in such a barren rascal.... Unless you laugh and minister occasion to him, he is gagged.' (1.5.71–2, 74–5). The centre of his characterization is that he is a spoilsport—against laughter and the festive spirit.[2]

However, the hostility he receives has connections with class and religious positions, though both of these are ambiguous for Malvolio. 'Art any more than a steward?' (2.3.102–3), Sir Toby asks condescendingly as Malvolio tries to break up his midnight revels with Sir Andrew and Feste. Sir Toby and Sir Andrew can stay up late enjoying themselves, and so can Feste; Malvolio has to work from the morning on to keep order in his employer's house.[3] But toward the end of the play we learn that he is not a commoner but a gentleman—on the privileged side of what Cristina Malcolmson calls 'the most significant boundary line in the society'.[4] He promises gratitude 'as I am a gentleman' (4.2.75–6) to Feste when he is imprisoned in the dark room, and Olivia later confirms his status (5.1.273). Furthermore, the opposition to him does not come only from the knights, but also from Maria and Fabian, lower-ranking than the knights—Maria, called by Olivia 'my gentlewoman' (1.5.145), is similar to him in class—as well as Feste. Stewards came from a variety of social ranks; the steward in a rich household was highest in status among the servants. Though he had a critical position of trust, it also required isolation—he ate at a table separate from everyone else. Correcting disorder in the household was among the obligations of the position.[5] The pleasure Malvolio has in rebuking others and the ambition he has to take on an even higher position so that he can rebuke them more securely lead to a general resentment. Even before he sees the forged love-note from Olivia, his fantasy about marriage to Olivia culminates in a dream of taking more 'prerogative of speech' (2.5.63) to say 'Cousin Toby... you must amend your drunkenness' (62, 65).

The personal wrong that Toby, Andrew, and Feste feel when he admonishes them takes on resonance of another issue when Toby follows 'Art any more than a steward?' with 'Dost thou think because thou art virtuous there shall be no more cakes and ale?' (2.3.103–4). Maria makes the link both explicit and ambiguous when she says, 'sometimes he is a kind of puritan' (2.3.125). Puritan was a term applied in England to those who felt the established church was not sufficiently holy and evangelical, and too tied to Catholic ritual.[6] It was at this time mainly a term used by those opposed to them, with negative associations, rather than one of self-identification.[7] For example, John Manningham, a law student whose diary records seeing a performance of *Twelfth Night* in 1602, says elsewhere, 'A puritan is such a one as loves God with all his soul, but hates his neighbour with all his heart.' Tensions around religion, for example how much reform there should be and how much ritual, were building in this time and would eventually contribute to the execution of Elizabeth's successor's successor, Charles I, and to the mid-century civil war and revolution.

The character who is most hostile to Malvolio on religious grounds is Toby's hanger-on Sir Andrew Aguecheek. Sir Andrew at once responds to Maria's word 'puritan' with 'O, if I thought that, I'd beat him like a dog' (2.3.126) without being willing to give any other reason. This line makes Andrew's attitude to Malvolio momentarily sound like Graziano's attitude to Shylock.[8] But Maria qualifies her analysis:

> The dev'l a puritan that he is, or anything constantly but a time-pleaser, an affectioned ass, that cons state without book and utters it by great swathes; the best persuaded of himself, so crammed, as he thinks, with excellencies, that it is his grounds of faith that all that look on him love him.
>
> (2.3.131–6)

Shakespeare has it both ways about religious conflict: if Malvolio both is and is not a puritan, stereotypes of both puritans and anti-puritans can be evoked, and Malvolio can be mocked in with religious language, but unlike *Merchant of Venice*, *Twelfth Night* stays on the social level and raises questions of dogma or conversion only in the register of wordplay. But this wordplay had much resonance for Shakespeare's early audiences.

The term puritan had rather loose boundaries, so it is not surprising that Malvolio could not be identified with it exactly, but his opposition to drinking and reveling was certainly characteristic of people who would be called puritans. A writer on their side, John Bate, presented and answered complaints against puritans that included their desire to have a society with 'no good friendship, no sports, no pastime, no not so much as upon the Sunday.'[9] And it is this aspect of Malvolio for which other characters are most immediately taking revenge. When Fabian joins in, he too has a grudge against Malvolio for complaints characteristic of those by puritans: 'You know he brought me out o' favour with my lady about a bear-baiting here' (2.5.6–7).

Other aspects of the images of puritans held by those more comfortable with the established church could also apply to Malvolio. The emphasis on Malvolio's close reading of a text to find a personal meaning in his interpretation could be seen as a parody of the detailed interpretations of Biblical passages made by puritans and other Protestant interpreters.[10] Perhaps his many references to Jove's doing are disguised references to evangelical belief in divine providence and predestination—shared with other Protestants, but not emphasized so much by them. For example, when Malvolio says of Olivia's supposed love for him 'I have limed her, but it is Jove's doing' (3.4.68–9), this could be a parodic reference to the puritan emphasis on God's planning marriages (as well as everything else), but referring to a classical deity with another kind of pretentiousness. And the revelation that this stern and apparently ascetic man is actually interested in wearing a 'branched velvet gown' (2.5.42–53) and a 'rich jewel' (2.6.54) reflects the frequent emphasis on hypocrisy in other satires on puritans written at the time.[11]

Puritans certainly felt that they were the targets of prejudice. Several of their polemical dialogues portrayed their spokespeople as the target of resentment from someone we might call an antipuritan—a character whom Christopher Haigh describes as 'the downmarket dim-witted despiser of religion, who excused his ignorance by calling the zealous "puritans."'[12] 'Godly authors,' he says, 'presented antipuritans as the dregs of society, as "cup companions, alehouse banterers who spent their time in swearing, gaming, drinking, surfeiting, revelry."' In other words, people who behaved much like Andrew and Toby. 'Do ye make an alehouse of my lady's house?' (2.3.80–1), demands Malvolio.

Sir Andrew is also like the stereotype of the antipuritan in his swearing, though just as his violence is only verbal, his oaths are mild. He uses far more oaths than anyone else in the play: he repeatedly swears by 'Faith' (1.3.87, 101; 2.3.9, 13, 22, 41, 51, 64; 2.5.167; 3.2.1), 'Before me' (2.3.157), 'Marry' (3.2.4, 3.4.288) (by Mary), and ''Slight' (2.5.28, 3.2.10), ''Od's lifelings' (5.1.178), and ''Slid' (3.4.353), which meant, respectively, 'By God's light', 'By God's little lives', and 'By God's eyelid'.[13]

Sir Toby is of course known for his drinking, even more than is Sir Andrew, but his name may have also identified him with the antipuritan side in religious terms. A bishop first of Durham, then of York, named Tobie Matthew, was so well-known as a wit that it became a Yorkshire saying 'to a bold man, a jocose fellow, "Thou art a Tobie"'.[14] Shakespeare's Toby is of course a joker of lower comedy, as his surname Belch suggests, but the allusion might still have had some weight for the original audience. Matthew was a friend of Francis Bacon and James I and would not have been congenial to puritans.

Furthermore, the punishment for Malvolio's madness that Sir Toby and Maria devise is particularly galling for a puritan—they describe him as possessed by the devil and in need of exorcism, and this was a ritual that puritans (as well as Catholics) often practiced.[15]

They are echoing his own supposed attitudes and presumed language back to him when Sir Toby asks, 'Which way is he, in the name of sanctity?' (3.4.77) and when Maria says, 'Get him to say his prayers, good Sir Toby' (3.4.107). This kind of mockery continues when Feste disguises himself as a clergyman and calls him 'thou dishonest Satan' (4.2.28).

Some readers and spectators might become sympathetic to Malvolio when they see how often the other characters speak of violence against him, though this violence remains in the realm of fantasy. For more, sympathy may begin to turn toward Malvolio when Toby, Maria, and Fabian pretend that they see him as mad because of possession by the devil and try to exorcize him, and they may see Maria and Toby themselves as like puritan exorcists, but Malvolio is still self-confident enough to say to them scornfully, 'You are idle shallow things, I am not of your element' (3.4.111–12).[16] But when Malvolio appears locked up in a dark room, a treatment for madness often mentioned in plays, he is finally shaken. Productions vary in how much emphasis they give to Malvolio's suffering in confinement, but the text suggests that at this point he should be taken seriously. Quite likely, as Malcolmson argues, he would have received more sympathy from the early audience because of the revelation at this point that he is a gentleman.[17] Malvolio speaks straightforwardly—'Do not think that I am mad. They have laid me here in hideous darkness' (4.2.26–7)—while Feste plays, often nonsensically, with words, voices, and old songs. More of the audience might well be drawn to Malvolio's side because he is so much easier to understand.

> *Feste*: Sayest thou that house is dark?
> *Malvolio*: As hell, Sir Topas.
> *Feste*: Why, it hath bay windows transparent as barricados, and the clerestories toward the south north are as lustrous as ebony.
>
> (4.2.27–30)

Earlier Malvolio had mocked Feste for his dependence on others; now he must acknowledge his own dependence on Feste, after he has put off his clerical disguise, for such simple objects as ink, paper, and light. As Camille Slights says, he has finally lost 'his presumptuous belief that he lives in a sphere above and beyond ordinary human relationships'[18] as he pleads with Feste. Three times he explicitly makes the plea based on similarity to others found so often in the language of Shakespeare's outsiders ('Hath not a Jew eyes?' *Merchant* 3.1.49–50)—nevertheless, as often happens, the claim is undercut. 'I am no more mad than you are' (4.2.42), he says to Feste, who is pretending to be Sir Topas; then 'I am as well in my wits, fool, as thou art' (4.2.80–1), to which Feste makes the obvious answer, 'Then you are mad indeed, if you be no better in your wits than a fool' (4.2.82–3). And the third time, he says, 'I am as well in my wits as any man in Illyria' (4.2.99). Illyria indeed includes many other characters who behave madly or feel they must be mad, or both. The universality of folly or madness was a commonplace reinforced by the popular satire *Praise of Folly* and frequently noted in comedies by Shakespeare and other playwrights. It can even be argued that Malvolio's particular kind of madness earlier in the play has been his belief that everyone else is mad and only he is sane: he greets the midnight revelers with 'My masters, are you mad? Or what are you?' (2.3.77).

In *Twelfth Night*, unlike *Merchant*, some acknowledgment that the punishment of the outsider is excessive is written into the text. Sir Toby himself says 'I would we were well rid of this knavery.... I am now so far in offense with my niece that I cannot with any safety pursue this sport to the upshot' (4.2.60–3), though Feste continues to mock the imprisoned Malvolio. Near the end Malvolio has an opportunity to make his case coherently to Olivia, and he does. For the first time in the play, he speaks in poetry, or at least blank verse, like the aristocrats.

> Why have you suffered me to be imprisoned,
> Kept in a dark house, visited by the priest,
> And made the most notorious geck and gull
> That e'er invention played on?
>
> (5.1.330–4)

Sympathy increases here because he speaks eloquently and usually the staging now makes him visibly diminished. For example, in Trevor Nunn's film he has lost his hairpiece and looks much older.[19] Olivia promises him that he can determine the punishment of his tormentors—'be both the plaintiff and the judge' (5.1. 343)—and concludes, 'He has been most notoriously abused' (5.1.366). Meredith Skura argues convincingly that when Malvolio exclaims

'I'll be revenged on the whole pack of you' (5.1.365), 'pack' clinches his resemblance to the bears frequently baited for amusement near the Elizabethan theatres by a pack of dogs, and that Shakespeare's use of this image pattern here and in other plays shows sympathy both for the bears and for the characters to whom they are compared.[20]

Although Malvolio has gained some sympathy, especially as his treatment has been linked with the history of abuse of those thought to be mad, the baiting and confinement of Malvolio has not given *Twelfth Night* the problematic status that the forced conversion of Shylock has given *The Merchant of Venice*.[21] Why not?

First, the threats in *The Merchant of Venice* are more serious than the threats in *Twelfth Night*. Both Antonio and Shylock are threatened with death, whereas at first the largest weapon against Malvolio as well as the largest he can wield is the threat of Olivia's disfavour. Locking Malvolio in a dark house and treating him as mad is more ominous, but he is released and given a chance to make a coherent protest against his treatment. And at the end Olivia and Orsino want a peaceful reconciliation with Malvolio, and don't demand that he leave his puritan behaviour.

Second, the persecution of the Jews has a longer and more violent history than the persecution of puritans by the established church in England, let alone antagonism to social climbers. When Sir Andrew talks about beating a puritan like a dog, it doesn't arouse the anxiety and historical memory that many of us feel at Graziano's calling Shylock a 'currish Jew' (4.1.287) or wishing that he were going to 'the gallows, not the font' (4.1.396), especially since Maria then denies Malvolio actually is a puritan, Andrew is seldom presented as physically threatening, and the humiliation of Malvolio is a practical joke involving the church only parodically and the state not at all. In *Twelfth Night* spectators don't experience a conflict between traditions of forced conversion and emergent ideals of freedom of conscience, though they may feel conflicted about Malvolio's humiliation for more general humanitarian reasons. It is arguable that both plays work variations on a religious opposition—in *Merchant*, for example, that Portia and Antonio do not show the mercy they claim is Christian—but in *Twelfth Night* the historical conflict of puritan and established church is treated less in religious than in social terms, so that it becomes primarily one between spoilsport and merrymakers. Through this social emphasis, *Twelfth Night* evokes a theme perennially relevant as an analysis of the attractive and potentially threatening place of the theatre and particularly of comic theatre. The audience in *Twelfth Night* is by its very presence on the side of the revelers as opposed to the antitheatricalists, though this does not exclude sympathy for Malvolio at the end.[22]

Third, though *Merchant* makes Shylock more threatening than Malvolio, it also humanizes him more throughout the play, not just at the end, adding to a more conflicted response. Shylock remembers his wife and loses his daughter. Precisely because the history of a community rather than the bad treatment of one individual is involved, his speech about the common humanity of Jews and Christians has more eloquence than Malvolio's parallel words, 'I am as well in my wits as any man in Illyria' (4.2.99). Even though class and religious prejudice are in the background of the play, Malvolio does not speak in those terms. It is hard to imagine him raising a protest on behalf of a group—such as 'Hath not a godly man eyes? If you scratch a steward, will he not bleed?'

Thus in *Twelfth Night*, by contrast to *The Merchant of Venice*, Shakespeare constructs a less troubling comedy of revenge. He diminishes sympathy for the outsider in some ways, but allows Olivia to express it, as no one does in *Merchant*. Less is at stake and Malvolio's tormentors have their own ridiculous sides as well. The ambiguity about whether Malvolio is a puritan is partly because of the ambiguity of the concept of puritan—but, as Jeffrey Knapp has suggested, Shakespeare may have carried that ambiguity further in Maria's remark because he was trying not to be divisive in his opposition to divisiveness.[23] Difference in religious belief and practice among English Protestants could be a very ordinary occurrence, a question of degree, and the isolation of the steward was a structural feature of a rich household. So tensions around Malvolio were exaggerations of tensions that were very familiar.

Antonio

Antonio is one of the three characters in *Twelfth Night* who are situational outsiders—they literally arrive in Illyria from outside, after a shipwreck. All three are more generous than the self-loving

Illyrians, and Sebastian and Viola catalyze changes in Olivia and the Duke which lead to the final marriages.[24] Antonio's plot works differently. Like his namesake in *Merchant of Venice*, he is monetarily generous to a younger man.[25] However, instead of the one melancholy man in a group of chatterers, he is a social, more than temperamental, outsider, because of his history of battle with Orsino's ships, and he has met the young man by saving him from drowning, not through kinship ties. He speaks of his love with less restraint than *Merchant*'s Antonio, but with less disparagement of other relationships. And at the end of the play, his situation is even more ambiguous than that of his namesake.

Antonio himself says that he has 'many enemies in Orsino's court' (2.1.39) and hence will be in danger when he goes there; this warning introduces him as more of an outsider than *Merchant*'s Antonio without specifying the reason. Later he explains that he fought against Orsino's ships, and Illyrian officers arrest him on Orsino's demand, and in the last act Orsino calls him 'Notable pirate' (5.1.63), though Antonio denies it. In early modern and classical times, Illyria, near modern Croatia, did indeed have a reputation for pirates.[26] Warren and Wells say that his refusal to return the spoils in the sea-battle with Orsino technically makes him a pirate.[27] But piracy was itself an ambiguous identity at this point: as Su Fang Ng writes, 'One man's pirate is another's hero: take Sir Francis Drake or Sir Walter Raleigh for example.... Antonio becomes defined as a pirate because he enters Orsino's lands.'[28] Furthermore, the charge is not made until we have already seen Antonio's courage and generosity, and even Orsino has said of his role as a sea-captain 'very envy and the tongue of loss | Cried fame and honor on him' (5.1.52–3).

Either piracy or willingness to spend a long time at sea in all-male company would suggest strong male-male bonds and the possibility of sodomy in Shakespeare's day, and Smith points out how frequent male same-sex attraction appears in early modern stories about shipwrecked youths.[29] When Antonio pursues Sebastian through the streets of Illyria, he says, 'I do adore thee so | That danger shall seem sport' (2.1.42), and that last phrase, an appropriate motto for a pirate, can also, as Valerie Traub writes, 'allude to the perils in early modern culture of an exclusively homoerotic passion'.[30]

Antonio's attitude toward Sebastian is certainly passionate and it appears exclusive. In an early scene, one of the few until the end where one person expresses love to another he or she knows, Antonio uses imagery that has recognizable sexual connotations when he speaks of his 'desire | More sharp than filèd steel' (3.3.4–5).[31] He also uses what sound like clichés of love poetry and neoplatonic theory in speaking to Sebastian, e.g. 'If you will not murder me for my love, let me be your servant' (2.1.30–1), though he may also be asking 'to be allowed to be his companion's servant, literally speaking.'[32] The image of murder appears in love poetry, such as that parodied by Phebe in *As You Like It*, with the idea that the beloved who rejects the lover by that action murders him, but also, as I will discuss later, in the love discourse of another potentially homoerotic tradition. When Antonio joins the other characters in confusion about the identity of his beloved, in trying to save Viola/Cesario/Sebastian from the duel, he defines himself in terms of love, courage, and restraint: he is one 'that for his love dares yet do more | Than you have heard him brag to you he will' (3.4.281–2). He uses Petrarchan imagery of worship, both when he resolves to look for Sebastian because 'I do adore thee so | That danger shall seem sport' (2.1.41–2), and later, when Viola/Cesario denies having seen him before, he claims to have shown 'sanctity of love' (3.4.325) and done 'devotion' (327) to his 'image' (326) and exclaims 'How vile an idol proves this god!' (329) This imagery is used of heterosexual love in plays such as *Romeo and Juliet* and *Midsummer Night's Dream*, and, like the financial imagery used by *Merchant*'s Antonio, of same-sex love in Shakespeare's sonnets.

Although critics used to discuss the relationship between Antonio and Sebastian as friendship, clearly it is more passionate, at least on Antonio's side, than that word generally suggests today; when the play was written 'friend' was ambiguous enough that it could include passion. For most of their scenes, Antonio is the one with intensity and desire. He speaks of love; Sebastian instead says, for example, 'I can no other answer make but thanks, | And thanks' (3.3. 14–15), implying regret, perhaps for being unable to reciprocate emotionally, perhaps for being unwilling to commit sexually, perhaps just for not having money with him to give Antonio gifts in return. However, the lines he speaks at his final reunion with Antonio are more emotional: his greeting is

> Antonio! O, my dear Antonio,
> How have the hours racked and tortured me
> Since I have lost thee!
>
> (5.1.210–12)

This is much more intense than what he says to Olivia after this, a joke about her double betrothal.

It is certainly plausible to imagine these characters regularly sharing a bed, since that was common in Elizabethan times, as well as embracing and kissing. Perhaps, as Joseph Pequigney argues, there is much more sexuality in the relationship of Antonio and Sebastian than there is in that of Antonio and Bassanio. He notes, accurately, that *Twelfth Night*'s Antonio speaks more of Sebastian's physical beauty than *Merchant*'s Antonio does of Bassanio's, and uses more eroticized language, and that Antonio and Sebastian are spoken of in the text as lodging together while Antonio and Bassanio are not.[33] However, this remains ambiguous.

Does Antonio say anything to suggest a sense of a minority sexual identity, or membership in a dissident group? He apparently is the only one still endangered as a result of his sea-fight with Orsino, but does not see himself part of a group like 'thief or pirate' (5.1.68). When he speaks of Sebastian's ingratitude, he makes an emphatic ethical statement: 'In nature there's no blemish but the mind. | None can be called deformed but the unkind' (3.4.331–2). Traub calls this 'the closest thing we have to an antihomophobic statement in an early modern text.'[34] In the immediate context this specific meaning is not explicit—but if Antonio is speaking of his own self-assessment, it certainly contrasts with the way the other Antonio calls himself a 'tainted wether' (4.1.113). *Twelfth Night*'s Antonio's point is that important norms are ethical and not physical, and kindness is the highest ethical value. Unlike his namesake, he provides no evidence that he sees himself as blemished.

Antonio's last line in *Twelfth Night* may be a slightly clearer reference to a text supportive of same-sex love. Upon seeing Viola and Sebastian together, he says, 'An apple cleft in two is not more twin | Than these two creatures' (5.1.216–17). This may be an obvious comment to make about identical twins (who in real life could not

Outsiders and the Festive Community in Twelfth Night 59

be of opposite sexes), but it is also an echo of an important literary/philosophical text. In Plato's *Symposium*, Aristophanes explains the origin of love by saying that every pair of lovers began as a whole but were split 'like a sorb apple that is halved for pickling.'[35] He includes here both heterosexual and homosexual lovers. Who in the audience would have known this text? Perhaps some interested in the neoplatonic love tradition, used in Elizabethan love poetry and developed by such authors as Ficino, whose language about love Antonio uses when he says to Sebastian much earlier, 'If you will not murder me for my love, let me be your servant' (2.1.30–1). The image of the apple halves is Antonio's last line in the play, and while it is entirely appropriate for the reunion of twins, it also could evoke a more general validation of love between those who appear more similar than different.

At the end of the play, Antonio's situation is even more ambiguous than that of Venice's Antonio, who finds out that his ships are safe and is put in his place as someone who can continue friendship with Bassanio but must give priority to Portia. For the last 181 lines, *Twelfth Night*'s Antonio neither speaks nor is spoken to, and for some of them he may be still flanked by the police officers who arrested him in Act 3, Scene 4, and bring him in at line 54 of Act 5, Scene 1. Roger Warren and Stanley Wells write, 'Presumably his renewed friendship with Orsino's future brother-in-law and his "kindness" to Viola (l. 60) ensure his release, but there is no reference to it, or indeed opportunity for it, in the text.'[36] In 1815, J. P. Kemble inserted in his performance version some lines for Orsino, just before 'Cesario, come' (5.1.372), freeing Antonio and encouraging him to be 'ever near' Sebastian.[37] Alan Sinfield, writing in 1992, says, 'If I were directing the play, I would show Antonio delighted with how it all turns out.'[38] If Toby could bring Sir Andrew to live in the household, Sebastian could bring Antonio. Olivia, unlike Portia, has shown no signs of wanting to limit the future role of her husband's friend, but Sinfield's conclusion, possible with the fluid sexuality of Shakespeare's time, according to which Antonio might benefit from his friend Sebastian having a rich and high-ranking wife, has persuaded few directors thus far.[39] According to Warren and Wells, 'Directors often make Antonio leave, freed but isolated, in a different direction than the lovers.'[40] In the Trevor Nunn film, he leaves as Feste sings "Gainst knaves and thieves men shut their gate' (5.1.382). The strangest ending for Antonio I have seen described is in Cheek by Jowl's touring production of 2001: here he seems to be pairing up with Feste![41] Antonio's ending in *Twelfth Night* may be less troubling as written than the one in *Merchant* because *Twelfth Night* allows for a multitude of such possibilities. Valerie Traub writes that Antonio's 'relation to Sebastian is finally sacrificed for the maintenance of institutionalized heterosexuality and generational continuity', in effect making him a scapegoat for 'the homoerotic energies of Viola, Olivia, and Orsino'. The play as written does not need to sacrifice that relation, but as performed it usually does.[42]

Are Women Outsiders in *Twelfth Night*?

The women of *Twelfth Night* exemplify the ambiguity of the positioning of women in many of Shakespeare's comedies. Olivia's household, which comes to encompass most of the characters, can be seen in two ways—as a community of order and as a community of festivity. At the first scene in that household, Maria invokes order and Toby festivity. But very soon it is clear that the relevant community in the play is the community of festivity, Maria joins in, and Malvolio, officially one of the doorkeepers of the household, is not in the party.

Negotiations about admission to Olivia's court are one of the most obvious situations in which a literal outside vs. inside conflict enters *Twelfth Night*. Olivia's household is difficult to get into.[43] Early on we hear that she will admit no suit and has rejected a messenger from the Duke. While in her first appearance her mood, like Malvolio's, seems to make her an outsider on the comic stage, as she declares 'Take the fool away' (1.5.33), unlike Malvolio she is drawn into participation in Feste's catechism. Centre of a court in which Feste now has a secure place, she rebukes Malvolio for his 'self-love' (1.5.77), sends him to deal with Cesario, and contrary to her court's expectations, lets 'him' in and is drawn into conversation and even fascination with 'him'.

It may seem that she becomes an outsider again as she loses her self-control in her lovesickness: when Maria describes Malvolio as 'tainted in's wits', Olivia says, 'I am as mad as he, | If sad and merry madness equal be' (3.4.14–15). By contrast to Malvolio, she is in contact with reality: still, after, as the head of the household, she says, 'Let some of my people have a special care of him' (3.4.58), she calls for Toby, showing that she has no idea that the hostility between the two of them makes Toby one of the last people who should look after a disturbed Malvolio. However, when Toby draws his sword on someone she thinks is Cesario, she takes over again, angrily dismissing Toby and inviting Sebastian, as it turns out to be, to her house. Sebastian soon testifies that she can

> sway her house, command her followers
> Take and give back affairs and their dispatch
> With... a smooth, discreet and stable bearing.
>
> (4.3.17–19)

She quickly proposes marriage, gets a priest, calls him in the last scene to testify to the marriage when Cesario denies it, handles the appearance of the injured Andrew and Toby, and offers to Orsino to host a double wedding when the twins' identities and who loves whom are sorted out. She presides over much of the last act and no one objects to her authority.

Jean Howard argues that as a woman in authority in her household Olivia is a threat to the patriarchal gender system.[44] However, not all of the original theatregoers might have felt that she needed to be humbled for this position. Not only had a queen reigned for decades, but at least 16 per cent of households in the theatre district of Southwark were headed by a woman, and at any given time most adult women in their society were not married.[45] 'Aristocratic women at the time managed great estates and wielded economic power comparable to that of the head of a large modern corporation.'[46] John Manningham, whose diary gives us one of the earliest examples of spectators' responses to Shakespeare, assumed she was a widow, one of the positions in which women were more likely to have relative power, and recorded the trick of making Malvolio believe that she was in love with him somewhat as he recorded gossip about real young men of limited finances like his own who married rich widows.[47] At the end, Olivia, who is rich and forceful, is not necessarily going to be disciplined in her marriage to Sebastian, who has responded positively to her plea, 'Would thou'dst be ruled by me!' (4.1.60).

Maria, though lower in rank than Olivia, is also an insider in her household. She frequently conveys Olivia's wishes, and she also joins in the merrymaking community, and even devises the plan that will accomplish their wish to humiliate Malvolio. Like the other two women in the play, she marries the man she chooses; and although Toby may not appear much of a catch, they have a companionable relationship, she can, like Cesario to Orsino, admonish him about how to behave, and his kinship to Olivia presumably assures her a continuation of her place in the household. She and Malvolio are apparently of similar ambiguous rank and in competition for Olivia's favour at the beginning; a gentlewoman was expected to be of gentle birth, but economically dependent on her position in service. But unlike Malvolio she interacts cheerfully with others in the household and represents what she presents as Olivia's wishes good-naturedly; she seems to be an orchestrator of events in the household, is clearly the winner of the competition with Malvolio, and probably replaces Andrew as Toby's favoured companion.[48]

Viola in *Twelfth Night* is a literal outsider in Illyria, arriving there after a shipwreck with no place to go, but in her disguise as a boy she is quickly admitted to more favour with Orsino than his longer-established servants. 'Already you are no stranger,' says her fellow servant Valentine (1.4.3). On one hand, she can speak more freely to Orsino than anyone else can, which sounds like an insider's prerogative; on the other hand her official job, it seems, is to carry his messages, and she is dependent on his approval and loves him while he woos someone else, which sounds like an outsider's situation. Viola is a liminal figure, and must listen to his condescending views comparing women to, for example, 'roses, whose fair flower | Being once displayed, doth fall that very hour' (2.4.37–8). However, from her own experience, in her disguise she can give Orsino messages from the other half of the human race:

> Say that some lady, as perhaps there is,
> Hath for your love as great a pang of heart
> As you have for Olivia. You cannot love her.
> You tell her so. Must she not then be answered?
> . . . .
> In faith, they are as true of heart as we.
>
> (2.4. 87–90, 105)

Viola as Cesario here is in the paradigmatic situation of the outsider trying to pass but still to present the outsider's viewpoint.

Her position as an outsider is also evident when Fabian tries to pressure her into dueling with Sir Andrew and when she thinks uncomfortably, calling herself 'poor monster' (2.2.32), about the tangle of misunderstandings and emotions that she has got into with her disguise. And yet she shares this analysis with the audience, taking them/us into her confidence, enjoying the paradoxical situation of being a kind of insider in the way she gives the audience analysis of the situation.

The doubleness of Viola's gender performance is another way in which the ending of *Twelfth Night* is open to interpretation. For their wedding to take place, Orsino and Viola agree, she must return to the women's clothes that she was wearing at the beginning, so she must find the captain who saved her, who has them. He, however, is in prison because of Malvolio—Malvolio would indeed oppose someone who collaborated in a cross-dressing disguise—and so Malvolio needs to be found. This plot detail is obviously a device for getting Malvolio back, and once he hears Feste's response to his own protest he leaves in rage before they can ask him about the captain. Thus at the end Viola is engaged to Orsino but they share the joke of pretending that she is still a boy, a parallel to the final joke that Bassanio makes to Portia, 'Sweet doctor, you shall be my bedfellow' (5.1.283). Orsino orders that Malvolio be entreated to a peace, but will he agree? The characters and most later readers and spectators expect that the marriage is going to take place (the Nunn version shows a final dance for which Viola has already changed into a dress), whether because, however unlikely, Malvolio will relent, or because they pragmatically realize they can get women's clothes elsewhere. But this ending, as critics have been mentioning since the 1980s, also gives a final visual image of a male-male couple, affirming on some level the homoerotic attraction that has been so important in this play.

Whirligigs and Mirrors

'The whirligig of time brings in its revenges' (5.1.364), says Feste to Malvolio, after echoing back to him the words with which Malvolio put him down near the beginning of the play. A whirligig is a toy in which, like a wheel, something moves around in a circle to a position opposite to where it began and then back. Revenge is, among other things, a structure in which a character mirrors to another the treatment he or she has received. As the revelers in the play take revenge on Malvolio, the sympathy which they receive when he attacks them gradually moves back to him in a movement that could be compared to a whirligig. Perhaps when Malvolio refuses to accept Olivia's sympathy and promises revenge, sympathy moves away from him again. But there are many other examples of mirroring and shifting sympathies in the play.

The intricate design of *Twelfth Night* provides a parallel between the two most obvious outsiders, Malvolio and Antonio, both of whom woo people whom they serve, and many other parallels between them and the characters who are or clearly become more accepted in the play's community. It has often been noted that Viola's love for her master Orsino is also, in class terms, a parallel to Malvolio's aspirations to his mistress Olivia—but the play also emphasizes that Viola, like Antonio, really loves while Malvolio is just ambitious, and Viola is aware of and sympathetic to other people's feelings while Malvolio is oblivious. Another parallel is made even more explicit when Olivia, returned to her stability and contracted to Sebastian, sees the resemblance between Malvolio's behaviour and what she remembers of her own when in love with Cesario.

> They say, poor gentleman, he's much [distract].
> A most extracting frenzy of mine own
> From my remembrance clearly banished his.
>
> (5.1.273–5)[49]

She sympathizes with Malvolio—her last words in the play are 'He hath been most notoriously abused' (5.1.366)—and perhaps this, as well as his desire to get Viola's clothing back, motivates the Duke to his order that someone should pursue Malvolio and entreat him to a peace. This moment of acknowledged kinship between the lucky-in-love insider and the humiliated and enraged outsider may pass by quickly, but it assures those in the audience who feel for Malvolio encouragement that their viewpoint is represented in the world of the play. Mirroring can suggest scapegoating, but Olivia's acknowledgment of similarity undercuts the scapegoating structure.

Resemblances (and also contrasts) between Antonio and other characters could have the effect of making him too seem less of an outsider. Shakespeare's comedies often implicitly make comparisons among heterosexual couples; here the comparisons also cross gender lines. Antonio's feelings about Sebastian have some similarities to those of both Orsino and Olivia about Viola, though Antonio knows the gender identity of the person he loves. The parallel between Orsino's pleasure in Viola's companionship and Antonio's delight in Sebastian's is explicit when each of them claims that the youth has been with him for three months. Orsino calls Antonio a pirate but, when he threatens to kill Cesario, compares himself to a legendary 'Egyptian thief' who was also a pirate.[50] Also, Viola's combination of service and love of Orsino is comparable to Antonio's service to Sebastian. Similarly, just after Antonio gives his purse to Sebastian, Olivia thinks about giving money to Cesario, and says, 'Youth is bought more oft than begged or borrowed' (3.4.3). The play suggests that if we can accept Olivia's use of money here we should accept Antonio's also. If we compare Antonio and Sebastian to two other men who are often seen together, Toby and Andrew, it is much clearer that Toby is exploiting Andrew than that either Antonio or Sebastian is exploitative, though of course Antonio and Sebastian are written as less comic.

Andrew too may end up as an outsider in *Twelfth Night*. Earlier an insider in the festive group who mock Malvolio, he now for the first time receives rage and open scorn from Toby, who blames him for the wounds they both has received from Sebastian. Since he was present in Olivia's household as a friend of Toby's and supposedly her wooer, now that both pretexts are gone he must leave, unless we see Toby's words as a momentary outburst he might later repent (an interpretation it is hard to find any production using).[51] Andrew might seem too shallow a figure to be missed. But recent productions often play up Toby's cruelty at this point, so the audience may care. It is a typical Shakespearean pattern that this character who has had the most fantasies of violence against Malvolio also mirrors him as a ridiculous suitor who arouses no romantic interest in Olivia. Analogously, though Toby's main characteristic in the play has been his drunkenness, just before denouncing Andrew he says, speaking of a doctor mentioned by Feste, 'I hate a drunken rogue' (5.1.193–4).

Feste too mirrors Malvolio. He mirrors all the characters of the play in his professional role of the fool who shows them their folly; he also sings songs that usually mirror their particular kind of folly. But he also mirrors Malvolio specifically as a dependent in a court, and as one the play most clearly shows as a solitary character. He is the one who echoes Malvolio's words about dependency on approval in shortened form, 'An you smile not, he's gagged' (5.1.363–4), back to him at the end. And after he exults 'Thus the whirligig of time brings in his revenges' (364), Malvolio in turn mirrors him, promising his own revenge. In Nunn's film, where Ben Kingsley plays Feste, their mirroring is even clearer as bald Feste wears and then removes Malvolio's hairpiece and Malvolio's own baldness and aging is revealed.

At the end of the play Feste is alone on stage singing the epilogue. With its refrain 'Hey ho, the wind and the rain', the song is easy to read as placing him literally outside, and the melancholy of that situation was emphasized in the Branagh-directed film of 1988, in which snow comes down, Anton Lesser as Feste has holes in his gloves that emphasize his poverty, and Fabian locks the garden gate to keep him out. However, in the Trevor Nunn production, Kingsley, whose narration has framed the play, enjoys his freedom as he leaves Olivia's court and runs toward the sea. 'We'll strive to please you every day' (395), he sings, and he laughs. 'Every day! Every day!' Is he a fool against whom men shut their gates, or is he one of the many involved in 'our play' (394) that is now done? It is part of the strength of *Twelfth Night* that, like so many questions about it, this one can be answered either way.

If we take the latter interpretation, it is just a step to remembering that Malvolio too is also a role in a comedy. While critics who have interpreted the play primarily in political terms have seen his revenge in the midcentury English Revolution which led to a civil war, the execution of Charles I, and a temporary government that, influenced by puritanism, banned the public theatre, in another sense he has had his revenge in becoming for centuries the most popular role in the play.[52] But that sense of revenge turns on its head the opposition to comedy of the character within the play. Another whirligig?

In his onstage humiliation, Malvolio is one of the characters in Shakespeare most likely to be considered a scapegoat. According to some definitions, a scapegoat must be both like and unlike the others in the community he represents.[53] Critics have often compared his self-love, first observed by Olivia, to her own self-love and that of Orsino, from which, arguably, they are both released in the course of the play. However, these characters are totally ignorant of the plot against him, which comes from Maria, Toby, Andrew, and Feste, and they are the least involved in scapegoating at the end, as Olivia compares her madness to his and says he has been abused and Orsino orders that he be entreated to a peace. Structurally, perhaps the most accurate way to describe Malvolio as a scapegoat may be to say that he is an opponent of comedy who has always been foolish in his pretensions but, in his response to Maria's letter, turns into a clown. In his folly, he is acting like all the others; in his opposition to folly, his inability to laugh off humiliation, he is different. Yet Shakespeare softens the scapegoating possibilities with Olivia's and Orsino's words, just as he leaves open the possibility of Antonio staying friends with Sebastian. 'We'll strive to please you every day' (5.1.395), sings Feste in the last line, and the subtitle is *'What You Will'*. *Twelfth Night* can be performed to suggest that however ridiculous people may look, whatever pain they may hide, if they want to be in the festive community, anything goes! Yet it can also be performed to show a festive community that is willing to include Malvolio only as long as he is useful, or that excludes Antonio, or Feste, or, most clearly indicated by the text, Sir Andrew.

Many recent influential productions of both *The Merchant of Venice* and *Twelfth Night* end by suggesting the loneliness of the unmarried characters and/or the potential unhappiness (often loneliness as well) of those who are paired off.[54] It seems that directors and perhaps audiences as well are now interested in even more outsiders in the comedies than previously. Sometimes the interest is satirical, but as the emphasis on Jessica's regrets comes partly from a more multicultural and postHolocaust society that takes a rejection of Judaism more seriously, the emphasis on the Antonios, as well as on potential unhappiness of the marriages, comes partly from the greater acceptance of same-sex love as having validity equal to heterosexual love, especially in urban areas where there is the most interest in theatre, as well as the expectation that sexual identity is fixed or that heterosexual and same-sex bonds would make competing demands.[55] An

Antonio today who loved a man as Shakespeare's Antonio loves Sebastian might well feel that even if Olivia weren't threatened by him, her demands on Sebastian as a husband would create too much conflict. And on the other hand, an Olivia might feel that Antonio's demands on Sebastian would create too much conflict. Northrop Frye wrote about comic structure, 'The logical end is festive, but anyone's attitude to the festivity may be that of Orlando or of Jaques.'[56] He may have never anticipated that any reader or spectator would identify with Shylock, Antonio, Jessica, or Olivia. But the plays are written in a way that, much of the time, makes such identification possible. So while some theorists of comedy maintain that comedy needs outsiders because a society needs outsiders to define itself against by laughing at them, some theatre practitioners are staging plays to encourage identification with more outsiders, even if, as with Andrew, the audience may laugh a lot at them before they sympathize.

3

Women as Outsiders and Insiders in Shakespeare

Why does this book, which has already considered Portia, Jessica, Viola, and Olivia, and will discuss the women of *Othello*, *Lear*, and *The Tempest*, have a separate chapter on women? While many of the other kinds of outsiders discussed here appear in only one or two plays, women appear in every one of Shakespeare's plays, as of course women do in every nation, ethnic group, and class.[1] But when they are outsiders, they are outsiders of a special kind. No woman, for example, leaves a Shakespearean comedy with the humiliation of Shylock or Malvolio, and many women in the plays are more privileged than those characters. Is Leslie Fiedler wrong when he groups women together with Jews, Moors, and Indians in his study of Shakespeare's 'private mythology', *The Stranger in Shakespeare*?[2]

No, Fiedler's grouping has merit, though his analysis of female characters is unreliable. There is something to be gained by considering Shakespeare's women together with other characters who are markedly different from the majority in their play's society, although women are obviously not the same kind of outsiders as the others he considers. Simone de Beauvoir writes of women, in *The Second Sex*, 'They live dispersed among the males, more attached though residence, housework, economic condition, and social standing to certain men—fathers or husbands—than they are to other women.'[3] Often it seems that the proper image for women's subordination is confinement rather than exclusion. But it is too simple to see them as having only the kind of outsider status that must 'threaten destruction', as

Fiedler says about women in the early plays.[4] In Shakespeare's plays, a woman can be the kind of outsider who provides a fresh perspective, the kind whose protest about exclusion arouses assent, or she can be, to a greater or lesser extent, an insider. Especially with the help of the kinds of feminist criticism that consider variables such as race, class, and religion and their intersection with gender, we can see that like Shakespeare's other outsiders, his women sometimes have considerable power, especially in comparison with other characters further outside.[5] Sometimes women seem to have special abilities to speak to other kinds of outsiders, and even to see their similarities—but sometimes one or the other or both are destroyed by their relationship.

Were women outsiders or insiders in Shakespeare's time? They were both. Queen Elizabeth was officially the most powerful person in England, but she had to calculate her rhetoric carefully: in one of her most famous speeches, she declared, 'I know I have the body but of a weak and feeble woman; but I have the heart and stomach of a King.'[6] Presenting herself as specially chosen by God, she did nothing intended to benefit other women. 'In Shakespeare's time, women were excluded from the universities and the learned professions [and] married women lost the right to their own property unless special provisions were made to preserve it.'[7] By education and custom women were told to practice virtues of chastity, silence, and obedience that were not demanded of men. They did not necessarily follow these commands, but they were conscious of them and could evoke the rules to get social approval, like Shakespeare's Margaret in the *Henry VI* trilogy, who says that she couldn't speak of all her love for the royal husband betrothed to her in an arranged marriage sight unseen, without saying 'more than beseems a woman' (*Henry 6, Part 2*, 1.1.26). In maintaining their own right to speak their mind and to pursue their own wishes, they risked disapproval for leaving their own properly subordinate role.

Universities in England, which excluded women, also excluded men of other religions than Protestant Christianity from receiving degrees. There were formal and informal restrictions on Jews and on the behaviour and clothing of people according to class. England had room for women, Jews, men who loved men of the right kind, and stewards who stayed in their place, though it was limited.

On the other hand, while 'women were barred from certain locations and institutions reserved for men...women's role in the gendering of space was not merely negative. They created their own culture, in part, by demarcating and controlling their own space... The household was a female-dominated milieu.'[8] It was also a place in which women might be working at crafts as diverse as millinery, silkmaking, brewing, and printing. And contrary to the advice books by conservative authors such as Vives, who counseled women to stay at home to preserve their reputation, women went to market, visited friends, gossiped at taverns, and attended the theatre.[9] A woman who was securely positioned working at one household as a maid, like Maria in *Twelfth Night*, was free to travel to another.[10]

It is striking how often Shakespeare's plays suggest a localized space in which a woman presides—in some cases, her own court or household, as with Olivia, Portia, the Countess of Roussillion, Cleopatra, and Paulina; in others, her husband may be nominally in charge, but we see her hosting and holding authority over who stays and who goes—Hermione and Goneril, and at a lower social level, Mistress Ford and Adriana. At a lower level yet, the Courtesan in *Comedy of Errors* and Mistress Overdone in *Measure for Measure* all host male characters in houses, as do Bianca in *Othello* and Mistress Quickly, the Hostess at Eastcheap Tavern in the history plays with Falstaff and his memory and Dr. Caius' housekeeper in *Merry Wives*, though these two nevertheless receive a lot of male mockery. Furthermore, there are a number of scenes that present what looks like a female space—a space entirely or predominantly inhabited by a group of women without a male authority figure present: the scenes among the ladies of *Love's Labour's Lost*; the marriage planning and female eavesdropping scenes of *Much Ado About Nothing*; the witches on the heath in *Macbeth*; Iras, Charmian, Cleopatra, and the eunuch Mardian; Hermione's ladies; and scenes between two women, sometimes with family ties as with Rosalind and Celia or Helena and the Countess of Roussillion, and sometimes including mistresses and their maidservants, such as Portia and Nerissa, Katherine of France and Alice, Desdemona and Emilia, or Juliet and the Nurse. While many of these scenes involve discussing absent men, nevertheless there is often a warm, intimate feeling in them which the actual presence of the man discussed would remove. Scenes like this give another perspective on the relativity of the term outsider by showing women as insiders in a female community.

With regard to their position as outsiders, Shakespeare's plays rarely, if ever, show explicit protest by women against exclusion from the universities or loss of their property rights. Some of the women who speak of women as a group even acquiesce in the clichés about women's weakness that are used to justify such exclusions. But the plays do show women—aristocratic, relatively privileged white women, who know that they face restrictions that men of their class do not—confronting customary limits on geographic mobility, ambition, violent behaviour, speech, sexual behaviour, free choice in marriage, and credibility. The issue is not simply exclusion from public power, but discrimination on the most personal level, including the difference between the sexual restrictions on women and the sexual restrictions on men, known as the double standard.

The plays show women who violate some of these limits receiving verbal abuse comparable to what some male outsiders receive. For example, Katherine in *The Taming of the Shrew* angrily objects to the way her father is trying to marry her off. The names that she gets because of her angry resistance show that some of the characters put her, as some characters in other plays put Shylock or Othello, in a separate category than human. Cultural prejudice turns her into not just an angry woman, but, for Hortensio and Gremio, a shrew, a devil, a fiend of hell, or, at least, a wildcat. Similarly, just as Brabanzio doesn't believe that Othello is really a Christian, but considers him a pagan, many male characters doubt women's faithfulness and any words that they say defending it.

But hostility, mistrust, and condescension to women are often contested. Just as Shylock argues that he and other Jews share common humanity with Christians, Emilia, as the next chapter will discuss further, argues that women share many qualities with men and therefore should have the same rights in marriage. Indeed, more women in Shakespeare say something like, 'O that I were a man!' than characters in any other outsider group express a comparable speculation.[11] (Malvolio's imagining what it would be like 'To be Count Malvolio' is the closest but has a different effect.)

For Beatrice in *Much Ado*, 'O that I were a man!' (4.1.300–1) is an expression of a wish to be able to fight a duel to defend her cousin

Hero's honor, but the expansion of possibilities they want is not always in violence. Cressida says to Troilus,

> Though I loved you well, I wooed you not—
> And yet, good faith, I wished myself a man,
> Or that we women had men's privilege
> Of speaking first.
>
> (3.2.116–18)

It's not the anatomy but the right to take the initiative in courtship that she wants. Characters such as Rosalind and Desdemona show that it is possible for a woman with sufficient imagination to circumvent custom in this regard—though Rosalind's first attempt at this simply leaves Orlando tongue-tied and Desdemona's ultimately leads to her death. Rosalind has better luck in involving Orlando in conversation when she disguises herself as a boy, and Viola takes a similar course, though she also has immediately practical reasons for her disguise—the easiest way for her to survive in Illyria is to get a position as a manservant to Orsino. More women in Shakespeare pretend to be male than members of any other outsider group play at a different identity, and their disguise is sometimes accompanied by predictions of how well they will hold up their part: for example, Rosalind says to Celia,

> We'll have a swashing and a martial outside,
> As many other mannish cowards have,
> That do outface it with their semblances.
>
> (1.3.114–16)

Not only comedies but also tragedies can raise issues of women's similarity to men contrary to social customs. Consider Othello's memory of Desdemona saying, 'She wished | That heaven had made her such a man' (1.3.161–2) and his fond name for Desdemona, 'My fair warrior' (2.1.178). Desdemona in turn insists that she will be Cassio's solicitor—lawyer—and that Othello's 'bed shall seem a school, his board a shrift' (3.3.24). Thus she imagines herself in the then equally male professions of law and religion as well as a teacher to her husband, which also went against the usual expectations that a woman would teach only other females, though a husband might teach his wife.

What would Shakespeare's original audiences have thought about these explicit or implicit protests against limits on women? No doubt there would always have been a range of reactions, but 'nontraditional' possibilities for women were thinkable. Clergymen were preaching against parental enforcement of marriage choice, and freedom for women on this issue was greater outside the aristocracy. In spite of the strength of law, custom, and official teachings, by the time Shakespeare's plays appeared many writers were protesting the subordination of women. While the protest often made a general claim about women's similarity to men, it frequently focused specifically on the sexual double standard. In the early sixteenth century, in Italy, Castiglione's influential book, *The Courtier*, translated into English in mid-century, imagines one of the characters arguing against the difference in sexual liberty acceptable in men and women.[12] Another Italian writer, Cornelius Agrippa, wrote *In Defence of the Excellency of Womenkind*, a treatise that while in some portions satirical, nevertheless makes a very similar point against the double standard, relating, as Castiglione's speaker does, to the fact that laws enforcing it were made by men, not women. In 1568, in a dialogue entitled *The Flower of Friendship*, written by Edmund Tilney, one of the characters says, 'Women have souls as well as men, they have wit as well as men.... What reason is it then, that they should be bound, whom nature has made free?'[13] In 1588, a pamphlet writer with the good English name Jane Anger—probably a pseudonym—also protested against the double standard.[14] And in Venice, in the historical year of 1600, a respectable woman named Moderata Fonte published a dialogue in which a female character says to a man, 'You know full well that we were born with the same substance and qualities as you, and that we were given to you as companions in this life, not as slaves.' She adds, 'Many men see the world in a blinkered way, and are so firmly convinced of the unwarrantable fallacy that they are created women's superiors, and so incapable of seeing past this lie that they believe themselves fully justified in treating women as tyrannically and brutally as they like.'[15]

Just a few years later, an Englishwoman named Aemilia Lanyer wrote a poem, *Salve Deus Rex Judaeorum*, in which the following words are addressed to men in general on behalf of women:

> You came not in the world without our pain,
> Make that a bar against your cruelty;

> Your fault being greater, why should you disdain
> Our being your equals, free from tyranny?[16]

And in the next decade, another Englishwoman who took the name Esther Souernam would protest against the double standard as presented in a misogynistic pamphlet written by George Swetnam.[17] An anonymous pamphlet titled *Haec Vir* would imagine a woman saying of her sex:

We are as freeborn as Men, have as free election and as free spirits; we are compounded of like parts and may with like liberty seek benefit of our Creations.

Many of Shakespeare's plays show the operations of the double standard, and several of them include characters who implicitly or explicitly protest it. Such protest is closely linked with the representation of unwarranted male suspicion of women's fidelity, something that Shakespeare's plays show with what may seem like obsessive repetition but also with development. In *Much Ado*, the silent and obedient woman, Hero, suffers most from the outsider position of women. Claudio readily believes Don John's stories about her, and in the wedding ceremony reveals her position in his mind as basically damaged goods when he says to Leonato, 'Give not this rotten orange to your friend' (4.1.30). When Hero faints at the accusation, even her father believes in her so little that he says he hopes she is dead. The most important kind of prejudice displayed against Shakespeare's women is shown here—the ease with which some men believe in their sexual promiscuity. In this comedy, Hero is vindicated after a few days, and so is Mistress Ford in *Merry Wives of Windsor*, but the results are more serious in the tragedy *Othello* and also in *Winter's Tale* and *Cymbeline*; in the late romances too the accused wives suffer more than in the comedies, and the suspicious husbands must do more to atone.

It is remarkable that most of the Shakespearean men who believe they are cuckolded are wrong. And in one of the few plays where a woman is unfaithful, *Troilus and Cressida*, Cressida's infidelity is shown to be pressured by a situation in which she is sent into an opposed military camp with no trustworthy protector, in a culture in which she was always suspect. Even her oath of fidelity is framed in terms of what will happen if she is false, as opposed to Troilus' oath promising to be true, and his promise of faith to her begins

> O that I thought it could be in a woman—
> As, if it can, I will presume in you—
> To feed for aye her lamp and flames of love...
>
> (3.2.145–7)

All Shakespeare's plays about self-styled cuckolds include protests against men's quick suspicion. Usually the jealous man sees the woman as a moral outsider while the audience sees her sympathetically as an innocent falsely accused. Such protests come from Beatrice, the Friar, and Benedick; from Desdemona, Emilia, and Lodovico; from Camillo, Antigonus, and Paulina in Leontes' court. Eventually, in *Cymbeline*, even the suspicious husband, after he thinks he has had his wife murdered, questions the importance of adultery: 'You married ones | If each of you should take this course, how many | Must murder wives much better than themselves | For wrying but a little' (5.1.2–5). Some critics assume that Shakespeare shared suspicion of women because he so often dealt with it in his plays; but the outcome of most of these plays suggests that, rather, he tended to treat such suspicion as a delusion to be exploded.

While the vindication of women suspected of infidelity occurs across genres, the result for female characters who actually do challenge customary limits varies. In tragedies and histories women who seek power usually have a sad end. However, most of his comedies show, in different ways, that such women can be insiders, whether after some trials or apparently more easily.

Earlier chapters have shown the success of some of the comic women who take on masculine disguise: they often function very well in the masculine world to which their disguise admits them: Viola as the Duke's attendant, Rosalind, in *As You Like It*, as Orlando's tutor about love, and, most obviously, Portia as a lawyer. It is true that Rosalind and Viola eventually confront the limits of femininity, as their society saw it; Viola cannot fight a duel and Rosalind faints at the sight of her wounded lover's blood. However, Rosalind quickly recovers and Viola looks better than Sir Andrew, a man who cannot fight a duel either, or Sir Toby, who fights the wrong person too quickly. Rosalind, Viola, and Portia all help to bring about a happy ending to their play—without Viola's maneuvering in disguise, the

Duke and Olivia would languish forever; without Rosalind's play-acting, so would Orlando, Silvius, and Phebe, and without Portia's skill in the courtroom, Antonio would die. In their masculine disguise these three characters bring an outsider's insight to characters who are stuck in romantic clichés, fantasies, or legal dilemmas.[18]

Why is it mostly women among Shakespeare's outsiders who engage in border-crossing disguise and the rhetoric of identity switching? Perhaps one reason is the fact that women were played by boy actors, and the related fact that in one influential way of looking at gender in the early modern period, women and boys were grouped together in opposition to men.[19] Two of Shakespeare's characters most known for their role-playing make explicit this grouping: Cleopatra (who is much like a comic heroine, though in a tragedy, and reminisces about a cross-dressing game with Antony) says to Dolabella, 'You laugh when boys or women tell their dreams' (5.2.73). Rosalind, in her disguise as Ganymede, describes herself to Orlando as having acted, in a previous performance as a woman to cure a love-lorn suitor, as 'for every passion something and for no passion truly anything, as boys and women are for the most part cattle of this colour' (3.2.368–70). Boys and women were both thought of as being more changeable and more emotional than men, and also more dependent.

Of course white Christian women were more familiar to the mass of male Londoners than were ethnic or religious outsiders. And at the same time boy actors were also familiar sights to the mass of Londoners. They had been carefully trained so that they could take on the gestures and intonations of women. Shakespeare knew, and his audience too could be reminded, how skillfully boy actors (outsiders, but often admired ones, because of their youth and their profession) could play the roles of women, and this could contribute to a further sense of how the differences between the sexes were not really inevitably and unbreachably great.

Two women of Shakespeare's comedies notoriously protest against expectations for women in their society without going into masculine disguise: Katherine in *Taming of the Shrew* and Beatrice in *Much Ado about Nothing*. While *Taming* is often seen, whether regretfully or with celebration, as showing the defeat of a woman's protest against male dominance, it actually evokes considerable sympathy for that protest, and can be argued to compensate Katherine for her public capitulation by giving her insider status at the end.

Though there were many women called shrewish in earlier literature and folklore, Shakespeare was the first to stage one in relation to her father's marriage plans for her.[20] In his Padua fathers bestow their daughters; men choose women, and women apparently have little choice. This was not the inevitable procedure in contemporary England, though it was a practice often followed by the aristocracy.[21] Baptista claims he will consider Katherine's own wishes but he believes Petruccio's account of them when she doesn't speak, and he wants to sell Bianca to the highest bidder.

Katherine gains some sympathy from other characters in her protest. Her initial behaviour can be seen as motivated by anger against the way her father treats her. In her first line she protests against being made 'a stale ... among these mates' (1.1.58)—a laughingstock, humiliated because the men around are all competing for her sister and none interested in her. Later, Katherine is not the only one to speak out against Petruccio's treatment of her—male characters protest too, an important theatrical technique to suggest that spectators might sympathize with her. When Petruccio is late to their wedding, and she complains 'I must forsooth be forced | To give my hand opposed against my heart' (3.2.8–9), even her father says, 'I cannot blame thee now to weep' (3.2.27). When Petruccio refuses her food, even his friend Hortensio, who earlier called her a devil, sympathizes and says, 'Signior Petruccio, fie, you are to blame' (4.3.48). When he also refuses her the cap that the haberdasher brings, her eloquence about her need to protest goes beyond the apparent triviality of the issue:

> My tongue will tell the anger of my heart,
> Or else my heart concealing it will break.
> And rather than it shall I will be free
> Even to the uttermost as I please in words.
>
> (4.3.77–80)

In the last scene, however, as Katherine gets social approval for her long speech and her marriage to Petruccio looks more stable than those of the other couples, she has turned into a comparative insider by contrast to Bianca and the Widow, whom she calls 'froward and ignoble worms' (5.2.173).

Much Ado about Nothing, written many comedies after *Taming of the Shrew*, uses a very different strategy in portraying a woman resisting marriage and speaking critically of her society's customs. Beatrice's primary identity is not as a shrew but as a woman whose wit is enjoyed by her family and friends. When Leonato tells her, 'thou wilt never get thee a husband if thou be so shrewd of thy tongue' (2.1. 16–17), she laughs this off. She has a sense of the expected power relations in marriage—she would be 'overmastered with a piece of valiant dust' (2.1.51–2) and forced to 'make an account of her life to a clod of wayward marl' (52–3)—and wants to avoid them, as in fact a surprisingly large number of women in Shakespeare's society did. In early modern England, more women were without husbands (this includes widows) than with them, and the percentage who never married may have been as high as 30.[22] Beatrice might be considered an outsider who is also on the inside, who can get away with criticizing a central institution in her society, even telling her cousin Hero that, with regard to her own marriage, she should curtsy and say to Leonato, 'Father, as it please me' (2.1.47). The good nature of her criticism and the general enjoyment of her wit is further emphasized in the Kenneth Branagh movie of this play, which shows Beatrice walking arm in arm with Leonato, his brother Antonio, Hero, and friends. But it is already in Shakespeare's text that the visiting Prince, Don Pedro, proposes marriage to her himself, before she gracefully turns him down.

Furthermore, Don John's eavesdropping plot deceives Benedick just as much as it does Beatrice. So it does not mark women as outsiders so much as it targets marriage resisters of either sex. When Beatrice and Benedick at the end promise to join in marriage, those who like can see hints that Beatrice is going to keep on talking and will not really have to make an account of her life to Benedick.

The structure of both of these plays works to give greater interest to the woman who goes outside conventional limits in her speech and criticizes the conventional marriages of her society. As Camille Wells Slights has written, these comedies present unflattering versions of social power and show that male authority is 'an arbitrary human authority unjustified by natural superiority'.[23] However, their endings show women who gain social power—become relative insiders—entering the institutions they have criticized.

Consideration of the degree to which women are outsiders in Shakespeare's plays shows that in this case, likewise, the difference between being an insider and being an outsider is not unbreachably great. Katherine, an outsider at the beginning, becomes a sort of insider who can frame other women as more outside than she is at the end. In other plays, women move back and forth between the roles of outsider and insider. Often their relative insider position appears by contrast to a male outsider, or perhaps a male they can put in the position of an outsider. Portia is an insider in her home at Belmont by contrast to Morocco, Aragon, and all her other stereotyped suitors. On the other hand, she is an outsider in the sense that, as she complains about in her first scene, her rights are limited, she is bound by the terms of her father's will to marry whichever of them chooses the right casket. In the court of Venice, disguised as a boy prodigy in law sent from Rome, she is more of an insider than Shylock is, though, with some detachment from Venice, she is more willing than anyone else in the court to say that he has a case in justice, and her position as a female in a world of bonding between Christian males emerges during the speech in which Bassanio says he would give her up to save Antonio. But when they return to Venice again, she is an insider who makes Antonio feel uncomfortable and give up his claim to first place in Bassanio's heart.

Beatrice's social criticism seems good-natured by contrast to the misanthropic outsider Don John, whom she mocks. When he accuses Hero of promiscuity and the other men believe him, it may seem that he is an insider in comparison to the women. But when the Watch reveal the truth and Borachio confesses, Beatrice and Hero are vindicated and Don John is an outsider again, left to the 'brave punishments' (5.4.122) Benedick promises to devise.

Like *Merchant*, *As You Like It* juxtaposes a woman who begins in bad spirits and soon recovers with a man who is temperamentally melancholy or at least pretending to be. Among the many witcombats of this play is one in which Rosalind's wit defeats Jaques' complaints. Under her orchestration, the play converts him to giving good wishes to most of the couples married at the end. Jaques is the most harmless of outsiders and sets off Rosalind's role as a kind of life force.

In *Merry Wives of Windsor*, the ne'er do well knight Falstaff is more insulting to the middle-class Mistresses Page and Ford in his attempt to get his hands on them and their money. They cleverly humiliate him by leading him on until he has to hide from the jealous Ford, first in a laundry-basket and then in a female disguise, and then they lead him on to a kind of ritual festive pinching in the woods, mostly by children. Ford's jealousy is plainly portrayed as irrational, and he repents; Falstaff too is finally forgiven, and the two women's friendship and their domestic authority are confirmed. These comedies in which women are portrayed as insiders by contrast to one or more men culminate in *Twelfth Night*, and in Maria's orchestration of the practical joke that defeats Malvolio and humbles him so much he leaves in rage.

While in the comedies, the romances, and many tragedies women move between the position of outsider and insider, in many histories and some tragedies such mobility for women is more difficult. In the history plays, many women are marked as doubly different from the beginning by their ethnic origins. Queen Margaret is not just an ambitious queen but an ambitious French queen. The group that rebels against Henry IV includes Mortimer and his wife, who speaks no English—yet she does sing a beautiful Welsh song which appeals to the English rebel Hotspur and presumably to many in the audience. And the outsider position of Katherine of France in *Henry V* is mitigated because the play gives her scenes with her maid which help us imagine her point of view, and because in the final scene France is given dignity as its King and Queen present their wishes for the marriage of France and England as well as that of the English husband and the French wife.

In *Julius Caesar*, Brutus's wife Portia and Caesar's wife Calpurnia never leave their role as outsiders excluded from the political world with which the play is concerned, and several characters repeat the rationale that women can't keep secrets. But in the later Roman plays the situation for women is different. Although Volumnia cannot fight or participate in politics herself, she has such an active role as a representative of Rome's militaristic values, and someone who has educated her son in them, she clearly has a place of honor in Rome— even when the tribunes call her 'mankind' (4.2.18) because of her vocal anger at banishment of Coriolanus she refuses to see this as an insult:

'Was not a man my father? Hast thou foxship | To banish him...?' (4.2.20) *Antony and Cleopatra* relativizes the values of Rome by including many scenes set in Egypt, with a whole different supporting cast and different customs, rather than presenting just one African outsider as occurs in *Othello*. Though Romans occasionally refer to her as a gypsy, Cleopatra revalues her dark skin by saying that she is 'with Phoebus' amorous pinches black' (1.5.28).

In tragic women's plots, Lady Macbeth is the prime example of woman as moral outsider; her desire for power is not confined to saying 'O that I were a man', but becomes 'unsex me here' (1.5.39), her prayer to evil spirits to remove her capacity for compassion, which she associates with womanhood. However, in Act 1 she can speak like a social insider to Duncan, and she and Macbeth have a close bond of their own; they are insiders to each other. In Act 1 Scene 7 pronouns that link the two of them echo repeatedly: 'Screw your courage to the sticking-place | and we'll not fail' (61); 'What cannot you and I perform upon | Th'unguarded Duncan?' (69–70). At this point their relationship is a kind of parody of the closeness that Viola and Rosalind develop with their husbands-to-be while in masculine costume—but Viola and Rosalind deflate the men's romantic fantasies with their realism, while Lady Macbeth encourages Macbeth's fantasies of assassination just as do the witches who are her symbolic reflection.

After the murder takes place, their harmony quickly breaks down and the two moral outsiders are little comfort to each other. Macbeth goes against their shared plan in killing the grooms whom they frame for the murder, and like Julia in *Two Gentlemen of Verona* when men seem to be deciding her destiny without her consent, she faints. But unlike Julia's, this faint has no impact on the plot. She is ushered away and Macbeth joins most of the other men in 'manly readiness' (2.3.128). He plans Banquo's killing with hired murderers (now perhaps his symbolic reflection), not with his Lady, and when he says 'we', it is often apparently the 'royal we', referring to himself alone, for example speaking of his refusal to 'eat our meal in fear' (3.2.19). Like Brutus in his first scene with Portia, he refuses to tell her his plans, and unlike Brutus, he never shakes in this decision.

The banquet scene presents Macbeth visually as an outsider, as he refuses to sit while he sees Banquo's ghost in his chair. Lady Macbeth echoes some of her earlier goading of Macbeth—'Are you a man?' (3.4.57). She acts like a concerned wife and hostess, trying to keep up appearances with their guests, but her role-playing cannot return her to either to the role of social insider, which she played earlier, or to her former closeness with Macbeth. From this point it is clear that he will never tell her what he is going to do. The last time we see her she has descended into the isolation of madness, as her past attempts to comfort her husband return and her guilt about their victims emerges for the first time in the language of her sleepwalking scene.

Goneril and Regan have a similar beginning—at first apparently social insiders because they behave as Lear wants them to, although they know that he has always loved Cordelia most. Having been given their halves of the kingdom, they make Lear into an outsider by challenging the behaviour of his men. However, their development, especially their blinding of Gloucester, reveals them as moral outsiders, and they die as social outsiders also in their competition over Edmund.

Tragic heroes are always at least temperamentally outsiders of a sort that I am mostly not considering here, because they feel and express more than other characters do, but in some of the tragedies, the central female and male character maintain for longer a kind of space of their own, like what Lady Macbeth and Macbeth have at the beginning, so that, whatever else happens, they are, for a while, insiders in a relationship. We see this in *Romeo and Juliet*: the tragic ending returns them to a space of their own. Antony and Cleopatra and Othello and Desdemona have such a space, lose it in different ways, and try to recover it in their deaths. There is a suggestion that Ophelia and Hamlet had such a relationship in the past, but during the play it is hard to see Ophelia as any kind of insider, particularly as she descends into madness.

Both Goneril and Regan fantasize a bond with Edmund. Goneril has a brief ecstatic kiss with him onstage and it is possible that he may be moved, not just ironic, when he says, just before his decision to try to save Lear and Cordelia, 'Yet Edmund was beloved' (5.3.238). It is hard to think of Edmund and either sister as heroic lovers against the rules of their society; nevertheless, the Richard Eyre film (1998) takes him seriously here and shows him trying to hold on to the hand of Goneril's dead body as he is carried away.

A shared space between lovers frequently occurs in comedy and romance, for example when Portia first welcomes Bassanio to Belmont, and gives him a musical key for the right casket. It may occur even if one of two lovers is in disguise, as Rosalind is in many of her scenes with Orlando. In the romances it may occur between lovers, as with Perdita and Florizel in *Winter's Tale*, or as powerfully between reunited father and daughter, as in *Pericles*.

At the end of some of Shakespeare's tragedies, women's place is clearly marked: either they die in a love relationship and, as symbolic insiders in their love, are valued by the other characters onstage, or else they die alone as moral outsiders. However, there are exceptions: Volumnia, when she last appears, is praised as Rome's saviour and patroness, but we don't see her reaction to her son's death, and are left to wonder about whether she rejoices in it as she expected to, because it is a death in battle, and whether, if so, we should consider her a moral outsider even if Roman society does not.[24] Gertrude drinks from the poisoned cup Claudius meant for Hamlet, but Hamlet acknowledges only the self-destructive aspect of her drinking, rather than seeing it as her testing Claudius' intentions for him, saying, 'Wretched Queen, adieu!' (5.2.276). At the end of most of Shakespeare's comedies most women are married, the ritual condition of admission to adulthood in his society, in spite of the social reality of the large number of unattached women. He seldom calls attention to a woman's singleness as he does to that of Antonio in *Merchant*, or Don Pedro in *Much Ado*, who is told by Benedick, 'Prince, thou art sad, get thee a wife' (5.4.117). At the end of *Winter's Tale*, after all the family reconstitutions, Paulina proclaims herself 'an old turtle' (5.3.133), a solitary widow with nothing left but mourning, and Leontes immediately matches her up with his counsellor Camillo. With a little more foreshadowing for the 'compulsory heterosexuality' of the ending, Rosalind pairs the formerly resistant Phebe to her devoted Silvius.[25]

One play, definitely an exception to this rule, however, is *Troilus and Cressida*, where Cressida is just a spoil of war and after being moved from the Trojans to the Greeks can't resist giving up her faithfulness to Troilus when she is besieged by Diomedes, and the audience sees her capitulation through Troilus' eyes. Written close to this in time is another possible exception. *Measure for Measure* shows

Isabella, who as a would-be novice in a corrupt society has always been an outsider, having the chance to become an insider by marrying the Duke. But the play does not give her an answer to his proposal.[26] *Troilus and Cressida* is, of all Shakespeare's plays, the hardest to place generically, and *Measure for Measure* is usually called a problem comedy or tragicomedy; one undoubted early comedy, *Love's Labour's Lost*, ends with many unmarried women, but it is because they have turned down the men's marriage proposals and set them trials to endure for a year or more before they get another chance.

The most celebrated social bonds for women in Shakespeare's plays are marital and familial; nevertheless occasionally there are more transient moments when characters form more tentative connections. While I have discussed earlier in this chapter how often women confirm a place as relative insider by contrast to someone who is more of an outsider, there are other occasions when relatively privileged women speak of or to outsiders with a sense of kinship or sympathy. In *Love's Labour's Lost*, the highest ranking woman, the Princess of France, expresses her sympathy for one of the actors in the pageant performed by characters of lower rank: 'Alas, poor Maccabeus, how hath he been baited!' (5.2.619) in words that anticipate Olivia's to Malvolio, although here the sense of particular similarity that Olivia expresses is lacking. It is part of Rosalind's appeal that, in her exile in the Forest of Arden, she feels kinship with Silvius, whose 'wound' in love she sees as like hers—though it is sobering to feminists who like her that she doesn't acknowledge that she might be similar to Phebe too.

The love of Desdemona for Othello can also be seen as an example of the affinity of a female insider for an outsider—or, alternatively, as an example of the affinity of a female outsider for a different kind of outsider.[27] When Desdemona says, 'she wished | That heaven had made her such a man' (1.3.161–2), affinity is the clearest message, whichever kind we think is dominant, though in the world of *Othello* that affinity is impossible to sustain except in death.

Women in Shakespeare are sometimes social insiders and can turn others, men and women, into outsiders, and when moral outsiders, do worse than that. Yet Shakespeare's plays often encourage us to see the similarity of characters from different groups, outsiders and insiders, different kinds of outsiders. The voice of judgment on outsiders is frequently accompanied by the voice of fellow-feeling, and some directors are suggesting such sympathy even when it is not written in the text—viewers and readers do not have to give up feeling for outsiders to appreciate the plays. Is that sympathy unthinkable even in a character who does not speak it? A 2011 Broadway *Merchant of Venice* production, directed by Daniel Sullivan, suggests that Portia is hostile to Antonio partly because of his forced conversion of Shylock. In almost its last image she looks out of her balcony with concern for Jessica, who discards the deed of gift of Shylock's possessions and sits alone on stage. Can the previously xenophobic Portia make a connection with Jessica? As a stage image, at any rate, it is very moving.

4

Othello and Other Outsiders

In her important book *Shakespeare, Race, and Colonialism*, Ania Loomba states, 'Any sympathy for Othello reinforces the misogynist sentiments mouthed by some characters, and any sympathy for Desdemona endorses the view that Othello is a "gull, a dolt, a devil."'[1] If these words mean that it is impossible to feel sympathy for both, I disagree. Part of the power of this play is that a reader or viewer may very well feel sympathy for both Othello and Desdemona, and may be even further torn by responding to the appeal of Iago. Some recent critics downplay this sympathy and suggest that the dominant impact of the play is racist and pornographic. However, while the play shows prejudiced characters, behaviour, and language, and can be seen in a pornographic way, this chapter, while reviewing some historical and literary context of the representation of outsiders in the play, will show through specific details that it humanizes Othello, gives Desdemona compelling speeches, and offers at one point, at least, an explicit critique of a patriarchal perspective on women.

'In Venice they do let God see the pranks | They dare not show their husbands' (3.3.205–6), says Iago in one of the key lines, calling up Othello's sense that he does not understand the adultery and deceit of the women of the city he is defending and therefore of his own wife. Struck with anxiety, Othello contemplates three different reasons for the rejection he thinks Desdemona has given him— 'Haply for I am black, | And have not those soft parts of conversation | That chamberers have; or for I am declined | Into the vale of years...' (3.3.267–70). Why does the play include this exchange? Why does Othello give other explanations for losing Desdemona besides his colour? Critics have focused on his blackness or, recently, his condition as a Moor, and the particular associations of these categories in his society are important to the play. Yet it shows how fluid the outsider position in Shakespeare can be that Othello is not certain whether his blackness is more important than his age or his inexperience in high Venetian society, and it is not clear here whether he thinks his blackness might present anything beyond aesthetic disadvantage, like aging (unpleasant enough, but not the same as being considered evil). Rather than an Othello and a society where race-consciousness trumps everything, the play gives us an Othello who has been highly honored in Venice earlier, though under Iago's pressure he can imagine several reasons for insecurity—who may really be, as the title calls him, a 'Moor of Venice' as opposed to being a Moor temporarily in Venice.[2] It gives us a Desdemona who somehow braves her society's controls on women with an insider's confidence, even as her confidence provokes Othello to see her as a moral outsider. And in Iago it gives us a class outsider (whose name, ironically, also suggests he is an outsider to Venice) who arouses Othello's insecurities largely because of his claim to insider knowledge about Venice. It gives us an Emilia who, similarly, has more knowledge of her world than Desdemona but along with that a clearer knowledge of the way she is deprived of rights in that world. The interplay of insider and outsider here and the complexity of Othello's outsider position as a foreigner who is admired contributes to the sympathy that many viewers have given Othello even as they deplore his shocking murder of Desdemona. Once more, an important aspect of the experience of this play is the shifting point of view as we first see Othello as an outsider through Iago's eyes, then see how he refutes Iago's image, then how he gradually approaches it as Iago makes him see Desdemona as an outsider, then how he kills the outsider in himself while Iago is revealed to the other characters as the real moral outsider.

Othello

The representation of Othello is double from the beginning of the play. On one hand, Othello's position in Venice and his reception in the Senate Council scene show more clearly than any plays so far discussed that an outsider can be admired. The senators and the Duke of Venice greet Othello as 'valiant' (1.3.48) and in the next act the man he is replacing as governor of Cyprus describes him as 'a worthy governor' (2.1.31), 'full soldier' (37), and 'brave' (39).[3] We see his narrative of his life fascinating the Senate as we hear about its fascination for Desdemona—indeed, the Duke says, 'I think this tale would win my daughter too' (1.3.170). However, the first picture of Othello in the play comes not from the Senate but from Iago, and his description begins with an attack on him for pride and bombast and moves on to call him 'an old black ram' (1.1.88). Roderigo speaks of 'the gross clasps of a lascivious Moor... an extravagant and wheeling stranger | From here and everywhere' (1.1.127. 137–8).

Calm and civilized on his actual appearance, Othello is quite different from the man Iago and Roderigo have described.[4] He faces those who would arrest him with an argument about keeping swords beautiful—'Keep up your bright swords, for the dew will rust 'em' (1.2.560). He is dignified enough that Emrys Jones finds this scene reminiscent of the mystery cycle portrayal of the arrest of Christ, who also responds to a nighttime attack with openness and calm peace-making.[5] Othello does not fulfill the expectation, discussed by Ian Smith, that cultural outsiders, sometimes called barbarians, would make linguistic errors, known as barbarisms. Many critics agree that Othello in his 'sheer power of speech claims a subjectivity that makes it impossible for the audience simply to distance himself as a racial other.'[6] In spite of the fact that he claims to be 'rude... in my speech' (1.3.81), his language is image-filled and resonant. It refutes the stereotype of the inarticulate barbarian, but Iago calls it 'bombast' (1.1.13). Classical rhetoricians might call it Asiatic (as opposed to Attic), a term suggesting ornament rather than brevity, hinting at a speaker somewhat foreign to preferred European style, and thus making his outsider position re-emerge.[7] More precisely, Robert Watson has shown that Othello frequently pairs neologisms with familiar words, in a code-switching 'making him a kind of familiar stranger... both exotic and accessible.'[8] His hybrid language expresses his double identity and shows his alienation, but helps him appeal to his audience.

Some of Othello's self-presentation may well have sounded less like insecurity to his early audience than it does now. Othello's self-characterization, 'Rude am I in my speech, | And little blessed with the soft phrase of peace' (1.3.81–2), fits with the polite courtiers' and humanists' convention of beginning with an apology about one's limitations, now known as the 'modesty topos'. When he promises to retell the story of their courtship 'as truly as to heaven | I do confess the vices of my blood' (1.3.22–3), which some readers now see as already hinting at guilt connected with his race, the dominant impression left earlier may have been of a Christian belief in the Fall, which affected all humanity, accompanied by confidence in heaven's forgiveness.[9] When Othello tells of the wonders he has seen on his travels, he speaks of them as if he were a European voyager like Hakluyt or Mandeville, or like Robert Greene's romance hero Orlando, who, like Othello, has travelled past the Anthropophagi.[10] Though he uses exotic words, he does not exoticize himself to the extent of the twentieth-century character who says 'I am Othello' in the Sudanese novel *Season of Migration to the North* and calls himself 'a naked, primitive creature, a spear in one hand and arrows in the other'.[11] Shakespeare's Othello, by contrast, claims he wants Desdemona with him to be 'free and bounteous to her mind' (1.3.264), not out of the heat of young passion. Nevertheless, Othello's self-containment and general respect cannot erase the memory of Iago's hostile words. If they now appear false, nevertheless they show that from early on his position is under threat.

Showing Othello from the beginning as a character with a bitter and clever enemy, from this perspective, helps to humanize him. So does his modesty, however conventional, and the way he presents Desdemona's love for him—not for his achievements but, more humbly, 'for the dangers I had passed' (1.3.166). Thus the play gives several ways to see Othello, to imagine his feelings. One of the main questions the play presents is how much the admiration or identification Othello invites near the beginning remains given the play's increased emphasis on his difference (from himself and from the Venetians) as he becomes jealous.

That term Moor was itself ambiguous; while it always suggested some kind of an outsider, according to Michael Neill it could refer to 'the Arab-Berber people of the region variously called "Mauretania" or "Barbary"...; sometimes it might extend...to all the inhabitants of Africa...[or could] be used as a blanket term for Muslims of any nationality. At still other times it might...be applied to any people of colour, regardless of geographical origin or religious affiliation.'[12] What colour and religion should Othello be? When he rebukes his soldiers, 'Are we turned Turks?...For Christian shame put by this barbarous brawl' (2.3.153, 155), and when Iago later refers to Othello's baptism, it is clear that he is now a Christian, which would be appropriate for a defender of Venice against the Muslim army of Turkey. However, in the early modern period (and not only then) the sincerity of Christian converts from Islam, and even of their descendants, was often suspect, and Brabanzio may well think of him as a pagan, judging from his warning to the Senate about the consequences of leniency about his marriage: 'Bondslaves and pagans shall our statesmen be' (1.2.100).

His colour may be even more ambiguous: In spite of all Iago's references to him as black, and Brabanzio's reference to his 'sooty bosom' (1.2.71), 'black' was often then used to refer to skin darkened merely by suntan. A tawny colour, writes Julia Reinhard Lupton, would emphasize his Islamic background more, and make him seem more alien to an English audience; however, she sees the play as leaving open, at least early in the play, the possibility that he is a convert from an African polytheistic or animist religion, which black skin might imply.[13] But along with his colour, his religious history is one of many facts about Othello that the play leaves ambiguous, not telling us when he became a Christian, what, if any, was his previous religion, how he got to Venice, where he came from. Perhaps his uncertain position adds to his power as well as his mystery, its instability making him more strange and possibly more terrifying.[14]

Attitudes toward Africans and Moors in Shakespeare's society were mixed, and the play shows traces of several currents. As Ania Loomba and Jonathan Burton have shown in their anthology, 'the idea that Africans are lustful is ubiquitous' in early modern Europe, though association with violence doesn't receive as much emphasis.[15] The negative images of Othello that come from Iago and Roderigo focus more on association with lustful animality rather than violence, though the two are related. *Othello* has more animal imagery than any other Shakespearean play, and it begins with Iago's labeling Othello an 'old black ram' (1.1.88) and a stallion who will give Brabanzio horses for grandchildren. Iago also describes him to Roderigo as lascivious and changeable, and in one soliloquy imagines him usurping his place in bed with Emilia. One of the most influential early modern writers about geography and character, Jean Bodin, regards Africans as 'more easily inflamed to passion, more jealous, and more sinful than "northern people."' However, he also gives Africans credit for 'letters, useful arts, virtues, training, philosophy, religion, and lastly *humanitas* itself', though he notes that these contributions were not widely recognized in his own time, and this observation has been one of the less influential portions of his own thought.[16]

The complexity of ideas about Africans at the time may reflect the fact that the modern concept of race, as well as the modern stereotype of the African, was still in the process of consolidation.[17] The term 'race' itself referred most often to 'familial groups and lineage', though it could be used to identify larger related groups such as Africans. Furthermore, images of Africans were themselves in flux. Mary Floyd-Wilson documents that in the early modern period ideas about the calmness and wisdom of Africans (based on beliefs about the influence of geography on the body's humors) competed and sometimes combined with the now more familiar belief in their extreme passions.[18] Calmness indeed characterizes Othello at the beginning, and Desdemona's view of him before she realizes how he has changed. And in an early soliloquy even Iago contradicts his descriptions of Othello as passionate, lustful, and changeable: 'The Moor... is of a constant, loving, noble nature' (2.1.275–6). But the more negative strand of ideas about Africans justified slavery, became the dominant trend in European culture, and has influenced reactions to Othello (and much else) ever since.

Previous representations of Moors and Africans were also mixed, though the dominant picture was again negative. The morality plays of the Middle Ages, still being played in Shakespeare's childhood, had a long tradition of portraying devils as black. In the secular theatre, all previous black characters in plays, such as Shakespeare's own Aaron, were villains and were clearly identified as Moors. The one good Moor, Abdelmalec in *The Battle of Alcazar*, is not described as black, though that term is used of the bad Moor, whom he fights. However, there were a few genres that presented black and/or Moorish figures more positively. The London Lord Mayor's pageant of 1585, for example, includes a Moor whose function is to pay tribute to the widely known fame of London and its queen.[19] And in the visual arts, black kings appear in a number of paintings before the date of Othello—a long tradition has it that one of the three kings or magi who travelled to Bethlehem from the East to worship the Christ child, probably Balthasar, was black.[20] So there were traditions associating blackness with both good and evil.

A Geographical History of Africa, written by Leo Africanus, another Moor turned Christian, appeared in John Pory's English translation just four years before *Othello* was first performed. Some of his descriptions of Africans and Moors sound as if Shakespeare drew on them: of the people of Barbary, he writes, 'most honest people they are, and destitute of all fraud and guile; Likewise they are most strong and valiant people.' On the other hand, 'No Nation in the World is so subject unto Jealousy; for they will rather lose their lives, than put up any disgrace in the behalf of their women.' Furthermore, he writes: 'Whithersoever they go, they are most honourably esteemed of; for none of them will profess any Art, unless he hath attained until great exactness and perfection therein.'[21]

Shakespeare had portrayed two Moors earlier, Aaron in *Titus Andronicus* and Morocco in *Merchant of Venice*. Aaron is a witty plotter of evil but he is not simply evil. He embraces his blackness in defiance of morality: 'Let fools do good, and fair men call for grace: | Aaron will have his soul black as his face' (3.1.203–04). But late in the play his colour pride becomes fatherly love of his newborn son with Tamora. He protests against racist descriptions of the baby and determines to save him against threats from Tamora's white sons and others, identifying with him as

> The figure and the picture of my youth.
> This before all the world I do prefer.
> ....
> Look how the black slave smiles upon the father,
> As who should say, 'Old lad, I am thine own.'
>
> (4.2.107–9, 120–1)

While he dies unrepentant of his evil deeds, his love of his son is an appealing quality in a play where the nominal hero, Titus, not only seems glad to have 25 military sons killed in battle but also kills his daughter himself.

Aaron never worries about Tamora finding his blackness unattractive, but in *Merchant of Venice*, Morocco begins his wooing of Portia by saying, 'Mislike me not for my complexion' (2.1.1). He is willing to have his blood tested against that of the 'fairest creature northward born' (3) for its redness, that is, for his courage, and brags that his face has frightened brave men and won the love of 'the best regarded virgins' (10) of his land. However, before he ever appears, Portia imagines that he has 'the complexion of a devil' (1.2.109–10), and when he loses the casket test, because he can't imagine that the referent of 'what many men desire' could be death and not Portia, she is relieved: 'Let all of his complexion choose me so' (2.7.79). Portia, who makes fun of most of her suitors in terms of ethnic stereotypes, is clearly no Desdemona.

Others of Shakespeare's earlier plays, as well as his later sonnets, also show an interest in the issue of blackness and its appeal or repulsion. In them, however, passages describing or denying 'blackness' as a barrier to love usually refer to blackness in a woman, and the word is usually taken to refer to a dark-haired, dark-skinned or tanned 'white' woman.[22] In *Love's Labour's Lost* Biron defends the beauty of his love Rosaline against the taunts of his friends that 'Black is the badge of hell' (4.3.250). *As You Like It*'s Rosalind, in her disguise as Ganymede, sounds a little like Portia as she disdains attraction to Phebe's 'inky brows' (3.5.47). Most famously, in the sonnets Shakespeare plays with the conundrum of how a man can be attached to a woman whose darkness does not fit his traditional ideas of beauty—in some, through the paradox that she is true beauty's heir because she is wearing black to mourn it, in others simply because he is foolish or mad, for her outward blackness expresses her inward evil: 'I have sworn thee fair, and thought thee bright, | Who art as black as hell, as dark as night' (sonnet 147).

So Shakespeare had long imagined characters using 'blackness' language not only to insult but also to question dominant ideals of beauty and how love relates to them, and he had begun to explore the protest of the dark speaker who is excluded by those ideals. But not until *Othello* does he explore an arc of psychological development in the voice of a black man who begins with pride in his ancestry as well as value to a new community and cannot maintain both, or the voice of a white woman who loves across race and defends her love of the individual, rather than a man who makes jokes about his non-traditional love as do Biron and the sonnet speaker. And in none of the earlier plays is there a character who uses the language of race so persistently and maliciously as Iago.

Venice was an obvious setting to explore the tragic psychological development of a Moor in an ambiguous insider/outsider situation. Not only was it known in England to be an international city, a city dependent on the trade of many nations (a theme previously used in *Merchant of Venice*), it was thought to be a place where diverse people, including people of non-Christian religions, were allowed relative freedom. And according to Contarini's *Commonwealth and Government of Venice*, translated into English by Lewis Lewkenor in 1599, and echoed by Shakespeare in some of his details, Venice had the tradition of appointing foreigners as captain general to its armies![23] However, this custom doesn't exactly make such a general an insider in every respect: it still builds on the advantages to the state of a foreigner's greater vulnerability in this position of power. David McPherson hypothesizes that the reason for this custom was to prevent military coups d'état, and if the position of the foreign general was analogous to that of the foreign vizier frequent in the medieval Mediterranean discussed by Sharon Kinoshita, foreignness would also have made him dependent on his Duke and less likely to have a family who would take vengeance if he were removed from power.[24] Still, most of those generals were from other Italian city-states; Lewkenor mentions a 'foreign' general from Bergamo. Venice's military records show soldiers and sometimes captains from France, Germany, Switzerland, Spain, Dalmatia, and Hungary. But the limits of the historical Venice's cosmopolitanism may appear in events of 1510, when some horsemen referred to as Turks joined the cavalry, and were ostracized and accused of crimes ranging from theft to assault and kidnapping of young boys.[25] These events did not get into Contarini or Lewkenor.

A few years after his first play about Venice, probably around 1603, Shakespeare found, or returned to, a story of an unnamed Moorish Captain in Venice in a collection of novellas he had just used for the main plot of *Measure for Measure*, Cinthio's *Gli Hecatommithi*. Though Cinthio's story also focuses on a noble Moor 'very dear to the Signoria' and described as 'valiant' but hated by his Ensign,

Shakespeare's play changes it in a number of ways.[26] Many of them contribute to possible sympathy for and humanization of Othello. Much as he did in adding anti-Semitic language from Antonio, Salerio, Solanio, and Graziano to his sources in *Merchant of Venice*, Shakespeare makes explicit at length race/religion-based hostility to Othello voiced by his invented characters Roderigo and Brabanzio, and his newly named and transformed Iago. The play adds the narrative of Othello winning Desdemona through his stories of suffering, adventure, and marvels, much of it resembling the description of Leo Africanus in Pory's introduction to the English translation of his book. It adds Desdemona's declaration that she saw Othello's visage in his mind, and changes her source character's belief in the jealousy of Moors to her (unfortunately wrong) belief that because of the sun's drying effect on the humors of jealousy he is calm, a belief widely circulating at the time.[27] And it adds Othello's changing views of his own race, from his initial pride in his descent—though this is expressed as pride in ancestors who were 'men of royal siege' (1.2.22), not in specific racial terms—to his later response to Iago's hint that Othello as a foreigner doesn't understand 'our country''s women's promiscuity—'Haply, for I am black...she's gone' (3.3.267–71). Thus the play gives several different angles on Othello's position with which a variety of readers and viewers might identify—pride in ancestry, anxiety about not understanding the codes of a new community, fear of being found inadequate for some unknown reason.

However, as the play proceeds, Othello's blackness increasingly takes on allegorical associations with evil. This occurs in speeches by Othello himself especially in Acts 2 and 3. His blackness is not simply an aesthetic reason for possible unattractiveness (as in 'Haply, for I am black') but associated with shame, when he says that either his name (in the Folio text) or Desdemona's (in the second Quarto) 'is as begrimed and black as mine own face' (3.3.391–3). Michael Neill finds a pattern in which when Othello calls, 'Arise, black Vengeance' (3.3.451) he becomes associated with that allegorical figure, and when he says his 'best judgment' has been 'collied' (2.3.189) his blackness is linked with irrationality.[28] Leah Marcus has similarly argued that overall 'What Othello does, and much more explicitly and powerfully in F [the early Folio text] than in Q [the early Quarto text], is to enact a process by which skin color comes to be associated even by Othello himself with innate differences that demand his subordination or exclusion.'[29] 'Even by Othello himself' is significant. After the initial impetus from Iago, it is mainly Othello himself who makes these associations. Emilia condemns him as a 'blacker devil' (5.2.140) when she finds that he has killed Desdemona, but at this point she doesn't know about Iago's role. Iago is, instead, the character who ends up being the most associated with the devil. Thus the play itself doesn't finally present blackness as demanding social exclusion as much as it shows Othello feeling that it does.

It is worth considering what the play does not do with the association of Othello and stereotype. Though Othello links his face with dirt and shame, he does not speak of particular vices for which his origin or colour would make him suspect. He does not go from 'Arise, black Vengeance', to an explicit race-related social expectation that he will be jealous or vengeful. Such self-consciousness is expressed by the transformed version of Othello as an adolescent basketball player in the 2001 US film *O*. But Othello himself does not say this. When Othello fears that Desdemona no longer loves him, he does not say that she thinks because he is a Moor he is violent, nor, when he plans to kill her does he speak about others' expectations of Moors' jealousy. He never speaks of struggling against expectations he will be violent, lustful, or jealous, though his early emphasis on his self-control can be read as countering such prejudices.

Perhaps if Othello showed a critical awareness of stereotype, it might contribute to a clearer anti-racist interpretation of the play, as opposed to the racist interpretation that he murders Desdemona because Moors really are more jealous and violent. What if Shakespeare had Othello at some point make a charge like that of Shylock—'Thou call'dst me dog before thou hadst a cause, | But since I am a dog, beware my fangs' (*MV* 3.3.6–7)—and say that he is behaving in a way that responds to others' insults or follows the behaviour others have used to him? Shylock's charge shows that the idea of the self-fulfilling prophecy, including the likelihood of people taking on bad characteristics expected in them, was available in Shakespeare's time—but on the other hand, *Merchant* criticism also shows that a character who explains himself in this way can still be interpreted according to the stereotype. On the other hand, perhaps Othello doesn't mention the stereotype because it hadn't yet been consolidated (as we have seen, others shared Desdemona's view that Africans were calm). As a tragic hero, he may believe that he has been up against destiny—'Who can control his fate?' (5.2.272), he exclaims in the last scene—but it might make him seem too sociological and too undignified if he suggested that his behaviour was heightened by others' beliefs about Moors or Africans. Most importantly, by omitting reflections from Othello about others' views of him, the play puts the focus more specifically on his jealousy of Desdemona. He thinks more about what her infidelity means to him than about what others expect of him as an African or a Moor.

During the time that leads up to the murder, Othello is framed as a cultural outsider by his description of the magical handkerchief, given to his mother by an Egyptian charmer, and, as Joel Altman says, by his apparent belief in the uncanny magic he is reporting.[30] And in some of these scenes his emotions overcome him and the language he once used so beautifully falls into pieces—and he becomes the inarticulate barbarian from which his earlier behaviour so differentiated him, or the split subject who moves in one speech from 'let her rot and perish' (4.1.174) to 'O, the world hath not a sweeter creature' (176). Even more importantly, as someone who is plotting murder, to the audience he becomes a moral outsider. He tries turning to a community of men, and making Desdemona the outsider: 'O curse of marriage | That we can call these delicate creatures ours | And not their appetites' (3.3.372–3). Nevertheless, the community of men who feel wronged (which of course includes Iago) is not a consoling one. At a deep emotional level, Othello's view of Desdemona as the outsider alternates unstably with his view of himself as an outsider in relation to her. Othello is concerned with having been 'discarded' by Desdemona, as he calls her 'the fountain from the which my current runs | Or else dries up' (4.2.61–2).

However, as the dramatic tension increases after the long scene during which Iago arouses Othello's jealousy, which includes the passage about his face as 'begrimed and black' and ends with summoning up 'black Vengeance from [his] hollow hell', and his pledging to persist in his resolution like the Pontic [Black]Sea, neither Iago nor Othello makes any more reference to Othello's 'blackness'. Othello has the reference to a handkerchief given his mother by an Egyptian, to be sure, with its exoticism, but there are no more words from Othello about his race or his Moorishness until his suicide speech. It is as if the explicit statements of Act 3 Scene 3 are where the racial images of the play have been moving—and once they have been made explicit, Shakespeare, unlike the scriptwriters of *O*, has no need to repeat them during the time leading most directly to Desdemona's murder. During this time, Othello does not care about whether he is an outsider in any other way once he is convinced that he is a cuckold. Once Desdemona found his stories of life outside Venice appealing, but now it seems he is outside her love, which is more important to him. As he eloquently speaks of Desdemona as 'there where I have garnered up my heart, | Where either I must live or bear no life' (4.2.58–9) readers and spectators may well identify with his suffering.

Othello could be seen as humanized further by his jealousy, since he is preoccupied by what apparently was such a common male anxiety at the time and his suffering is so obvious. At the same time we see that the play's actual community of men, including Venetian visitors, is shocked by his behaviour. Othello hardly cares about this male disapproval, but as he goes to kill Desdemona he thinks 'She must die, or she'll betray more men' (5.2.6), making his loyalty to an abstract male community more explicit. He no longer thinks of himself as acting out of vengeance, but rather out of desire for justice, and his eloquence has returned. Thus his position continues to be double. He is killing his wife, acting as a moral outsider, yet he thinks he is behaving justly.

Before Emilia he tries to retain the position of moral authority— 'She's like a liar gone to burning hell' (5.2.138)—but Emilia returns to the language of colour and race, giving them both the names that allegorical tradition would have given them from the beginning, identifying Desdemona as too good for this world and Othello as too evil for it: 'O, the more angel she, and you the blacker devil' (140). But as Othello comes to understand how wrong he has been about Desdemona, he appears less a devil, especially because, unlike Emilia, readers and audience members have seen how Iago has deceived him. Marcus argues that lines like 'Be not afraid, though you do see me weapon'd' (5.2.273, only in the Folio) 'require the on-stage audience to recoil in horror from Othello's person.'[31] However, readers and viewers know more about him than does the on-stage audience, and might identify with him to the point of feeling how terrible it is to see that people find you so dangerous. The intensity of his pain for his wrongdoing is clear as he imagines himself in—indeed, asks for—hell-like suffering: 'Whip me, ye devils, | From the possession of this heavenly sight. | Blow me about in winds, roast me in sulfur' (5.2.284–6).

Othello's suicide speech is his only return to exotic language since he told Desdemona about the Egyptian source of the handkerchief. The world outside Europe evoked here includes ignorance, as in the 'base Indian' (Neill makes a good explanation why this reading is better than 'Judean') but it also includes healing.[32] Othello weeps, as Desdemona had before, and the tears are like the 'medicinal gum' (5.2.360), myrrh, of Arabian trees. The possibility that grief and repentance could be restorative, which will become real in the romances, surfaces for a moment. But then Othello returns to the fraught world of religious/political warfare with its polarities of good and evil, and reenacts how he has become its battleground. As B. J. Sokol has observed, earlier in the play he and most of the Venetians spoke of his Turkish opponents with respect, but here he not only aligns himself again with the Venetian state (and Shakespeare's expected audience), but also speaks with contempt for the one punished in Aleppo as well as for his own recently erring self as well as killing them both in one gesture: 'I took by th' throat the circumcised dog | And smote him thus' (364–5).[33] Whereas earlier he killed Desdemona to defend males, now he is killing himself to defend Venice. In the same move he tries to resolve the ambiguities of his identity, empowering the loyal Venetian in himself to kill the alien also within him. But finally it is reunion with Desdemona that he wants most: 'No way but this: | Killing myself to die upon a kiss' (368–9). For him, there is no other way to be reunited with Desdemona, no other way to atone, but in suicide. Does his death establish his posthumous rehabilitation for the characters within the play?

At this point Iago's evil, his status as a moral outsider, is finally revealed to the characters, and their judgments on him are clearly harsher than their judgments on Othello. Emilia refers to Othello as a villain in 5.2.179, asking Iago to disprove Othello's explanation, but every use of the word 'villain' after that—by Emilia, Montano, and Lodovico, as well as Othello—refers to Iago. Othello is called 'this rash and most unfortunate man' (289) but Iago is a 'viper' (291), 'most heathenish and gross' (321) 'demi-devil' (307) who is 'hellish' (378) and a 'Spartan dog' (371). This is a reversal of the animal imagery Iago originally directed as Othello, and might suggest that in contrast with the attitude to Iago, Othello is in death relatively accepted by the onstage community. However, for most of the surrounding characters, there is only omission to show this acceptance. Lodovico mentions him to declare that the Venetian Graziano, Desdemona's uncle, will inherit what he calls 'the fortunes of the Moor' (365)—and perhaps to refer to him as part of 'the tragic loading of this bed.... The object poisons sight' (373, 374).

Cassio, however, gives Othello the final tribute—'he was great of heart' (371). Cassio's forgiveness of Othello for plotting his murder is remarkable: all he says about it is 'Dear general, I never gave you cause' (305). He is a voice for the feeling in the audience that would sympathize with Othello at the end. This is a brief tribute to Othello at the end by contrast to tributes to Hamlet, Anthony, and Brutus, for example, but in Shakespeare shorter is not necessarily less powerful. Nevertheless, it is true that most of the other tragedies include a more general mood of admiration for their hero among the surviving characters.

Some of Shakespeare's outsiders, such as Shylock, or in this play Emilia and Bianca, have speeches that claim similarity to those in the majority. But as the object of persecution near the beginning, Othello maintains not his equality but his meriting a high position because of his descent from 'men of royal siege' (1.2.22). The movement in the play that counters Iago's hostility begins not by presenting Othello as similar to ourselves, but, in the tradition of tragedy, as superior. And even as he falls apart with jealousy, Lodovico recalls him as 'the noble Moor whom our full senate | Call all in all sufficient' (4.1.261–2). He falls a great deal from that height.

But he never becomes as much a moral outsider as Cornwall is when he puts out Gloucester's eyes or Lady Macbeth when she prays to the spirits of evil. Othello kills Desdemona thinking that she is evil. Terrible as such an act is, it may have been, if atoned for, more forgivable to an audience of the time than those of some of Shakespeare's other characters.

Perhaps as much as any character, Othello exemplifies how polarizing reactions to an outsider can be in Shakespeare, with the play's great interest—and indeed *Othello* was from the beginning one of the most frequently performed and written about—resulting from strong and often opposite emotions. One of the reasons for these opposite emotions may be that the disgust Iago solicits for Othello stays in our minds even though a rational appraisal of the play shows us Iago's unreliability: 'the play thinks abomination into being and then taunts the audience with the knowledge that it can never be *unthought*'.[34] This is supported by recent experimental psychological research, which shows that if people read a number of statements and are told that some are unreliable, they are still more likely, when tested later, to remember a statement they have read in this experiment as true.[35] Thus, in a way analogous to the effect of the play Neill discusses when he says we can't forget Iago's words, the propagandist technique of the Big Lie repeated many times works, and thus it seems plausible that readers and audiences of all historical periods can't help remembering Iago's charge that Othello is an animal.

Yet Othello kills himself in atonement. His suicide is one of the most significant changes Shakespeare made from his source, in which the Moor denies everything under torture and is banished and then killed by Desdemona's relatives. How much more heroic is it that Othello acknowledges what he has done and punishes himself for it!

However, the recent critical history of the play shows that Othello's intended act of atonement does not put him sufficiently in the category of tragic hero to save the play from charges of racism. By his suicide and the language surrounding it, Othello has proved that he has a human, self-judging sense of justice, but many readers and spectators can't help remember his killing of Desdemona more vividly than his killing of himself.[36] Or they regard his suicide not as atonement but as a weak way out or, like Daniel Vitkus, as a sure path to damnation.[37] Is atonement possible for someone who has committed a murder? Is the feeling that it is not possible for Othello conditioned by our racial history since Shakespeare's time? Or, more recently, by prejudice against Muslims?

In the mid seventeenth century, Abraham Wright, a clergyman who read plays, praises the characterization of 'Othello for a jealous husband'.[38] Against our current expectations, most of the early responses pay little attention to race. Race becomes explicitly important in comments later in the seventeenth century. Most likely, as Loomba and Kim Hall have written, this change occurred because the development of the transatlantic slave trade made race more salient and linked blackness more explicitly to godlessness, servitude, and moral inferiority. However, even at this time not everyone reacted to Othello's race in the same way, with the racist critique of the play by Thomas Rymer itself soon answered by Charles Gildon.[39]

At this point I want to contextualize reactions to Othello in the light of another kind of research by experimental psychologists. This research, which presumably would have different results in different societies, shows that many people who consciously avoid acting in a racist way nevertheless have an unconscious racism that can be triggered by visual or verbal testing. Thus, for example, psychologists found that an ambiguous shape held by a black man is much more likely to be judged as a gun than a similar shape held by a white man.[40] People do vary in their degree of unconscious racial associations—but for many people, it seems, the image of a black man as a killer of someone else fits their previous assumptions better than the image of him punishing himself. Furthermore, when directors interpret a play in the light of these associations, the associations are heightened for everyone who observes that version. So Oliver Parker's film of *Othello*, featuring Lawrence Fishburne, who had recently played the wife-beater Ike Turner, gives Othello jungle background music in his first scene with Desdemona and shows him walking toward her menacingly. In such contemporary productions, much of the ambiguity of Shakespeare's text is resolved in favour of a simpler version of Othello as a threat from the beginning.

Responses to a complex play and its performance cannot be exhaustively explained by the simple association tests of social psychologists. And even the majority of those who showed unconscious racism also showed a conscious belief in racial equality, so they are really more complex than the word and image association tests show. Nevertheless, these lines of research raise the question of whether any work of literature dealing with race in a society with a history marked by race-based slavery—with the possible exception of a didactic work like the 1967 pro-integration film *Guess Who's Coming to Dinner*—can be free from being read as exemplifying racist ideology.[41] This does not mean that every work of literature dealing with race in such societies is racist. Rather that, as the ambiguously shaped object held by a black man is seen as a gun by many who are not consciously racist, but who have probably seen more photographs, movies and TV images of black men with guns than of black men with cell phones, the racism of associations in, for example, American culture and the English language makes it hard not to associate Othello's violence against Desdemona with Othello's race, whether directly, or as an aspect of a stereotype he resists, or unconsciously. Because of the long impact of slavery, the image of the violent black man—from its Jim Crow use to justify lynching to the black-created form of gangsta rap—has much more currency today than it did in Shakespeare's time. And so, probably, since the World Trade Centre attack of 2001, has the image of the violent Moor, another outsider who is threatening rather than admired. Shakespeare's presentation of Othello is not this simple, but it is easy for viewers and readers to fit it into a simple paradigm that they have seen many times elsewhere, especially if the production is also influenced by that paradigm.

Desdemona, Emilia, Bianca

This play deals not only with Othello's place in a society where he is always marked as different, it also deals with how women are marked as different as well, and the ambiguity of their position as in some ways insiders and in some ways outsiders, and often moving from one position to the other.[42] Just as *Othello* shows a polarized attitude toward Moors, with Desdemona's love and Venice's original admiration of Othello combined with Iago's hatred, it also shows a polarized attitude toward women. Othello and Cassio both idealize Desdemona, but the hatred of women that only Iago shows early in the play communicates itself to Othello as he comes to see Desdemona as a whore and Emilia as the madam of a brothel, and something like it surfaces in a milder form in Cassio's casual contempt for Bianca. Indeed, at some point every woman in this play will be called a whore by the man closest to her.

From very early in this play, the way Iago treats Emilia exemplifies the position of women as outsiders. She is introduced with an insult, as Iago's first comment on her is to complain that she talks too much, a common Elizabethan stereotype of women. She protests, 'You ha' little cause to say so' (2.1.112), but the conversation proceeds with Iago making jokes about different kinds of women, and insulting them all. The frequent language of anti-feminism here contributes to the impression that, though Othello is the character most often seen as an outsider, the play deals with a culture to which women can never fully belong.[43] There is a clear expectation that women will be subordinate, and yet somehow they often inexplicably escape control. Iago heightens the suspicion of Desdemona as a changeable and untrustworthy woman in the minds of Brabanzio, Roderigo, and finally Othello, and his scene with Desdemona as they both wait for Othello to arrive in Cyprus shows the tissue of misogynistic proverbs which he can use. For women's changeability, untrustworthiness, and lust are not ideas unique to Iago—as we have seen in the previous chapter, there is a strong current in European culture emphasizing these beliefs as reasons to keep women in a subordinate and confined place.

Like Othello, Desdemona does not bother to argue her audience out of beliefs that may be held against her, but rather speaks eloquently of her love. By this time Shakespeare had imagined many comic heroines who earn audience admiration by their open love, and Desdemona has much charm and generosity in common with them.[44] But as the play continues Desdemona is an outsider in a way most of them are not; she is living in a military world, and her attempts to reconcile Othello with Cassio show something of the clash of that world with the domestic and courtly society to which she is accustomed. As Othello's jealousy heightens, Desdemona's difficulty in admitting his limitations and even in admitting that some women do deceive their husbands make her seem further an innocent who comes from another world.

Desdemona, like Othello, is framed as a paradoxical outsider. She is at first a beloved pet—'a white ewe' (1.1.89)—and then a traitor who 'has made a gross revolt' (135) by marrying a 'stranger | Of here and everywhere' (137–8). Her position, even more than Othello's, is a complicated interplay of insider and outsider.[45] As Othello recalls their courtship, she is literally a Venetian insider by contrast to his travels, but on the other hand she is at first a woman hearing a conversation between men about the world of men, and sometimes having to leave to deal with 'house affairs' (1.3.146) until he tells the whole story to her alone. Fascinated by his 'strange' (159) story with its 'dangers' (166), she ambiguously seems to identify with it—'she wished | That heaven had made her such a man' (161–2).

Just as the Senate's high valuation and Othello's own self-confidence at the beginning conflict with the racism that Iago utters and evokes in Brabanzio and Roderigo, Desdemona's courage in the first half of the play conflicts with the misogyny in Iago's language. Before the Senate, she has an insider's assurance that she can choose her husband and accompany him to Cyprus. When she arrives there, she is deferentially welcomed by Cassio, and as a woman in a relatively powerful position, defends Emilia from Iago's insults about talking too much. Trying to distract Iago from arguing with his wife, as well as to distract herself from her anxiety about Othello's safety, she invites Iago to write her praise, and thus sets up the couplets that amplify his already announced scorn of all women, at their best able only to 'suckle fools and chronicle small beer' (2.1.162). She has the confidence to label his words, good-naturedly, as 'heavy ignorance' (145) and 'profane and liberal' (165), unaware of how his worldview will infect Othello and thus impinge on her, denies him the usual husbandly prerogative—'Do not learn of him, Emilia' (163–4)—and turns to talk with Cassio. And when Othello arrives and speaks of the precariousness he feels about their happiness, Desdemona once more shows an insider's security when she says, 'The heavens forbid | But that our loves and comforts should increase | Even as our days do grow' (190–2).[46]

Desdemona further shows her faith that her relationship with Othello gives her an insider's power when she tells Cassio she can reconcile the two of them. She even thinks that within the marital bond she can have the authority to speak to Othello associated with predominantly or totally masculine roles in Shakespeare's time: 'His bed shall be a school, his board a shrift.... thy solicitor shall rather die | Than give thy cause away' (3.3.24, 27–8). She is interfering in matters of military administration, which she admits for a moment—'they say the wars must make example | Out of her best' 66–7)—but basically sees her advice as comparable to advising Othello on his health. Thus Othello, and perhaps many in the audience, would see her as a presumptuous outsider at this point, though he still loves her. Her extravagant insistence that Othello should see Cassio within three days and that some day she will ask him an even larger request contributes to the ease with which Othello succumbs to Iago's hints later in the scene.[47] After the jealous Othello insists on the handkerchief with persistence like Desdemona has used about Cassio, however, Desdemona starts to see herself critically as an 'unhandsome [unskillful] warrior' (3.4.147), more of an outsider to Othello's military or political concerns—'in such cases | Men's natures wrangle with inferior things | Though great ones are their object' (139–41). Yet, even when he is planning her murder, Othello still has moments when he sees her as an insider—'She might lie by an emperor's side and command him tasks' (4.1.177). He can still think of her in his former idealized way—'The fountain from the which my current runs | Or else dries up' (4.2.61–2)—as well as feel pain that she has, as he thinks, turned into 'a cistern for foul toads | To knot and gender in' (63–4).

When the Venetian delegation arrives in Cyprus, Desdemona once again is hopeful: her cousin Lodovico can 'make all well' (4.1.218). Here the insider's confidence has turned into the outsider's naïveté that we see in her continued trust of Iago and her refusal to believe that any wives are unfaithful. Though she can say 'I have not deserved this' (236), when Othello strikes her, he is treating her as an moral outsider, a 'devil' as he calls her. As Othello's treatment of her grows more erratic, Desdemona thinks of another outsider, her mother's maid, Barbary (associated with Africa by her name) and identifies with her, singing the song she sang when 'he she loved proved mad' (4.3.26). As Penny Gay has pointed out, in singing at all Desdemona is further identified as an outsider, since 'major female characters don't sing in Shakespeare unless they are distracted—"mad" like Ophelia; or...of a foreign culture' (Mortimer's Welsh wife in *Henry IV, Part 1*).[48]

What I have been calling Desdemona's confidence has been minimized by many directors, especially in the Victorian period, analyzed by some critics as stepping too far out of women's place, observed admiringly by Carol Thomas Neely in one of the most influential pieces of feminist criticism from the 1970s, and more recently critiqued by Ania Loomba, and in effect by playwrights such as Paula Vogel and Djanet Sears, who exaggerate it in their rewritings of her, as showing her upper class white privilege.[49] Perhaps this is one tragic woman's modulation of the overreaching of Shylock and Malvolio. Unlike Shylock and like her husband, she never makes an explicit claim about her rights as a member of a subordinate group—it seems that in Shakespeare's world that would make her less tragic—but at times she can be seen as acting that claim out, and in one notable speech, Emilia makes that claim for her.

The early Emilia seems simply an oppressed, obedient wife as she takes Desdemona's dropped handkerchief saying 'I nothing but to please his fantasy' (3.3.302), in the only soliloquy in this play by a woman. In Act 3 Scene 4 she watches Othello explode in rage at Desdemona over the handkerchief without admitting anything. But she now sees the similarity between Desdemona's situation and hers, as she protests, about husbands, 'They eat us hungrily, and when they are full | They belch us' (100–2), lines symmetrical to Iago's prediction about Desdemona, 'Her delicate tenderness will find itself abused, begin to heave the gorge, disrelish and abhor the Moor' (2.1.226–7).[50] With her experience of Iago's jealousy, she tries to give Desdemona advice about Othello, and when he questions her she goes so far to promise to 'lay down [her] soul at stake' (4.2.14) for Desdemona's fidelity. Finally she does indeed give up her life defending Desdemona, first proclaiming Othello's murder of her, and then, braving Iago's threatening sword, his deceptive use of the handkerchief.

Bianca, who enters the play in the scene just after Othello has become jealous, exemplifies the social exclusion of women in a different way than Emilia—though like Emilia she protests against it. Cassio, who greets Bianca at first as 'sweet love' (3.4.166) and asks her to copy Othello's handkerchief, wants her to leave before Othello sees the two of them together, not wishing Othello to 'see him womaned' (190). Talking with Iago, he scorns her with the additional charge that she is 'a customer' (4.1.117), i.e., a prostitute whom he would never marry as she wishes. Iago has set up this dialogue for Othello to overhear it and assume Cassio is discussing Desdemona, and he does. The cultural bias with which Othello turns from loving Desdemona to calling her 'whore' may have something in common with Cassio's scorn of Bianca, as well as building on it. For, though Bianca is in an unusual position as an unmarried woman who can entertain Cassio in her house, in her last appearance she denies the judgment that others make on her, saying

> I am no strumpet
> But of life as honest as you that thus
> Abuse me.
>
> (5.1.120–2)

'Honest' is full of meaning here. Iago repeatedly calls himself 'honest', but also leads Othello to question whether Desdemona is, and here the word, as usual in regard to women in this culture, applies specifically to sexual fidelity. In Italian of this time, however, a related word, 'honesta', meant something more like 'honoured', and there actually was a Venetian category of 'cortigiana honesta', translated in English as 'courtesan', the term usually applied to Bianca in the dramatis personae.[51] But these women, 'supported by one or two wealthy clients at a time and living a life of splendid luxury', sound more privileged than Bianca seems. Is Bianca a courtesan or prostitute at all? The dramatis personae list was published after Shakespeare's death and he was probably not involved.[52] At any rate, she is here attacking the claims to moral superiority of Iago and Emilia, the characters who are at this point interrogating her suspiciously about the attack on Cassio. The most powerful impression Bianca gives in this scene is the strength of her love for Cassio. She responds to his cries when wounded, after Lodovico and Graziano, visiting from Venice, have hung back, fearing it is unsafe to approach. Arguably she feels more love for Cassio than exists in the marriage between Iago and Emilia, and some in the audience may well feel, giving another twist to an adjective so often used in this play, that this love makes her life more honest. She 'calls in question the value of the purely technical chastity by which the male world sets such frantic store.'[53] Emilia also acts against and verbally attacks patriarchal values; it is ironic that she nevertheless accepts the prevailing scorn of Bianca.[54]

This play parallels the unjustified jealousy of Othello with the unjustified jealousy of Iago and with everyone's condescension to and suspicion of Bianca. Both Desdemona and Emilia 'are seen by their husbands as women out of their place', as creatures (ironically, like Othello) 'of here and everywhere'[55]—though Iago's jealousy seems to have no love in it, only suspicion. We have never seen Emilia as an insider in a relationship, and now Desdemona has lost the one she had with Othello. The play also parallels the murders that Othello and Iago commit against their wives, and recalls the history of the sexual double standard, which considered women's adultery as a serious crime and men's adultery as an amusing pastime. This view was legally enshrined in Shakespeare's time, although there were reformers who were trying to impose laws to make it punishable (even by death) for both sexes.[56] In one of the most modern-sounding speeches of the play, Emilia explicitly challenges this double standard.

> Let husbands know
> Their wives have sense like them. They see, and smell,
> And have their palates both for sweet and sour,
> As husbands have. What is it that they do
> When they change us for others? Is it sport?
> I think it is. And does affection breed it?
> I think it doth. Is't frailty that thus errs?
> It is so too. And have not we affections,
> Desires for sport, and frailty, as men have?
> Then let them use us well, else let them know,
> The ills we do, their ills instruct us so.
>
> (4.3.91–101)

As I have discussed in the previous chapter, there was already a long tradition of literary attacks and defences of women. Some focused specifically on listing good women and arguing women's greater virtue than men's, but others, like Emilia, used similarity as a reason for better treatment of women. She notes the custom of allowing men much more sexual freedom, and argues that women as well as men have 'affections, | Desires for sport, and frailty' (5.1.98–9). In spite of all the social restrictions on women, there are enough jokes about cuckolds in Shakespeare's time to suggest that these restrictions didn't always work, and some women did indulge their desires. If Desdemona had actually committed adultery, Emilia is suggesting, it would have been fair retribution for the suspicion and violence with which Othello has been treating her—rather than an unforgiveable betrayal rightly, or at least understandably, punishable by death.

Othello kills himself because he eventually learns that Desdemona was innocent. He may never have gone beyond the view that he would have been justified in killing Desdemona if she had committed adultery. But the implication of Emilia's speech is that he would not have been justified, since male adultery was not considered a serious crime, women and men have the same feelings, and therefore female adultery shouldn't be punished so much more severely than men's would be. Examples of similar arguments in the previous chapter have shown that this argument was thinkable in Shakespeare's time. And perhaps of specific relevance to this play, William Painter's story 'Two Gentlewomen of Venice', translated in 1566 from the Italian writer and occasional source for Shakespeare, Bandello, includes an oration before the Venetian Council by Mistress Isotta, one of the gentlewomen of the title, who makes the parallel argument that female and male adultery are morally the same.[57]

Furthermore, the plot of the whole play, in which Othello is shown to be wrong in his suspicion of women, and Iago's fanning of such suspicion to be a diabolical plot, could be said to be a support for Emilia's speech. The double standard is ideologically closely connected with the suspicion of women as being more sexual than men and therefore more in need of close control, and Desdemona's behaviour refutes this.

Emilia's speech is a challenging one to many social traditions, and it was often cut in performance, especially in the eighteenth and nineteenth century. Furthermore, of the two different early texts of *Othello*, awkwardly for the importance of this passage, it is found only in the Folio text, not the Quarto. If the Folio is a later revision, its addition could contribute to a sense of its importance. On the other hand, the Folio text may have been earlier, and the Quarto a revision. Neill, drawing on Scott McMillan, argues that Q may have been a version cut for specific theatrical purposes. The largest number of discrepancies is in the parts of Desdemona and Emilia in Act 4, and possibly the boy actors of Emilia and Desdemona were not up to acting some of their speeches, including this one.[58]

Regardless of the Folio/Quarto issue, this speech not only prepares for Emilia's defiant exposure of Iago, it also resonates with other speeches in which Shakespeare's outsiders claim equality with insiders, mostly notably that by Shylock. Both argue largely on the basis of the body and its feelings, and both claim that the denial of equal rights justifies revenge.[59] Neither one seems to make an impression on the onstage listeners, but both can be galvanizing to listeners and readers. This one is particularly striking because it shows Emilia speaking in solidarity with Desdemona as well as standing up for herself. She says, if husbands

> break out in peevish jealousies,
> Throwing restraint upon us; or say they strike us,
> Or scant our former having in despite:
> Why, we have galls; and though we have some grace
> Yet have we some revenge.
>
> (4.3.87–91)

Iago's complaint that Emilia talks too much is written in the script, and we know from a soliloquy that he likes to nurture suspicion of her with Othello and Cassio to feed his sense of grievance, but it is only Othello that the text has so far shown hitting his wife and making a scene about her in public. Though their situation is similar and ultimately they die within a few minutes of each other, only Othello looks violent at this point, and to Emilia, Desdemona is in more trouble than she is and needs a defence more. Although previous plays have shown outsiders claiming similarity to those more privileged as part of arguing for their own rights, it is rare to find them also speaking on behalf of other outsiders. We will, however, find more of this in *King Lear*.

Iago

Ironically, Iago can also be seen as an outsider in Venice in spite of his claim to 'know our country disposition well' (3.3.305). It may show in his language when he refers to Desdemona as a 'super-subtle Venetian' (1.3.247) but other clues are even more important. His name is that of a Spanish cult-figure saint, a version of St. James, whose name in Spanish was Santiago and was particularly venerated under the title of Santiago Matamoros, in other words St. James Moor-killer. He was honoured for helping Spaniards defeat Moors in the legendary 9th century Battle of Clavijo. Why does Iago hate the Moor? His name suggests that hatred of Moors is his very essence. The name of his tool Roderigo, though Iago calls him 'this poor trash of Venice' (2.1.290), is also recognizably Spanish, as it was the name of El Cid, another legendary fighter against Moors.

How literally should we take these names as indicating the characters' nationality or ethnicity, and how much are they figurative? Perhaps they do not tell us that the characters are literally ethnic outsiders much more than Dogberry's name tells us he is literally an English policeman in Messina. Nevertheless, just as Dogberry's behaviour would be expected to be familiar to *Much Ado*'s English audience from their observation of incompetent and proud English policemen, Iago's name may be indicative that his viewpoint seems more Spanish than Venetian. During the time of this play Spain was more known for its opposition to Moors than was Italy, still a collection of city-states with different policies, and certainly more than at least ostensibly cosmopolitan Venice. Moors would be expelled from Spain in 1609, and the Inquisition was already testing converts or descendants of converts, suspicious that conversions were not sincere. But Venice and Spain were allies in battles against the Turks, and Spain controlled many of the Italian city-states, so probably to Othello and to many English in Shakespeare's audience, Venetians and Spaniards would seem closely enough linked, that though an national outsider to some degree, Iago would still appear an insider by comparison to Othello, and it wouldn't seem too strange that he can impress Othello as seeming to have insider's knowledge when he says, 'I know our country disposition well' (3.3.305). Furthermore, if Venice was cosmopolitan it certainly included many Spaniards as well as many Moors.

Though we learn Iago's name as early as the second line of the play, he never speaks of himself as an outsider by state or ethnicity. What preoccupies him more is exclusion by class and rank. Iago is only Othello's subordinate, and has been denied the favoured place of lieutenant by contrast to Cassio, who has more education and higher status. His resentment about this is clinched in his soliloquies at the end of Act 1 Scene 3 and Act 2 Scene 1. Furthermore, the play's dialogue, especially if the class-related uses of 'you' and 'thou' are noted, frequently shows Cassio, Othello, Brabanzio, and Desdemona condescending to him.[60] Thus part of the complexity of the play is that Iago is an outsider who can successfully manipulate some of the insiders. Since we as readers and audience members know what he is planning and Othello and Desdemona do not, we are mentally joined with him in our understanding of what is going on, no matter how much we loathe him as a character. Thus Shakespeare is making another paradoxical outsider/insider maneuver—in this dimension the insiders are Iago and the audience, who alone know what is going on, though he enjoys it and we (most of us, still) deplore it.

Neill writes, 'Iago identifies himself as a kind of "masterless man," part of that reprobate community of social exiles who haunted the early modern imagination.'[61] When Iago speaks of belonging to a group, it is more precisely the group of those who ostensibly have masters, yet 'throwing but shows of service on their lords, | Do well thrive by 'em' (1.1.53–4). This, like the community of 'masterless men', is only a community in the abstract, rhetorical sense, somewhat like the imaginary community of bastards Edmund will invoke in *Lear*. Like Edmund's, Iago's basic point is that he is out only for himself. And thus he also makes fun of official ideologies of loyalty and virtue.

In previous chapters we saw Shylock's acknowledged hatred of Christians, Antonio's and Graziano's hatred of Jews, and Sir Andrew's hatred of puritans, but a character strongly loathing two (or more) different kinds of people is unusual in Shakespeare, and encourages thought about the nature of prejudices—those 'ancient grudges' targeting groups, sometimes between insiders and outsiders, sometimes between various kinds of outsiders.[62] Iago's role in *Othello* is closely tied to the question of how ideologies that locate women and Moors as outsiders function in it.

Loomba has shown how closely connected are the histories of these ideologies. 'Analogies between sexual and colonial contact worked to define both in terms of male possession.... When Europeans first ventured abroad, alien races were routinely described in terms that were commonly used to describe women at home—as hypersexual, emotional, fickle, duplicitous, wild, jealous, and of inferior intelligence.'[63] And women could also be described in terms of alien races. For example, the anonymous tract *Hic Mulier*, writing of women thought to be dressing in an overly masculine way 20 years after *Othello*, says, 'If these be not barbarous, make the rude Scythian,

Othello and Other Outsiders 115

the untamed Moor, the naked Indian, or the wild Irish, Lords and Rulers of well-governed Cities.'[64]

But Iago's combination of expressed biases about both gender and race is exceptional among dramatic characters of the time, at least in Shakespeare. What ideas were in the air at the time about prejudice in the abstract as a concept, as distinct from specific prejudices? The most relevant may be the term 'custom' (used by Montaigne in its French equivalent and by the anonymous author of *Haec Vir*, when s/he writes, responding to *Hic Mulier*, 'Custom is an idiot.... We are as freeborn as men.' However, neither this author nor others anthologized and discussed in *Half Humankind* nor those discussed by Constance Jordan in *Renaissance Feminism* makes any analysis of prejudices about both race and gender.[65] Just before issues of sexism and racism were widely discussed or linked, Maynard Mack identified as Iago's poison that he has 'learned to "sickly o'er" the central and irreducible individual with the pale cast of class and kind', following this with examples of Iago's generalizations about women and Moors. More recently, Joel Altman similarly analyzes 'I know our country disposition well' as an example of a 'rapid shift from the individual to the species'.[66]

More to the point may be Pechter's analysis, which draws on Werner Sollors' discussion of how 'ethnic, racial, or national identifications rest on antitheses, on negativity', and discusses gender as well.[67] It may seem obvious to say Iago is a man because he is not a woman, but beyond this, as Pechter says, he moves from differentiation to hatred. This is where the echo in his name of Santiago Matamoros becomes particularly relevant. Though he never speaks of himself as Christian, his namesake's essence is killer of Moors because of opposition of religions. Iago never speaks of himself as white, but his dominant attitude to women, blacks, and Moors shows that his identity is not based just on differentiation but on hatred. His early line to Desdemona, 'I am nothing if not critical' (2.1.121), is an understated hint of this; to those who are marked as different, he is not merely critical but actively hostile. His rhymes about different categories of women, like his suspicion of his wife, show his belief that all women are deceitful, which is his justification for this hatred, just as his claims that Othello has wronged him by promoting Cassio and seducing Emilia are among his justifications for his hatred of

Othello. Pechter points out that the play calls attention to the general mechanism of 'difference experienced as hostility' when Iago moves from mocking women to 'Nay, it is true, or else I am a Turk' (2.1.117).

Shakespeare's previous plays have presented characters who define themselves as in opposition to other groups and social structures, including those to whom they appear to have loyalty, such as Richard III, Aaron, and (more trivially) Don John. These versions of the stage Machiavel justify themselves with regard to a characteristic they have from birth—deformity, illegitimacy, melancholy temperament doomed by the stars. With Iago, there is no such explanation: the identification of his name with the legendary Moorkiller has a different status. He looks like an ordinary man on stage, with an ordinary man's resentments. At the same time as he accuses Moors of jealousy and changeability and women of duplicity, he is himself jealous, changeable, and, above all, duplicitous.[68] Indications of such projection are not so unusual in Shakespeare, but the phenomenon of projection of qualities onto such outsiders is so frequent that some audience members might not notice it.

Nevertheless, Shakespeare complicates Iago's attitude to Desdemona and Othello beyond these generalizations. In soliloquies, he says that the Moor 'is of a constant, loving, noble nature' (2.1.276) and that Desdemona can be subdued 'In any honest suit' (2.3.315), admitting that he will 'turn her virtue into pitch | And out of her own goodness make the net | That shall enmesh them all' (334–6). To Roderigo, he says that Desdemona and Othello are changeable and will tire of each other, but these passages show that he would not expect this to happen without his intervention. Iago knows that some of the stereotypes that he uses to influence others are false. But he does not care.

This doubleness in Iago's attitudes toward Othello and Desdemona has led to other speculations about underlying causes of his hostility to them. Perhaps, even though he sees Desdemona as virtuous, he resents that virtue, whether because of its association with her upper-class status or because it represents a counterexample to his cynical view of the world. When he says that Cassio 'has a daily beauty in his life | That makes me ugly' (5.1.19–20), perhaps this may hint at his attitude to her. Other critics have argued that Iago resents Othello marrying a woman he feels belongs to his own race, or that Iago is conflicted about his own unacknowledged attraction to Othello.[69]

Perhaps most suggestive, however, is the fact that Iago enjoys exerting power over people, especially to destroy them.[70] He knows he can influence them, and he plots for his 'sport and profit.... Let me see now, | To get his place, and to plume up my will | In double knavery' (1.3.375–6). His use of stereotypes in which he does not necessarily believe, as well as his interest in swaying opinion and his frequent success, could be compared to that of some political staffers and radio talk show personalities today—but is he also a little like a playwright, and like characters such as *Measure for Measure*'s Duke and *The Tempest*'s Prospero? Extraordinary as he is in many ways, it may be his most extraordinary quality is the ability to influence people—both the characters in the play and the members of the audience, partly for reasons discussed near the end of the Othello section.

Iago speaks, whether in dialogue or in soliloquies, as if with an insider's knowledge about what is really happening.[71] Nevertheless, at the same time as he draws the audience into complicity by sharing his plot, his interest in this kind of power is partly a vengeful response to his position as a social outsider, and he reveals that he is more of a moral outsider than Othello ever becomes. Pechter analyzes the play in René Girard's terms of the need for a scapegoat. It may look at the very beginning as if Othello is the scapegoat, the character to be sacrificed to purge Venice—then Othello thinks of killing Desdemona as a sacrifice, trying to make her a scapegoat (the term does not necessarily imply innocence). Are the two of them sacrificed for Venice? Lodovico, the figure of order who has the last speech, focuses much of it on denouncing Iago. Yet the play has deliberately shown Iago surviving Othello's sword, and Lodovico promises him torture, not prison or execution. Perhaps the play is denying the possibility of getting rid of Iago and the attitudes he represents.

Both Pechter and Neill, surveying stage and critical history, find that from the twentieth century on, Iago is likely to dominate the play in performance, and critics are generally more likely to take a view close to Iago's in analyzing the other characters.[72] This may correlate, in part, to a general turn toward skepticism, and perhaps in particular the populist skepticism of resentment. Similarly, Leah Marcus and Patricia Parker, as well as Neill, have argued that not just Iago's speeches but also other aspects of the play show a voyeuristic preoccupation with women's 'secret place' and the bed of miscegenation.[73]

But just as the psychology experiments referred to earlier in this chapter show that viewers' reactions may lead to racist interpretations not justified by the visual evidence, responses to the play as pornography are also not inevitable. If a viewer (or even more, a reader) empathizes with the character of Desdemona, then s/he will not experience the pornographic reduction of Desdemona to her sexual orifices so much as s/he will experience Desdemona as struggling against this interpretation. Similarly, if readers or spectators empathize sufficiently with Othello, they will not accept the racism that the imagery of some speeches, even Othello's, may suggest, but see him as trapped by racist linguistic traditions as well as by Iago. And to the extent that viewers/readers identify with Desdemona and Othello in seeing their love as not just a matter of lust, they will not see the tableau of the two on the bed, with or without Emilia, as pornographic.[74] If the characters/directors have followed Emilia's request to 'lay me by my mistress's side' (5.2.244), the three people on the bed do not create the triangle that Iago imagined before, of Othello sexually involved with two women, but rather a different triangle, showing Desdemona loved by both Emilia and Othello. If we empathize with the characters, we see that like Othello, Emilia dies atoning for her earlier transgression against Desdemona (in her case stealing the handkerchief and not confessing earlier). Empathy and identification are not the only elements in reading/playgoing, and careful critics who read with empathy notice other dimensions of the play and may revise their overidentifications. But clearly the importance of empathy and its related quality sympathy in literary and dramatic response differs for different people, and this makes for different experiences.[75] The more a viewer or reader identifies with both Othello and Desdemona, the more painful the play is. Identification with Iago and turning the experience of the play into a pornographic one, which includes satisfaction at the destruction of Desdemona and Othello, might defend against this pain, but those for whom these are the main reactions to the play surely miss much.

'The Pity of It'

Perhaps for many, the play is painful partly because they respond to the great speeches of the lovers as well as to the skepticism of Iago as he predicts and brings about their doom, and as the interplay between outsiders and insiders of different sorts contributes to the play's toll. Othello says, famously, 'She loved me for the dangers I had passed, | And I loved her that she did pity them' (1.3.165–6). The love of Desdemona for Othello can be seen as an example of the surprising affinity of a female insider for an outsider—or, alternatively, as an example of the affinity of a female outsider for a different kind of outsider—Desdemona's 'desire to break the claustrophobic patriarchal confine'.[76] When Desdemona says, 'she wished | That heaven had made her such a man' (1.3.161–2), affinity is the clearest message, whichever kind we think is dominant, though it can be argued that the play shows that affinity impossible to sustain except in death.

Emphasis on the outsider/insider contrast in this play, or the surprising sense of affinity between two different types of outsiders, dramatizes the idea of marriage as a heroic adventure, which can be found in a surprising number of sermons at the time.[77] This play shows both the risks and the beauty of love between characters as different as Othello and Desdemona. Contrasted with Iago's hatred for whoever is different from himself (which ultimately means everyone), Desdemona's sympathetic curiosity about a traveller from another world is compelling, as is Othello's willingness to give up his freedom for her.

But, from another point of view, even without Iago, Othello is framed by a world that alienates him from himself when he thinks he is accepted, where 'black' and 'Moor' are always possible to turn into epithets, where it is not surprising he ends with suicide. Desdemona is victimized by a plot in which she can live only vicariously and a society in which everyone is pruriently fascinated by her sexual behaviour. Against this framing, Othello and Desdemona can still be seen as heroic and their marriage as the 'impossible achievement'—impossible to maintain in their society—that constitutes tragic heroism.[78]

Can two people break down the barriers between the two of them and trust each other in spite of their roles as outsider or insider? What about two different kinds of outsiders? These are the most intense versions of the issues many of us face in a diverse, multicultural, class-stratified society. Its urgent and eloquent version of them is part of why *Othello* is a great play.

5

King Lear: *Outsiders in the Family and in the Kingdom*

In *King Lear*, unlike most of the plays discussed here so far, the most obvious insider/outsider contrast is not between people of different ethnicities or religions, but between people in the same family, especially parents and children. Two of the outsiders it presents are a difficult elderly father and an unwanted illegitimate son, and at various times it encourages us to sympathize with both parents and children. It shows two families in which, as Meredith Skura writes, 'father and child are both sinned against and sinning' as they 'attack, humiliate, and abandon each other'.[1] But through the trajectory of both fathers and another son, it goes beyond immediate family issues to consider also the situation of the homeless poor and the mad as outsiders.

The characters who focus most of the attention on poverty—Lear, Edgar, Edmund, Gloucester, and Cordelia—are only recently or temporarily poor and homeless, and because their dispossession results from family conflicts, this play, more obviously than most of Shakespeare's, shows apparent insiders becoming outsiders, partly because of their own and/or another's stubbornness, pride, lust, greed, cruelty, or negligence. In most of the conflicts there is some wrong on both sides, and the behaviour of adult children is framed from the beginning by their fathers' folly.

The play moves us to a larger look at the outsiders in its world because Lear himself, when exposed to the storm, thinks of other 'poor naked wretches' (3.4.29), and responds with a kind of metaphysical shock—'Is man no more than this?' (3.4.94–5)—to Edgar's appearance in the guise of Poor Tom. Later, Lear makes even more explicit denunciations of the injustice experienced by the poor, who are more severely punished for their misdeeds than the rich: 'Plate sin with gold, | And the strong lance of justice hurtless breaks; | Arm it in rags, a pygmy's straw does pierce it' (4.6.159–61). Partly because the homelessness of Edgar, Lear, and Gloucester results from the behaviour of their family members, as does the social alienation of Edmund, the play encourages us to make the link that Lear does when he says 'I have ta'en | Too little care of this' (3.4.33–4) about the homeless in his kingdom and urges the wealthy to 'shake the superflux' (3.4.36) to wretches—to believe that poverty in the kingdom is the result of human behaviour which can be changed.[2] While Lear is wrong to believe that Poor Tom's poverty comes from his daughters' cruelty, the homelessness of the character who plays Poor Tom does come from family members' actions, and Lear's intuition hints at an analogy between the responsibility of family members for one another and the responsibility of the rich for the poor.

That the play deals with outsider issues with regard to poverty and illegitimacy is obvious. In the first conversation of the play, Gloucester marks his son Edmund as outsider, by focusing on the embarrassing circumstances of his birth, and attempts to dismiss him: 'He hath been out nine years, and away he shall again' (1.1.30–1). Imagery of being literally or figuratively an outsider is crucial throughout the play. Lear himself becomes an outsider, most visibly when he 'abjure [s] all roofs' (2.4.203), walking out of Gloucester's castle onto the heath, vulnerable to the storm as 'a poor, infirm, weak and despised old man' (3.2.19), in exile, poignantly, in his own country.[3] The lack of hospitality from Regan and Cornwall that precipitates his departure is a change from Shakespeare's source play, producing the tragic version of the frequent comic technique of the lock-out.[4]

Critics such as Kate McLuskie have argued that the structure of meanings in King Lear is patriarchal and misogynist. 'In order to experience the proper pleasure of pity and fear, they [the audience] must accept that fathers are owed particular duties by their daughters and be appalled by the chaos which ensues when those primal links are broken.'[5] However, this generalization about the structure leaves out too much, including how the play relates to attitudes about the elderly and poor in its time. McLuskie herself writes that Cordelia's 'resistance to her father gains audience assent through her two asides' and that research on the attitude toward and position of the elderly in England when the play was first performed suggests that some in its early audiences may well have been conflicted about performing such duties, a point that has not been as often quoted as the earlier part of her analysis.[6] More recent historical work has provided a further sense of these tensions. Half the population was under 20 and only 7 per cent were between 40 and 50, fewer older, but men in their forties, and those who held on longer, had most of the power.[7] On the other hand, old men were 'discouraged from retiring and not contributing to society, yet criticized for wishing to stay in positions of authority'.[8] In spite of the biblical and classical literature encouraging respect for the elderly, literature and popular culture frequently presented them critically. There was a polarized picture of the aged—sometimes wise, sometimes foolish, sometimes too strong, sometimes too weak. Perhaps this is analogous to the polarized views about other kinds of outsiders in the family, women and bastards, as we will see.

Generational conflicts between grown children and aging parents apparently were frequent in early modern England. Contrary to some nostalgic myths, this was not a time of many harmonious multi-generational households. Only 5 per cent of elderly parents with married children lived with them, and only 2 per cent of widowers did.[9] Popular culture is full of complaints of adults about the demands of their aging parents and the complaints of aging parents about the neglect of their children. Sermons warned parents that if they neglected their parents, they might be neglected in turn—obviously the sermons were thought to be needed. There was discussion of the need for aging parents to get their adult children to sign contracts to provide them maintenance. And although poor laws demanded that parishes care for the old without children—most of the poor on relief were old—those demands were resented as well—as were the laws about parish responsibility for bastards born within their geographical limits.[10] As Nina Taunton writes, 'In Northern Europe, the place and role of the elderly in the nuclear household... indicates that the ideal of reciprocal giving... that children have a duty to look after parents when they are old and infirm and as a result can expect to be looked after in their turn was one that no longer reflected the complex nature of reality.'[11]

The old were a much smaller percentage of society than they are today, but the tensions we are now seeing about how much the rest of society should contribute to the elderly had their forerunners in this time. Thus the issue of care of a bastard child in the family, raised at the beginning of the play, is soon paralleled by the issue of care for a difficult aging parent, which in *Lear*'s main plot, as frequently historically, devolves on women.[12] Critics have often discussed Shakespeare's plays with regard to distrust between the sexes; *Lear* gives the most attention of any of Shakespeare's plays to another large and emotional social issue with a base in the family, distrust and resentment between generations.[13]

The issue of social contributions to the dependent was heightened because of the general economic conditions of Shakespeare's time. As William Carroll writes,

Hunger and privation never disappeared in the Tudor-Stuart period, even when harvests and other economic conditions were good; and when such conditions were bad, the poor died in the streets, and the beggars and vagabonds of the kingdom multiplied—like vermin, it was said, in 'swarms.'[14]

Shakespeare had dealt with poverty to some degree in many earlier plays: *Henry VI, Part 2* shows a revolt of the poor, *Taming of the Shrew* builds the induction around a poor drunken tinker, the apothecary in *Romeo and Juliet* sells poison because of his poverty. But *King Lear* is unique in the extent to which it brings the experience of poverty home to its audience by the way it hits the central characters. Poverty in Shakespeare's day was marked, among other ways, by the increased visibility of bastards, elderly poor, and beggars—represented in Lear by three characters who most thoroughly play the role of outsiders, Edmund, Lear, and Edgar.

Edmund

'Bastard' was a term of abuse in Shakespeare's England in an extended sense, as it is still today. There were popular beliefs about the disadvantages of bastardy to a child's body, mind, and soul. Most literary and legendary bastards were thought to be deformed and devious, though some in literature and recent history were heroic.[15] Births out of wedlock had been rising in Shakespeare's time, reaching their peak a few years before *King Lear* was written; apparently under the influence of legal and religious reformers worried about economic and moral disorder, the stigma of bastardy had recently been increasing.[16] Being born out of wedlock had long had legal consequences. However, in Shakespeare's time bastards of the aristocracy often did have provisions made for them by their father's will. According to Alison Findlay, 'bastards who were publicly acknowledged by kings or aristocrats could be admitted into the legitimate family as long as it was on the family's terms.'[17] However, they would still be marked as outsiders by their different last name, the bar sinister on their coats of arms, and their exclusion from holy orders (unless the family paid for a dispensation) and some other institutions. Edmund's outsider status is clear at the beginning, and Gloucester, though he claims to love both his sons equally, does not grant Edmund an inheritance until Edmund tricks him into disinheriting Edgar.

Edmund is not the first of Shakespeare's bastard characters to be self-conscious about his identity. His earliest bastard, the character in *King John* who is initially called Philip but prefers to be known as the son of King Richard Coeur de Lion and takes a new name of Richard from him, declares 'I am I, howe'er I was begot' (1.1.175).[18] The bastard Don John of *Much Ado about Nothing*, though he does not use the word 'bastard,' similarly explains his melancholy by saying 'I cannot hide what I am. . . . it better fits my blood to be disdained of all than to fashion a carriage to rob love from any. . . . I am a plain-dealing villain' (1.3.10, 22–3, 25).

John's reticence about the word 'bastard' might be considered another example of Shakespeare's ambiguity about the reason for a character's status as an outsider, but stage directions repeatedly identify him as 'John the bastard', and speech headings in the early texts call him sometimes 'John' and sometimes 'Bastard'.[19] The only time the word appears in the script is when Benedick, after the abortive wedding, sees through the plot against Hero and says 'The practice of it lives in John the Bastard' (4.1.187), making a kind of punch line that identifies Benedick's accuracy about Hero's innocence with his willingness to give John his epithet.[20]

Edmund is the only one of Shakespeare's bastards whose father also appears in his play—in fact in the very first scene. *Lear*, uniquely among Shakespeare's plays with bastards, suggests paternal negligence and insensitivity as a frame for Edmund.[21] In the first conversation of the play, Gloucester fails to introduce him until asked, and then, when asked, jokes about his illegitimate conception and birth, recalls often blushing to acknowledge Edmund, and concludes, 'He has been out nine years, and away he shall again' (1.1.30–1). Edmund, to his father, is a 'young fellow' (12), a 'knave' (20), and a 'whoreson' (33). Only his legitimate offspring Edgar does he call his son in this scene. The play thus evokes some sympathy for Edmund at the beginning, which helps prepare for his early soliloquy about his bastard position.[22]

Edmund capitalizes on this potential sympathy. Witty and satirical like the bastard in *King John*, Edmund is similarly self-conscious about his identity, saying 'I should have been that I am had the maidenliest star in heaven twinkled on my bastardizing' (1.2.120–2). Though he denies the conventional belief that stars determine temperament, he is quite ready to associate his temperament with the circumstances of his birth outside of wedlock (as the soliloquy about to be discussed will show). In *King John*, bastardy permits a rise to a connection with the royal family (though a loss of land); for Edmund it provokes other kinds of ambition.

Like Emilia and Shylock, Edmund has a long speech about his position as an outsider.

> Why bastard? Wherefore base?
> When my dimensions are as well compact,
> My mind as generous, and my shape as true,
> As honest madam's issue?
>
> (1.2.6–9)

Like Emilia and Shylock, he uses language claiming his similarity to those in the preferred group. But while Emilia and Shylock move from common humanity to revenge, Edmund has a middle term, his own excellence. He plays on the reference of the word 'base' to rank below the aristocracy as well as birth outside of wedlock, and it is clear that he scorns people of lower class as well as lower abilities. As he invokes a group of bastards to whom he belongs, he argues superiority, not just equality.[23]

> Why brand they us
> With base? with baseness? bastardy? base, base?
> Who, in the lusty stealth of nature, take
> More composition and fierce quality
> Than doth, within a dull, stale, tired bed
> Go to th'creating a whole tribe of fops,
> Got 'tween asleep and wake?
>
> (9–15)

Then we see where this is heading:

> Well then,
> Legitimate Edgar, I must have your land.
>
> (15–16)

He does not want to share the family inheritance of land with Edgar, just as he does not want to be seen as just as good as everybody else. He wants to reverse the hierarchy and take the land. As Jonathan Dollimore says, 'Edmund, in liberating himself from the myth of innate inferiority, does not thereby liberate himself from his society's obsession with power, property and inheritance; if anything that obsession becomes the more urgent.'[24]

Still, Edmund may maintain some audience sympathy at the beginning of his speech by identifying his case with that of the younger brother, which he also is. In England at the time, the rule of primogeniture, all inheritance going to just one brother, the oldest legitimate one, had received popular written attacks.[25] And it has been suggested that, since younger brothers of the aristocracy and gentry often went to London to seek their fortune, the theatre audience might be full of younger brothers.

But defences of bastards by others at the time tended to be less serious than defences of younger brothers or defences of women. John Donne praised the fortunes of bastards as a paradox.[26] Some people in Shakespeare's audience might know about the Irish custom of 'Gavelkind', which according to some sources permitted illegitimate sons to inherit as well as legitimate, but at least one author, Sir John Davies, blamed Irish factiousness and disorder on this practice. By the end of his speech, it is clear that Edmund is planning to go too far to avenge his wrongs. If he keeps audience interest it is not necessarily for being wronged, as much as for being witty, energetic, outrageous, and probably handsome. Still, he gets more audience sympathy than Iago, who has similar qualities, partly because Gloucester's treatment of him is dramatized while the wrongs Iago complains of seem more imagined or less serious.

However, it is easy to see Edmund's moral failings. He imagines himself as one of a group of bastards, but this group exists just to authorize him; he acts only for himself. He claims at the beginning of his speech that Nature is his goddess, playing on the fact that he would have been referred to as Gloucester's 'natural son', and in the speech quoted he aligns himself with nature, but this is only conceptually, in terms of identifying with natural fierceness against civilization. He stays in the aristocratic social world, unlike other characters who go out into the storm on the heath and confront external nature and the lives of those with more physical suffering. But that social world has plenty of fierceness and suffering, to both of which Edmund contributes. Like Iago, Edmund pretends honesty as he advises those he is betraying. He sets up a plot to make Gloucester suspect Edgar's loyalty, then takes Edgar's place in Gloucester's affections; then he betrays Gloucester to Cornwall, claiming that he regrets following his loyalty to Cornwall against the claims of blood. Has Cornwall touched his vulnerability in offering to be 'a dearer father' (3.5.21)? He forms sexual liaisons with both of Lear's two older daughters, Goneril and Regan, fulfilling the stereotypical seventeenth century image of bastards as, like women, deceitful and lustful.

Even as Goneril praises his bravery by contrast to her husband, he salutes her by saying 'Yours in the ranks of death' (4.2.24). Like Hotspur's speech before battle describing his men as sacrifices to the god of war, this suggests the dark side of military prowess. It also foreshadows the way loving him will lead to death for both Goneril and Regan; at this point Edmund seems as casual about having sworn love to both of them as Iago is about the result of the duel between Roderigo and Cassio that he has set up. Still, as Lars Engle says, Edmund 'does not seem full of the desire to hurt others, but rather of the desire to sweep aside obstacles to his acquisition of power.'[27]

In public, near the end, Edmund values rank and appearance in a way that contrasts markedly with Lear's insights on the heath. When Albany makes an accusation of treason against Edmund, and Edgar, hiding his identity with disguise, arrives to fight him, Edmund is willing to maintain his nobility by combat because, he says, Edgar's 'outside appears so fair and warlike' (5.3.141). And when he is defeated, Edmund says to Edgar, 'If thou'rt noble, | I do forgive thee' (5.3.164–5). While Edgar says he forgives Edmund also, he then places them once more as legitimate vs. illegitimate:

> I am no less in blood than thou art, Edmund;
> If more, the more thou'st wronged me.
>
> (166–7)

Edmund is clearly an outsider as at the beginning; as he says, 'The wheel is come full circle! I am here' (5.3.173), at the bottom of Fortune's wheel.

Nevertheless, at the end of the play Edmund suddenly changes. After hearing about the death of his father, he says to Edgar, 'This speech of yours hath moved me, | And shall perhaps do good' (5.3.198–9). Then, after seeing the dead bodies of Goneril and Regan, who killed each other over him, he remarks, 'Yet Edmund was beloved' (5.3.238), which sounds like mockery but is followed by his attempt to save Lear and Cordelia, saying 'Some good I meant to do | Despite of mine own nature' (5.3.242–3). Is this an echo of Lear's conclusion, earlier in this scene, that love matters more than exclusion or inclusion from the privileges of court?

The conversion to goodness that appears in Edmund at the end is anomalous in Shakespeare's tragedies, although his comedies and tragedies do often involve the repentance of minor characters such as Iachimo or Borachio, and major ones such as Claudio (in *Much Ado*), Caliban, and Leontes. But these conversions often occur during an investigation of an accusation, rather than being linked to revelation of the deaths of other characters close to the repentant one. One might wonder about its connection in Shakespeare's personal mythology, given the two conversions of wicked brothers in *As You Like It*, a play in which another kind of outsider, the melancholy Jaques, also suddenly decides to follow the converted Duke into a religious retreat. It might also be compared to two other surprising moments for outsiders in Shakespearean tragedy, the point in *Titus Andronicus* when we suddenly see Aaron's love for his infant son, and, even more relevantly, the point in *Othello* where Emilia, previously a figure of moral relativism whose handkerchief theft has fed Othello's jealousy, risks her own life to tell the truth about the dead Desdemona. But while Emilia's outburst is crucial to the resolution of the plot, the major effect of Edmund's conversion, in the context of the play, is its futility, since it comes too late. Yet, when he dies soon after, Albany's epitaph, 'That's but a trifle here' (5.3.295), may seem inadequate. Though understandable given Edmund's relationship with Goneril, it echoes too much the neglect of Edmund that Gloucester showed at the beginning of the play.

Lear

Lear is a potential outsider from his entry into the play because of his age, even though as king he is officially at the pinnacle of his society. This vulnerability is already evident in the conversation between Goneril and Regan at the end of the first scene of the play: 'The best and soundest of his time hath been but rash' (1.1.293).

Shakespeare had treated old men in earlier plays—Egeon and Gremio in early comedies, Polonius in the tragedies. In addition, characters such as Shylock and Brabanzio are usually played as old. However, Lear's age, his foolishness, and both his initial power and his fall are emphasized much more than those of any others. Indeed, he also becomes Shakespeare's most detailed treatment of madness.

Hostility to Lear, focusing on his age, is obvious in Act 1 Scene 3 when Goneril already thinks of him as just an 'idle old man' (16) whose behaviour shows that 'old fools are babes again' (19). The Fool quickly identifies him as 'one that's out of favour' (1.4.85) in speaking to Kent. 'Truth's a dog must to kennel; he must be whipped out, when Lady the brach must stand by the fire and stink' (95–6). If Lear no longer has the power of a king, and fatherhood gives him no power over his daughters, he is simply an old man, and he can imagine, though sarcastically, that in his society people might already think 'Age is unnecessary' (2.4.148). He wonders whether the gods have stirred his daughters against him: 'A poor old man, | As full of grief as age, wretched in both!' (2.4.267–8). He has already pledged to 'abjure all roofs' (203) and 'to be a comrade with the wolf and owl' (205). At this point he is about to face nature under the same vulnerable conditions as the homeless poor. He is no longer an outsider simply because he is a despised old man in his daughter's court, but also because he is a poor man without defence against the storm.

The outsider position is a fluctuating one and in this play perhaps even more fluctuating than most. Lear is an insider at the very beginning, but because he is old and gives up his land to his older daughters, even with the name of king he becomes something of an outsider in the court. While on the cusp of becoming a literal outsider himself, Lear makes three other characters of the play into outsiders, exaggerating a pattern seen in other plays in which potential outsiders struggle against each other for a place. Two he banishes literally as well as figuratively. He compares Cordelia to 'the barbarous Scythian' (1.1.166), justifying his cruelty with this image, as Linda Woodbridge and Lars Engle have analyzed.[28] He now holds Cordelia as 'strangered with our oath' (1.1.205) and sees her as almost (oddly, not quite) similarly rejected by nature, 'ashamed | Almost t'acknowledge [Cordelia] hers' (214–15). Both his attitude and the one he attributes to nature recall issues in Gloucester's initial treatment of Edmund. Lear exiles Kent, calling him 'vassal, miscreant' (1.1.161), in the second term (which at the time meant 'unbeliever') placing him too outside of their culture.[29] And he more explicitly echoes the bastardy and anticipates the charges of bastardy in the Gloucester plot (in 2.1. 79 Gloucester will say of Edgar, under Edmund's influence, 'I never got him') when he calls Goneril 'Degenerate bastard!' (1.4.229)—though at this point he no longer has the power to banish her.

When Lear goes to the heath he dramatizes and intensifies his position as an outsider. Lear's calling to the winds in Act 3 Scene 2 could be seen as a parallel to Edmund's addressing Nature as his goddess—both seeking alliance with nature as opposed to humans—in their struggle partly with humans in their family. But soon the forces of the storm are not so much allies as better than his daughters because they are not ungrateful—then they become ministers of his daughters. Then he turns again to think of them as punishing guilty people, though dramatizing his outsider role as 'more sinned against than sinning' (3.2.37–8). Lear moves between the suffering of the storm itself and the suffering of the ingratitude of his daughters, which is more painful: 'This tempest will not give me leave to ponder | On things would hurt me more' (3.4.25–6).

Yet at this point Lear begins to think of other people's suffering, not just of his own. He urges the Fool into the hovel Kent has found, and prays for others without homes, sees his responsibility, says 'Take physic, pomp; | Expose thyself to feel what wretches feel' (3.4.34–5)—addressing his own past self at the same time as the audience. Then he sees someone who looks like one of those wretches—Edgar, in his disguise as Poor Tom. Though Lear himself has been showing us the effects of being homeless in a storm, Edgar's appearance puts the visual image of poverty on the stage in a more immediate way and asks the audience as well as Lear to think about what it means that a human being, 'unaccommodated' (3.4.98–9), can appear to be 'no more but such as poor, bare, forked animal as thou art' (99–100).

The more obvious kind of outsider status in Shakespeare comes from a character's birth into an ethnic, racial, or religious minority group. Usually such a character appears in the play as the only representative of that group.[30] Lear, by contrast, when old and no longer treated as king, comes to experience being an outsider in ways new to him, not resulting from his birth. And rather than being alone in his outsider position, he is joined on the heath by the Fool, Edgar, Kent, and eventually Gloucester and Cordelia—all of them characters who have suffered their own move to vulnerable outcast positions; nevertheless Lear has fallen the farthest. Linda Woodbridge has pointed out that there were prejudices in Shakespeare's time against the poor and homeless, who were often thought to be deceivers, or to have brought their suffering on themselves.[31] Lear shares those prejudices when he thinks of the storm as attacking a 'wretch, | That hast within…undivulged crimes' (3.2.49–50). But when he thinks of the suffering of the Fool along with his own, for the first time he uses the first person plural not with the royal 'we' but in a speech that suggests his fellow feeling with others in suffering: 'The art of our necessities is strange, | That can make vile things precious' (3.2.68–9). This scene is the beginning of the movement in this play towards a creation of a community of outsiders, the opposite of the struggle for position among different kinds of outsiders that occurs in many other plays and has occurred earlier in *Lear*.[32] As Woodbridge has noted, when Lear thinks of the poor, rather than arguing about whether they are deserving or undeserving, a matter of much discussion in texts about poor people in his time, he simply says that feeling what they feel should lead others to improve their condition 'and show the heavens more just' (3.4.37).

While on one level Lear's movement from the simple position of being homeless and poor to the further outsider position of madness is marked by his insistence that Poor Tom too must be suffering because of his daughters, his position as mad outsider is even more clearly framed when he enters wearing a crown of wild flowers and speaking with wild and incoherent free associations.[33] His claim 'I am the king himself' (4.6.83–4) both exemplifies his madness further and also suggests the idea, further developed when he says, 'Nature's above art in that respect' (86), that he, in a different way from Edmund, is critiquing human society, and prefers being king in a natural world far away from the court with its flattery. He now sees the deference given to a king as no more than the caution a beggar shows in running from a dog. The institutions of his society that are supposed to bring justice now look to him simply like the rule of the rich over the poor: 'The usurer hangs the cozener. | Through tattered clothes great vices do appear; | Robes and furred gowns hide all' (157–9).

Herman Melville found in such lines 'The sane madness of vital truth' and argued that Shakespeare uses Lear's madness as a mask to allow a critique of social injustice that could not otherwise be uttered.[34] Shakespeare's source character in the old play of *King Leir*, which some of his audience had recently seen revived, had nothing of this anger on behalf of the poor; this element is one of many changes that might have stood out against the audience's expectations. Lear's words in his madness are not uniformly full of insight—this scene contains many incoherent passages as well as a tirade against women's lust—but it is after the critique of the effect of money on the legal system that Edgar has the aside 'Reason in madness' (4.6.169).

At this point, the double plot becomes more than a suggestion of the generality of the father–child conflict and a hint to think about contrasts between Lear and Gloucester. When Lear meets Edgar in disguise earlier, the issue of poverty takes on more immediacy, but Lear never realizes who Poor Tom really is. Here for the first time he acknowledges recognition—the other old man on stage, blind, poor, and probably still bleeding, is his old courtier Gloucester. Just after he says, 'I know thee well enough: thy name is Gloucester' (171), he speaks again significantly not with the royal 'we' but with the 'we' of fellowship with Gloucester and indeed of common humanity. 'We came crying hither: | Thou know'st, the first time that we smell the air, | We waul and cry' (172–4). In these words he breaks down the opposition between old and young so important in this play. Though his words resonate with the theme of his return to a second childhood, they also show he knows that suffering is not unique to those who are poor or old, or something peculiar to those rejected by their daughters, but part of the human condition. Here fellowship in suffering may be a community in which there is no distinction between inside and outside. Everyone shares the experience of coming to a world that includes bad smells. Perhaps there is even a hint that everyone shares the sudden experience of becoming an outsider in leaving the womb to be born.[35] Lear repeats his point with a metatheatrical flourish as well as an acknowledgment of his own folly and of everyone's: 'When we are born, we cry that we are come | To this great stage of fools' (176–7). Age and youth are both included here: 'fools' was a word that often connoted 'children' in early modern English, but it was also often used of the elderly, and many in Shakespeare's audience might have thought at this point of Erasmus's *Praise of Folly*, in which Folly herself both asserts that all people are foolish and also makes some very sharp and specific social criticism (which is nevertheless masked because it is Folly who is speaking).

In a second Lear has lost this profundity and is imagining leading his troops in vengeance against Cornwall and Albany, but there is an even more important reunion with Cordelia in the next scene. Upon awakening he thinks he is in the ultimate outside location of hell—'bound | Upon a wheel of fire' (4.7.46–8). Then he realizes that his condition is the more ordinary one, which he can now acknowledge, of being 'a very foolish fond old man' (4.7.61). He is still confused and displaced: 'I am mainly ignorant | What place this is' (66–7). But it is

King Lear: *Outsiders in the Family and in the Kingdom* 135

the relationship with Cordelia that matters most. 'As I am a man,'—no longer the king that his loyal followers still call him—'I think this lady | To be my child, Cordelia' (70–1). Perhaps he hopes to be near her home: 'Am I in France?' Wherever he is, he does not feel that it is, as he is told, [his] 'own kingdom' (77).

When Edmund takes them in as prisoners, Lear prefers life with her in a cell to anything else. Again he speaks in a first person plural that is not the royal we. But now it is not a 'we' that easily blends with common humanity: it is the specific 'we' of his relationship with Cordelia—'We two alone will sing like birds i'the cage' (5.3.9). 'Who's in and who's out' (15) at court matters only as a subject for detached gossip. Wherever she is is where he wants to be. Being with her is the 'inside' that matters, even if it is inside prison. And at the end, as he looks at her dead body, any issue of outside or inside apart from the question of her life is irrelevant to him.

Is there any other Shakespearean outsider or tragic hero toward whom as much sympathy is expressed as there is for Lear? There are two most significant early texts for this play, the Quarto, which was published in 1608, and the version published as part of the First Folio including almost all his plays, in 1623. More of these expressions of sympathy are in the Quarto, but many of them are in both texts. (In this chapter I draw on the Norton's conflated text, but use almost exclusively the readings found in the Folio.) Desdemona can see that Othello, the most obvious outsider hero, is suffering when he is raging at her ('let our finger ache and it endues | Our other, healthful members even to a sense | Of pain' 3.4.142–4) and he is termed 'great of heart' (5.2.370) by Cassio after his death. There are admiring final judgments expressed on Brutus, Hamlet, Anthony, Cleopatra, and others. But none of these figures suffers visibly, in body and soul, for so long and so intensely as Lear does. In none of these other plays does a suffering community form around the central character as it does in *Lear*. Is there any other play in which the central character, so egotistical at the very beginning, turns to sympathy with others (when he cares for the Fool and prays for the homeless, when he preaches to Gloucester about universal suffering, when he repents before Cordelia) at such emphasized moments?

Lear's dying scene does not show him with the compassion for all that he expressed earlier: focused on Cordelia, he proudly says,

'I killed the slave that was a-hanging thee' (5.3.273), and he calls his loyal companions 'murderers, traitors all' (268), because they are not mourning Cordelia's death as expressively as he is, or perhaps just because they are alive and she is not. Nevertheless, they forgive him these lapses, and even though his behaviour recalls the imperious self-willed man he was at the beginning of the play, their forgiveness is a call for the audience to forgive him as well.

Edgar

While Lear's transformation from king to poor old man is central to the play, its treatment of poverty and sympathy is intensified by the role of Edgar. After Edmund frames Edgar as a villain, he like Lear becomes homeless and poor and thus another literal outsider. His disguise as Poor Tom, the beggar who either comes from or pretends to come from St. Mary's of Bethlehem/Bedlam Hospital, which specialized in care for the insane, is a paradoxical attempt to protect himself by taking on the identity of someone even more scorned than he is. Edgar describes his disguise, which involves muddying his face, mutilating his arms, wearing only a blanket, and pretending to be diabolically possessed, as 'the basest and most poorest shape | That ever penury in contempt of man | Brought near to beast' (2. 3. 8–9). As William Carroll has shown, Poor Tom was 'a social stereotype of the underclass', generally imagined as a fraud, and, like other beggars, a terror of the English in his time.[36] Though Edgar is not a beggar and has no literal association with Bedlam, Woodbridge writes, 'In a sense, Edgar's disguise is no disguise at all—he really has lost everything, and he really is homeless.'[37] These scenes of interaction between the two plots, in which a poor beggar vividly appears and is taken by Lear to be a source of wisdom, are Shakespeare's invention, though he has literary sources for both Lear's and Edgar's mistreatment within their own families. Poor Tom's appearance is unnecessary for the plot, but it puts both beggary and a need for sympathy more vividly before our eyes.

Like Edmund, conceptually, and Lear, more literally, Edgar turns to nature as an alternative to his family. But when Lear, the Fool, and Kent meet him on the heath, he joins their 'society of outsiders'.[38] In his disguise as Poor Tom, he invents a past as a serving man as well as blaming himself for his sins and complaining about the cold. As Woodbridge says, he 'adopts the orthodox early Tudor line on the causes of poverty', blaming the poor for their earlier extravagant and imprudent living.[39] But, as the play develops he also speaks, in his own person, in sympathy for Lear—first in an aside, 'My tears begin to take his part so much | They'll mar my counterfeiting' (3.6.35–6), and then in a whole soliloquy. Thus he moves, more consistently and for more of the play, in the same way as Lear does, from feeling for himself to feeling for others.

In this soliloquy, Edgar uses, as Lear has begun to, the first person plural of fellowship in suffering, here blending into a generalization about the human condition which nevertheless maintains a class contrast. 'When we our betters see bearing our woes, | We scarcely think our miseries our foes' (3.6.95–6). While Edgar has already revealed his sympathy for Lear, there is something inadequate about these pat couplets. On the one hand, seeing Lear's sufferings gives Edgar more perspective on his own; on the other hand, if he can really focus on how 'light and portable [his] pain seems now' (101), his sympathy with Lear is somewhat distanced. His kind of outsider position here constitutes Edgar as both within and without the fellowship of the suffering.[40] This is one of the soliloquies present in the Quarto but not in the Folio. Cutting it, if the Folio text is later, could be seen both as making the call for sympathy for Lear less coercive and more subtle, and also as putting less emphasis on Edgar's detachment, in the version in which he will emerge as the next king at the end.[41]

At his next appearance he is again trying to console himself, but now, instead of finding the suffering Lear, from whom he can distance himself while sympathizing, he finds the suffering Gloucester, from whom he cannot detach so easily.[42] At first, again he tries to find consolation for seeing his father 'poorly led' (most editions) or 'partieyed' (Norton 4.1.10, referring to the red of his bleeding eyes under white dressings; in either case another outsider now) in a first person plural generalization about human suffering: 'World, world, O world! | But that thy strange mutations make us hate thee, | Life would not yield to age' (10–12). But in Gloucester's plight there is no consolation. Again Edgar generalizes, but this time perhaps less glibly: 'The worst is not | So long as we can say, "This is the worst"' (28–9).

The context of some of Edgar's most explicit lines about sympathy exemplifies this problem of distance. He describes himself as 'a most poor man, made tame to fortune's blows; | Who, by the art of known and feeling sorrows, | Am pregnant to good pity' (4.6.216–18). Fine, but this is in answer to Gloucester's question, 'Now, good sir, what are you?' (215) And Gloucester has already said in his hearing that he has forgiven Edgar and that if Edgar were there he would 'say [he] had eyes again' (4.1.24). A number of critics have discussed at length and penetratingly the question of why Edgar never reveals himself to Gloucester until (offstage) just before his battle with Edmund; most plausibly, Janet Adelman suggests that he is angry because his father has so misjudged and mistreated him.[43] As Skura argues, his behaviour (and the anger it implies) once more emphasizes how characters in this play are not simply good or evil as in its source.[44] Though Edgar has put aside the role of Tom of Bedlam, he keeps himself in a different kind of outsider position by remaining in disguise (as also do characters such as Rosalind and the Duke of *Measure for Measure*).

After Edgar tells the story of his revelation and his father's death, even Edmund says he looks 'fair and warlike' (5.3.141), and Albany declares, 'Methinks thy very gait did prophesy | A royal nobleness' (174–5). Is Edgar, who has now returned to his position as Gloucester's heir, no longer an outsider? For some in Shakespeare's time, Edgar's name would recall that of a King of England (959–75), who established codes of law and founded monasteries after the period in which, according to Thomas Elyot in *The Governour*, the people were 'pursued and hunted like wolves or other beasts savage'.[45] Though many elements of the Folio text are bleaker, the emphasis on his future rule made by giving him the last lines may add some hope to its ending. This play which has so often seen young and old at odds with each other strikingly concludes in the Folio version with a young man paying tribute to the old: 'The oldest hath borne most. We that are young | Shall never see so much, nor live so long' (5.3.324–5).[46] The theme of generational reconciliation, only a prelude to death previously in the play, echoes here along with the sense of loss.

Other Outsiders

Many critics have noted how much Gloucester's trajectory, in his misjudgment of his sons, his betrayal by the one he trusted, his suffering in the castle and on the heath, and the care he receives from Edgar, parallels Lear's. Both of them move from insider to outsider to a community of outsiders, reunion with their loyal children, and death, and both of them call for a fairer distribution of the world's goods, though Lear falls from a greater height, is more active in setting up his downfall, probes more deeply into good and evil, and journeys into madness rather than blindness. But Gloucester does develop insight into his own negligence and, when deprived of his own house by Cornwall and Goneril, he leads Lear to shelter in service that shows a thorough change of heart.[47] Lear's two other loyal male companions, Kent and the Fool, make their own contributions to the play's treatment of outsiders, adding to its bleakness if we focus on the way others fail to pay attention to them but to its stress on fellowship in suffering if we observe their generosity to Lear.

Kent, the first person in the play to call Lear mad and foolish after the banishment of Cordelia, appears to accept his own banishment with less rage, but instead goes into disguise and continues to serve Lear, now as a literal servant rather than as a courtier.[48] His transition to outsider anticipates Lear's, as his own anger mirrors Lear's own though it is in defence of Cordelia rather than against her. And he mirrors Lear in still another way; though one of his first insults to Lear is to call him 'old man' (1.1.146), and he is sufficiently younger that he claims to be 48 in his disguise, yet he is called 'ancient ruffian' (2.2.54) by Goneril's servant Oswald, and says he is 'too old to learn' (119). Kent's angry defence of Lear is excessive: he trips Oswald when he annoys Lear, and in the next scene berates Oswald at great length and even draws his sword, creating so much disturbance that Cornwall orders him put in the stocks, a frequent way of punishing servants. Maynard Mack sees the tableau of Kent in the stocks an emblem of 'Virtue Locked Out'; on the other hand, as R. A. Foakes points out, Kent's uncontrollable anger has contributed to his punishment.[49] Kent participates in the play's pattern of showing all of its characters as imperfect. But once out on the heath with Lear, he never appears angry again as he loyally helps arrange shelter for Lear and his reunion with Cordelia. He subordinates himself to Lear dramatically as well as practically, except at one point near the end, when he tries to tell Lear who he is. In putting on his disguise, he hoped that his master would one day 'find[him] full of labours' (1.4.7) but in the event, Lear is too confused to understand. The promise of their reunion, like that of Edgar and Gloucester, and Lear and Cordelia, is blighted.

The Fool is present mainly to exhibit loyalty to Lear and to emphasize aspects of him. If we take 'family' in its original sense of household, he could also be seen as beginning as an outsider within the family. Like Shakespeare's Touchstone in *As You Like It*, the Fool follows loyalties into exile; like both Touchstone and Feste, he provides a critical reflection on the actions of other characters. He repeatedly stresses Lear's folly, sometimes getting Lear to unwittingly call himself a fool. Dependent on others, he speaks most directly about the hardships of being a homeless person exposed to the weather, echoes Feste exactly when he sings 'hey, ho, the wind and the rain' (3.2.73) in literal rain on the heath, and emphasizes the similar misery of the other characters when he says, 'This cold night will turn us all to fools and madmen' (3.4.75). Like Kent, the Fool dies without much notice being given to his death; his last words, 'And I'll go to bed at noon' (3.6.78), are not identified as his last words until it becomes clear that there are no further words written for him.

King Lear is the seventh of a succession of Shakespearean plays showing 'outraged fathers, abusing, rejecting, and even cursing their daughters.... in the last four, Shakespeare enlarges or alters the story he is working from so as to emphasize the possessive anger in the role.'[50] The daughters Lear curses later, Goneril and Regan, appear to be insiders in the community of the play at the beginning, unless we observe that as women they are also, in a sense, disinherited—they can't legally inherit land or power themselves, but only pass it to their husbands. Unlike Edmund, disinherited in a different way, they never complain about this inequality. Another inequality about which they might complain becomes explicit only for a moment, when Goneril says to Regan, 'He always loved our sister most' (1.1.288–9). But they are outsiders in a different sense: they almost always have little audience sympathy. Shakespeare gives neither of them a soliloquy, makes them seem less isolated than Edmund by doubling them, and makes Lear's behaviour to them seem less negligent, if more manipulative, than Gloucester's to Edmund. Their competition in love for Edmund can be seen as retribution for their competition in words of love for their father, but it is presented to emphasize their lust, rather than their humanity. After their cruel treatment of their father and their attack on Gloucester, Albany calls them 'Tigers, not daughters' (4.2.41) and there is little to counter that viewpoint in the play or in traditional criticism. This could partly come from residual prejudice on the part of critics—A. C. Bradley says that Edmund is the least detestable of the three villains partly because he 'is at any rate not a woman'—but the text itself does humanize Edmund more.[51]

It was a drastically new shift of emphasis—though one consistent with the range of perspectives in many of Shakespeare's plays—when Peter Brook's 1963 stage production for the first time portrayed Goneril's complaint about Lear's disorderly servants as justified, and emphasized her suffering at Lear's angry curses.[52] This shift continued in 1991 when Jane Smiley rewrote the plot of *Lear* in her novel *A Thousand Acres*, giving the undutiful oldest daughter a chance to tell the story, set on an American farm in the 1970s, and the Women's Theatre Company, similarly, in their 1987 play *Lear's Daughters*, co-authored with Elaine Feinstein, imagine for all three a past shadowed by Lear's tyranny and greed.[53]

In Shakespeare's version, Goneril's husband thinks he has the last comment on the two older sisters' dead bodies, placing them outside human sympathy:

> This judgment of the heavens, that makes us tremble,
> Touches us not with pity.

(5.3.230–1).

However, as we have seen, their deaths may matter to Edmund, callous about them as he has seemed earlier.

To modern readers of *King Lear*, Cordelia sometimes seems at the opposite pole from Goneril and Regan. But Shakespeare alters the story to make Cordelia's response to Lear's initial request for words of love more stubborn.[54] Her counterpart in the old play of *King Leir* at once replies to her father,

> I cannot paint my duty forth in words.
> I hope my deeds shall make report for me:
> But look what love the child doth owe the father,
> The same to you I bear, my gracious Lord.[55]

Cordelia, by contrast, answers Lear's question with 'Nothing, my lord' (1.1.86). Although many readers and viewers find Lear difficult enough that they sympathize with her brusqueness, especially considering the aside in which she promises to 'love and be silent' (1.1.60), the change from the source moves her further from conventionally ideal feminine behaviour and suggests less moral polarization between good and evil than will eventually develop between her and her sisters. Cordelia's reticence is early and understandable since Lear has asked, in Shakespeare's version, 'what can you say to draw | A third more opulent than your sisters?' (1.1.84–5), setting up an answer as greedy flattery, and Edgar's failure to reveal himself to Gloucester is late and more mysterious, but both details complicate their characters and invite more audience thought.

Cordelia's asides about the impossibility of speech have already marked her as an emotional outsider to the ritual requirements of the court, and when she speaks she intensifies this role also by attacking her sisters' hyperbolical words of love as insincere because they are married. When she refuses to participate in Lear's contest for words of love, she becomes disinherited, disowned, and cast out from her family and her country. She may seem unfamilial in her own behaviour, unwilling to make the compromises on which social harmony depends, but in this play those who provide expedient flattery are greater threats to the family. Upon her return to take care of Lear, she is clearly at the moral centre of the play because of her sympathy for him, even as they are both defeated in battle and sent off to prison and finally to death. She looks like an outsider onstage, but she is an insider to the play's value system. Her sympathy is not confined to family members, at least according to her language:

> Mine enemy's dog,
> Though he had bit me, would have stood that night
> Against my fire.
>
> (4.7.36–8)

But she certainly feels that Lear belongs with her, not with 'rogues forlorn | In short and musty straw' (39–40).

Cordelia's death must have been particularly devastating to his original audience, since in the previous chronicle versions as well as the recently revived *King Leir* she survives after her reunion with her father. The earlier play includes more scenes of her in France as well as scenes showing her as a poor outcast, and in other versions of the story she, or in the play her husband, inherits the throne.[56] Shakespeare's ending continued to be so painful that for centuries the play was staged only in Nahum Tate's Restoration adaptation, in which Cordelia survives and marries Edgar. The influential 18th century critic Samuel Johnson defended substituting this adaptation on the grounds that it gives the characters the happy ending they deserve, but from the romantics on, serious theatre has become more open to showing final suffering and injustice for its main characters, and as Foakes has written, *Lear* has, since 1960, come to be seen as Shakespeare's most profound tragedy.[57] Shakespeare could have written a version in which Cordelia survives Lear. When he anticipates living with her in prison like birds in a cage it seems as if he will, with the happy ending and 'her kind nursery' (1.1.124) he initially hopes for, but as it is the play takes him into further realms of loss. At its end Lear does not think of being socially outside or inside except with regard to whether Cordelia is still alive so he is still in his relationship with her. The audience focus at this point is so much on those two characters that memories of Cordelia's husband and of her choice to leave him in staying with Lear tend to vanish, though Janet Adelman has observed how this structure provides Lear at his death with the all-giving maternal daughter that he has always wanted, simplifying her psychology.[58]

'We came crying hither'

In this play where even Edmund ultimately turns out to show sympathy, it is a human quality, not simply a feminine one, as Shakespeare's language often makes it seem. In spite of the intensity with which the play presents Cordelia, much of its actual language of sympathy for outsiders comes from male characters. There is no other Shakespearean play in which we are cued so often to feel sympathy for other characters as we are in *Lear*. Gloucester, Kent, and Edgar express sympathy for Lear, Edgar and Kent express sympathy for Gloucester, Lear and Gloucester each express sympathy for the poor. Edgar talks about the process of learning to feel sympathy; he most of all discusses various effects of seeing someone else's sufferings while you are suffering, and some of Lear's most memorable lines are about the universality of suffering: 'We came crying hither' (4.6.172).[59]

In the four plays to which I have devoted chapters in this book, there is a progression in the degree of sympathy expressed by characters in the play for the most obvious outsider. No one expresses sympathy for Shylock at the end, though Portia has acknowledged earlier that he has a case. Olivia does express sympathy for Malvolio, and Orsino orders someone to attempt to pacify him. Cassio pays tribute to Othello at the end, as a number of characters have earlier. While Lear's faults are clearly noted from the first scene on, at the end the surviving characters, Kent, Edgar, and Albany, are united in their sympathy for him. In plays about other kinds of outsiders Shakespeare never makes the theme of sympathy so explicit; and it can be argued that it shows something of a bias in his vision, that the play which focuses on sympathy is one whose suffering outsiders are white, mostly male, English, aristocrats by birth, and religiously able to speak the language both of an archaic English pagan setting and Shakespeare's own Christian world. It may well be the case that Shakespeare's audience found it easier to sympathize with a homeless or poor person if they had seen him previously as an aristocrat. Nonetheless, to use this hypothesis to trivialize the expansion of sympathies asked of the audience in the play underestimates the extent to which most early modern English texts show a revulsion against the homeless and the poor—the outsiders they might find begging at their door. As Woodbridge writes, '*King Lear* is one of the only texts of the English Renaissance to give beggary tragic rather than comic or farcical treatment.'[60] Richard Strier has argued that *Lear* is a radical play in its treatment of obedience and disobedience; Woodbridge's evidence shows that it is also radical for its time in its treatment of homelessness.[61]

Furthermore, the issue is not only sympathy for Lear but Lear's sympathy for others. This is the only play of the four I discuss in which the central outsider is shown first to lack and then to develop sympathy for other characters. Not only do we see Lear earlier assuming that 'Our basest beggars | are in the poorest thing superfluous' (2.4.259–60), and then realizing that he has taken 'too little care' (3.4.35) of the poor in his kingdom, we also see him looking out for the Fool and, after he has banished her, realizing that he has wronged Cordelia. *Lear* is not just a play about homelessness, but also one about the pain and yet the importance of homes and families. Families can include people who make you feel like you are an outsider even in your own home as well as ultimately refuse you one. As the characters show, you may long for reunion with them anyway but not know how to behave when the chance arises. The play acknowledges deep flaws in both fathers and children; both can be considered responsible for the suffering it portrays, particularly the suffering of outsiders. Yet it draws readers and audiences into identifying with characters on both sides of the generational divide as it proceeds to its poignant reunions and its painful final bereavement.

Epilogue

The Tempest, *Outsiders, and Border Crossings*

Caliban is probably the Shakespearean outsider who is most invoked by political movements around the world. Not only British and US writers, but those who are 'French, Cuban, Nicaraguan, Barbadian, Canadian, Ghanaian, and Zambian', among many other nationalities, have applied his words or his situation to conditions in their own time and place.[1] His protest to Prospero against his enslavement, 'This island's mine, by Sycorax my mother' (1.2.334), has become a symbol of the complaint any people ruled by settlers of different ancestry can raise. His charge, 'You taught me language, and my profit on't | Is I know how to curse' (366–7), has been often repeated in relation to the imposition of a foreign tongue and educational system by conquerors. The frequent reference to him as 'monster' or 'disproportioned' can foreshadow the alienation that colonialism's imposition of different standards of aesthetics and behaviour can impose. But it is also important to the power and the relevance of this play that, as with the others discussed, Caliban is not the only outsider in *The Tempest*.

Interpretations of Caliban are multiple partly because, as with most Shakespeare plays, so much is ambiguous. First there is the location. The 'uninhabited island' of the stage direction is supposedly reached by travellers in the Mediterranean, including Antonio, the brother who usurped his title to Milan, and Alonso, the Duke of Naples, who assisted him, returning from Tunis to Italy and blown off course by a storm. But the play is full of hints of the New World. Caliban refers to Sycorax's god 'Setebos' (1.2.376), also the name of a god found in a Patagonian travel narrative.[2] The play has verbal echoes of the apparently providential salvation after a hurricane hit ships bound for Virginia from a company whose members included Southampton, one of Shakespeare's most important patrons. The behaviour of Caliban, hospitably welcoming Prospero and later becoming more aggressive, is similar to that of the Indians toward many colonists, and like the Indians in Virginia, Caliban continues to supply the colonists with food even after the situation has changed. And the play directly refers to English fascination with the

New World when the jester Trinculo says 'When they will not give a doit to relieve a lame beggar, they will lay out ten to see a dead Indian' (2.2.29–31).[3]

Caliban's appearance is also ambiguous. The Folio list of characters refers to him as 'a salvage and deformed slave', but there is no evidence that Shakespeare actually wrote this, or nor of what Caliban's deformity would be. The play includes no authoritative description of him. The unreliable Trinculo (part of the shipwrecked group, but washed ashore at a different place) identifies him as a fish from his smell, but says he is 'Legged like a man, and his fins like arms!' (2.2.31–2). The unreliable butler Stefano identifies him as 'some monster of the island with four legs' (2.2.62), but that is because the frightened Trinculo has crawled under the gabardine that is covering Caliban. When Trinculo rises, however, the monster identification sticks, and the two of them (no one else) call him 'monster' about 40 times in the play: very likely 'attempts by a jester and a butler to assert a modicum of superiority over their self-proclaimed "foot-licker"'.[4] It is particularly ironic—a kind of parable of projection—that Trinculo insists on this term, since it arises from Stefano's misinterpretation of Trinculo's legs as well as Caliban's extending from under Caliban's gabardine. In spite of their constant use of the epithet, however, once they realize he is not threatening them they are happy for his companionship, subservience, and knowledge of the island. Ironically, Caliban can offer to show them how to get food, as he earlier showed Prospero, and give them other advice because, in its sense of 'one who has knowledge', he is actually an insider on the island.

Three other characters comment on Caliban's appearance: upon first seeing him, Antonio calls him a 'plain fish' (5.1.269), Alonso says, 'this is a strange thing as e'er I looked on' (5.1.293), and Prospero, who has earlier called Caliban 'Misshapen knave' (271), replies, 'He is as disproportioned in his manners | As in his shape' (294–5). Probably Caliban should look different from the European characters, but the production, or the reader, has many possibilities of how to imagine him. Some directors have made him a kind of evolutionary 'missing link', but in recent years many have given him no particular deformity but, perhaps, body markings suggestive of Indian and/or African customs.

Like Othello, Shylock, and Malvolio, Caliban has abilities that the dominant people in his society use. As Prospero says, 'We cannot miss him. He does make our fire, | Fetch in our wood, and serves in offices | That profit us' (1.2.314–16). He is linked with Othello because Sycorax, his mother, is from Africa, in this case Algeria, but the outsider he most closely resembles is probably Shylock, though there are also likenesses to Edmund. While Othello is loyal to Venice, Caliban, like Edmund, Malvolio and Shylock, has a strong sense of having been wronged. He recalls the help he gave to Prospero and Miranda when they first arrived, by contrast to his current

Epilogue: The Tempest, *Outsiders, and Border Crossings* 149

confinement and forced work. He has a very specific plan to get rid of Prospero, as Edmund alienates his brother from his father to get the land he thinks he deserves, and Shylock takes advantage of the loss of Antonio's ships to plot taking his pound of flesh through the court. And for different reasons and in very different ways, he resembles the outsiders Othello and Malvolio in arousing hostility by violating boundaries around a woman of the dominant group.

The Tempest, like other plays of the romance/tragicomic genre, has comic elements and an ending with reconciliations, but includes within it a version of a tragic plot which it goes beyond. Caliban too has qualities that might link him with both tragedy and comedy. He shows the overt self-assertion that is the mark of the most obvious outsider in comedy, the kind who is openly punished or humiliated.[5] But he is unlike most of the comic outsiders, especially Malvolio and Shylock, in that he can be sociable, festive, carnivalesque, as in his scenes with Stefano and Trinculo. He is friendly to newcomers on the island, and rather than develop a solitary plot of revenge he enlists Stefano and Trinculo to help, imagining Stefano as a better master than Prospero and recommending Miranda to Stefano as a wife rather than still hoping for her himself. Although it eventually becomes obvious to him that he has misjudged his allies, it is possible that this instinct for collective effort, as well as his clear focus on his oppressor, is part of what has made him so appealing to various political movements. Caliban is also unlike Malvolio and Shylock in that he appreciates music: indeed, one of his most eloquent speeches declares, 'The isle is full of noises, | Sounds and sweet airs, that give delight and hurt not' (3.2.131–2). His sensitivity to beauty here, and his ability to create it in his own language, are other characteristics that make him seem to have more depth than most comic outsiders as well as his confreres in rebellion in this scene.

In one way Caliban is more isolated than most of Shakespeare's other outsiders: because of biography, not temperament, he has no link with a community of his own, as Shylock has and as even Othello has, with memories of his mother, his father, and pride in the 'men of royal siege' (1.2.32) in his ancestry. Caliban has only distant memories of Sycorax. No wonder he wishes he could have 'peopled… | This isle with Calibans' (1.2.353–4) and made it possible for him to rejoice, as does Aaron in *Titus Andronicus*, with offspring in his own image. The constant references to him as a monster reinforce the sense of his uniqueness and merge with suggestions of his repulsiveness to Miranda beyond the justification provided by the rape. Richard III, the Shakespearean character most clearly presented in terms of deformity, from his beginning (in *Richard, Duke of York/Henry VI, Part 3*), links his appearance with unattractiveness to women. For Richard also the disability is linked with his sense of aloneness—'I have no brother, I am like no brother' (5.6.81)—although Richard, unlike Caliban, actually has live relatives.

Again linking him more with the tragic world than the comic, Caliban's bitterness, unlike Shylock's, has more a sense of betrayal, like Lear's. He not only mourns the loss of the time when he was, as he says, 'mine own king', instead of Prospero's subject, he also mourns the loss of the affection that he once received from Prospero: 'When thou cam'st first, | Thou strok'st me and made much of me' (1.2.335–6). Though he is still a relative youth, he seems, like the Lear who wanted Cordelia's 'kind nursery' (1.1.124), nostalgic for the way he was treated in childhood, another quality that humanizes him in a different way than most of the outsider characters in comedy.[6]

Furthermore, he is also unlike those characters in that he seems to have learned from his experience and plans to change:

> I'll be wise hereafter,
> And seek for grace. What a thrice-double ass
> Was I to take this drunkard for a god
> And worship this dull fool!
>
> (5.1.298–301)

Although he has not committed errors as drastic as those of Othello and Lear, he shows signs of an ability to learn that could link him to Othello with his desire to atone and to Lear with the change in his values. In this way he is somewhat like the heroes of Shakespeare's other late romances such as Posthumus and Leontes, who reform after learning they were wrong to suspect their wives.

However, his ending is still open-ended, even more than the ending of the other outsiders. His repentance and rejection of Trinculo and Stefano might seem to indicate that he will return to Europe with Prospero, who has just acknowledged him as 'mine' (5.1.279). But Prospero simply asks him to fix up the cell for the guests from the shipwreck, and says nothing definite about Caliban's future. Aimé Césaire's *A Tempest* changes the ending so that he and Prospero both stay on the island, Caliban growing stronger as Prospero grows weaker: productions of *The Tempest* itself often now show Caliban returning to possession of the island. As Virginia and Alden Vaughan have written, the openness of Caliban's ending may have been one of the encouragements for later authors to use their own imagination about his future.[7]

Another character who plays the role of the outsider at the end is a moral outsider, not one who looks different from anyone else—Prospero's brother Antonio, who usurped his dukedom. Antonio, during the play, persuades

Epilogue: The Tempest, Outsiders, and Border Crossings 151

another character, Sebastian, to a parallel usurpation, and there is never a hint of his reformation; Prospero, as he removes Antonio from his dukedom, offers him the most unforgiving words of forgiveness in drama:

> For you, most wicked sir, whom to call brother
> Would even infect my mouth, I do forgive
> Thy rankest fault, all of them.

(5.1.132–4)

But Antonio at the end does not say anything about his pride in his evil deeds, as dramatic characters sometimes do, to assert his resistance to Prospero. All he does is maintain silence, a silence that moved W. H. Auden to write him some devastating imagined speeches in his sequence based on *The Tempest*, *The Sea and the Mirror*.[8] This silence is one of the few resemblances between this Antonio and the earlier Antonios. In all three cases it has something to do with not being included in the final celebrations. Antonio's loss of his dukedom, Stephen Orgel has suggested, takes on more permanent implications because the marriage between Ferdinand and Miranda, making Ferdinand, Duke of Naples, Prospero's heir, removes Antonio and his offspring, if any, from the line of succession to the Duchy of Milan, so in addition to his general resentment of Prospero he might have additional reason to feel affronted.[9] The other Antonios, by contrast, must deal with not having first place in their beloved's official kin, whatever this means unofficially, and could be silent just out of tact (or because dramatic structure focuses on the newly married or newly engaged couple). Nevertheless, it is strange that Shakespeare gives this Antonio, like the one in *Twelfth Night*, a male friend called Sebastian. It is as if their friendship, which in this play consists mainly in joint mockery and in Antonio tempting Sebastian to treachery, is a bitter parody of the friendship in *Twelfth Night*, whose Sebastian speaks of wishing for Antonio's counsel.

Miranda, like many of the other women in Shakespeare, can be seen as both insider and outsider. In the second scene of the play, Prospero initiates her into more knowledge of her history and history of the island. She herself has taken on the role of insider with regard to Caliban, teaching him language. The play repeatedly emphasizes her own ignorance of the world, but shows how this gives her a charming enthusiasm and responsiveness. She has no idea that Prospero has set up her marriage to Ferdinand and is just pretending to oppose it; thus she has the experience of spontaneity and free choice, even though she will unknowingly be aiding Prospero's political goals. When she is revealed playing chess with Ferdinand in the final scene, she suggests a bit more skepticism about him than she has shown before: 'Sweet lord, you play me false' (5.1.174), but this doesn't seem to lessen her love, or her enthusiasm about the other humans that she is seeing for the first time: 'How beauteous mankind is! O brave new world | That has such people in't!' (5.1.186). Both Miranda's inexperience and her ambiguous position sharing Prospero's privilege yet subject to his power in a way parallel to Caliban have made her a figure often reimagined by women writers.[10]

Ariel could be considered an outsider because he is the only character who clearly identifies himself as not human, though by saying that the suffering people he sees would receive compassion from him if he were, he provides a kind of model for Prospero to sympathize also. He could also be considered an outsider because he receives freedom from Prospero at the end, rather than taking the ship back to Milan with the others. Unlike an outsider such as Malvolio when he leaves the play's community, Ariel seems to have no ill will for it; he simply belongs somewhere else.

The most important complexity of the outsider condition in the play, however, is that Prospero, who appears as the most powerful and informed character and therefore an insider, is also an outsider, an exile from Milan and a newer resident of the island than Caliban or Ariel. Caliban points out that it was he who showed Prospero 'all the qualities o'th'isle, | The fresh springs, brine-pits, barren place and fertile' (1.2.340–1). Many previous plays of Shakespeare use changes between places to relativize who is an outsider: for example *Antony and Cleopatra* and *Henry IV, Part 1*. In *As You Like It* Jaques argues that the Duke taking refuge in the Forest of Arden is actually usurping the territory of the animals. But here the issue of who should have power over the island has more serious political overtones, and Caliban's protests are eloquent. When Prospero promises to leave the island, his plan has more implications about his possible lack of rights there than when at the end all the exiles in Arden except Jaques return to the court. The switch in Prospero's position is emphasized by his relinquishment of magic and the humility in his epilogue, where he 'puts himself in the position of Ariel, Caliban, Ferdinand, and the other shipwreck victims throughout the play, threatened with confinement and pleading for release from bondage.'[11] 'This thing of darkness I | Acknowledge mine' (5.1.278–9), he has said earlier, claiming Caliban, in lines that resonate with indefinite suggestions of hard-earned self-knowledge about his own failings, parallel perhaps to the suggestions he made earlier to Miranda of how his own focus on his secret studies led to the ease with which Antonio usurped the throne.

Who are the outsiders in *The Tempest*? Caliban, Antonio, Ariel, Miranda, Prospero? As in *Lear* and *Twelfth Night*, as I have discussed them, sometimes the term may seem to expand so much it includes everyone; sometimes it seems to refer to just a few marked characters. This ambiguity is actually part of the meaning of the term. Shakespeare's plays are structured so that the

Epilogue: The Tempest, *Outsiders, and Border Crossings* 153

most obvious outsiders reflect qualities of other characters. Increasingly in his career there is a contrast between the marked outsider, who is conventionally expected to be evil, and the moral outsider, who really is. The most visibly different outsiders who are consciously evil occur in relatively early plays, *Titus Andronicus* (Aaron) and *Richard III*. Shylock is already ambiguous, and the most marked later outsider in tragedy, Othello, turns out to be more human than Iago, the moral outsider who claims to be an insider. In *Lear* the apparently dutiful daughters become moral outsiders while Edmund, who scoffs at conventional morality, dies hoping that he can save the lives of Lear and Cordelia. In *Antony and Cleopatra*, the cultural outsider stages a glorious death that even Romans can appreciate, while in *Coriolanus* the apparent insider, the Roman who seems to operate by Roman military values, brings death on himself because he can find home nowhere, and in *The Tempest*, the 'born devil' (4.1.188), Caliban, promises to 'be wise and seek for grace', while Prospero's own brother is revealed as a moral outsider and Prospero, saying of Caliban, 'This thing of darkness I | Acknowledge mine' (5.1.178–9), hints at acknowledging darkness in himself. As a corollary to this, Shakespeare's plays don't show many satisfying killings or expulsions of scapegoats.[12] In addition to those I've already mentioned, Falstaff is admitted back into the community in *Merry Wives of Windsor*, and in *Henry V* his death is mourned and recalled in a way that casts a shadow on Henry's banishment of him. Malvolio is needed for the concluding marriages to happen, and Olivia wishes he could be back as her steward. Iago apparently can't be killed or expelled. Either the boundaries between good and evil, insiders and outsiders, are questioned, or execution can't get rid of evil.

This book is among other things an attempt to link a history in which groups and individuals are clearly marked with power differentials with a theatre in which those markings and those differentials are shaken up and similarities appear among characters in very different places. Shakespeare's theatre sometimes explicitly shows characters asking each other to imagine across boundaries. Sometimes they are boundaries of gender, as when Viola, in her disguise as Cesario, says to Orsino,

> Say that some lady, as perhaps there is,
> Hath for your love as great a pang of heart
> As you have for Olivia. You cannot love her.

(2.4.87–9)

She sees the similarity between Orsino's love for Olivia and her own for him.

Sometimes they are boundaries of the imprisoned sinner vs. the apparent saint, as when Isabella says to Angelo, who has condemned her brother to death, 'If he had been as you and you as he, | You would have slipped like him'

(2.2.66–7). Angelo soon will slip, in even a worse way than Claudio, perhaps partly because of the way his imagination is stirred by this appeal. Sometimes they are national boundaries, as when the Goth Tamora, in her first speech of *Titus Andronicus*, pleads for the life of her son this way with Titus, who is mourning the death of his:

> if thy sons were ever dear to thee,
> O, think my son to be as dear to me!
> . . . .
> O, if to fight for king and commonweal
> Were piety in thine, it is in these.
>
> (1.1.107–08, 114–15)

When later in the play Tamora behaves monstrously, as when she encourages her sons in the rape and mutilation of Titus' daughter Lavinia, the play leaves open the possibility that she does not begin as a monster but becomes embittered because Titus insists on the sacrifice of her son Alarbus.

The characters who try to get a specific person to imagine being in someone else's situation are mostly female, with some exceptions such as Thomas More, mentioned in the introduction. But both male and female characters speak about seeing resemblances between themselves and others. For example, in *Twelfth Night* Olivia says of Malvolio, 'I am as mad as he, | If sad and merry madness equal be' (3.4.14–15), as a prelude to her final sympathy for him. It is part of Hamlet's appeal that he sees his enemy Laertes as like himself at the end—they have both lost their fathers and are seeking revenge. Rosalind identifies with Silvius in his love of Phebe, and Viola with Orsino in his love of Olivia, though both are also detached enough to give advice. Edgar notes the analogy between his situation and Lear's, 'He childed as I fathered' (3.6.103). Then there are the more general equal rights speeches of Shylock, Edmund, and Emilia, the great generalizations of Lear on the heath, 'When we are born, we cry that we are come | To this great stage of fools' (4.6.176–7). Often outsiders of some kind are the ones who make the comparative or generalizing comments, in some cases because it is an argument for their dignity, but also sometimes because, as particularly with fools, they can see social patterns better from their position on the outside.

Many other similarities are unacknowledged by the characters, but hinted at by the structure and the language. In *A Midsummer Night's Dream* the lovers make fun of the events in the Pyramus and Thisbe play, in which characters act rather similarly to the way they themselves have. In *The Merchant of Venice*, Portia's behaviour punishing Bassanio for giving away her ring is a parody of Shylock's attempt to punish Antonio for not being able

Epilogue: The Tempest, Outsiders, and Border Crossings

to return his money. 'The bond!' he repeats—'The ring!' she insists. Olivia's behaviour with Cesario is like Antonio's behaviour with Sebastian. Lear's misjudgment of his children is like Gloucester's. Iago's influence over Brabanzio and Cassio is like his influence over Othello. Caliban, Ariel, and Prospero all want to be free.

The aesthetic pattern of resemblances and contrasts is one that also carries an ethical point. Every one of Shakespeare's significant characters could be considered an outsider at some time in some way, but outsiders in one situation may be insiders in another, and may feel or behave in some ways similar to those who are insiders in contrast to them. The ethical point could be generalized in the conclusion found in the words of one of Thomas More's hearers, as well as many other places, 'Let's do as we may be done by' (Add.II.D.153–54). But no motto can convey the galvanic experience in changing point of view and expanding imaginative sympathy that Shakespeare's plays can be. Even the outsiders who most evoke threatening stereotypes at some moments appear merely human.

Notes

INTRODUCTION

1. But see Ania Loomba, 'Outsiders in Shakespeare's England' in *The Cambridge Companion to Shakespeare*, ed. Margreta deGrazia and Stanley Wells (Cambridge: Cambridge University Press, 2001), 162, 'these plays explore the fragility as well as the tenacity of difference.'
2. Margaret Cavendish, *CCXI Sociable Letters* (1664; rpt. Menston: Scolar Press, 1969), 245–6; Elizabeth Montagu, *An Essay on the Writings of Shakespear* (1769; rpt. New York: Augustus M. Kelly, 1970), 36; John Keats, *Letters*, 2 vols, ed. Hyder Rollins (Cambridge, M.A.: Harvard University Press, 1958), 1: 386–7; Samuel Taylor Coleridge, *Biographia Literaria*, chap. 15, in R. A. Foakes, ed., *Coleridge's Criticism of Shakespeare* (Detroit: Wayne State University Press, 1989), 30; Stephen Greenblatt, *Will in the World* (New York: Norton, 2004), 'a certain capacity to conjure up the lives of others, an ability to identify even with despised and degraded humanity', 264.
3. William Hazlitt, *Characters of Shakespear's Plays*, in *Complete Works*, ed. P. P. Howe, 21 vols. (1930; rpt. New York: AMS Press, 1967), 4: 346–7.
4. See for example Arthur L. Little, Jr., *Shakespeare Jungle Fever: National-Imperial Re-Visions of Race, Rape, and Sacrifice* (Palo Alto: Stanford University Press, 2000), 92; James Shapiro, *Shakespeare and the Jews* (New York: Columbia University Press, 1996); Lisa Jardine, *Still Harping on Daughters: Women and Drama in the Age of Shakespeare* (Totowa, N. J.: Barnes & Noble, 1983).
5. Leslie Fiedler, *The Stranger in Shakespeare* (1972: Frogmore: Paladin, 1974). Fiedler argues that for all these character types Shakespeare 'in the main subscribed consciously to the values of the popular audience, which demanded their symbolic casting out' but this was not so with the 'odd man out'—'those equivocal lovers [such as the Antonios] excluded from the happy ending.' He also relates the stranger to the spoilsport and the fool (15–16), but does not discuss characters in these categories in depth.
6. Susan Amussen, *An Ordered Society: Gender and Class in Early Modern England, 1560–1725* (New York: Blackwell, 1988), Keith Wrightson, *English Society 1580–1680*, rev. ed. (New Brunswick: Rutgers University Press, 2003; Cristina Malcolmson, '"What You Will": Social Mobility and

Gender in *Twelfth Night*', in *The Matter of Difference: Materialist Feminist Criticism of Shakespeare*, ed. Valerie Wayne (Ithaca: Cornell University Press, 1991), 29–58.
7. I discuss the recent religious flux and its effects in my chapter on *The Merchant of Venice*. Steven Mullaney relates it to the development of drama in 'Affective Technologies: Toward an Emotional Logic of the Elizabethan Stage', in *Environment and Embodiment in Early Modern England*, ed. Mary Floyd-Wilson and Garrett Sullivan (New York: Palgrave Macmillan, 2007), 71–89. Also, for reasons sometimes related to religion but for many other causes, banishment and exile were threats that loomed large in the imagination of the time and in Shakespeare's plays: see Jane Kingsley-Smith, *Shakespeare's Drama of Exile* (Houndmills: Palgrave Macmillan, 2003).
8. Mario DiGangi, *The Homoerotics of Early Modern Drama* (Cambridge: Cambridge University Press, 1997), chapter one.
9. This and all subsequent quotations from Shakespeare's text come from *The Norton Shakespeare: Based on the Oxford Edition*, 2nd ed., edited by Stephen Greenblatt, et al. (New York: W. W. Norton, 2008).
10. On Sebastian, see Camille Wells Slights, *Shakespeare's Comic Commonwealths* (Toronto: University of Toronto Press, 1993), 216–35, 237; on the French in Shakespeare's history plays and, among other things, how their characterization is Orientalist, Linda Woodbridge, *The Scythe of Saturn: Shakespeare and Magical Thinking* (Urbana, Illinois: University of Illinois Press, 11–17; on children, Kate Chedgzoy, Susanne Greenhalgh, and Robert Shaughnessy, eds. *Shakespeare and Childhood* (Cambridge: Cambridge University Press, 2007).
11. Penny Gay, '*Twelfth Night*: "The Babbling Gossip of the Air"' in *A Companion to Shakespeare's Works*, ed. Richard Dutton and Jean Howard (Oxford: Blackwell, 2003), 440; Robert Weimann, *Author's Pen and Author's Voice: Playing and Writing in Shakespeare's Works* (Cambridge: Cambridge University Press, 2000).
12. Stephen Orgel, *Impersonations: the Performance of Gender in Shakespeare's England* (Cambridge: Cambridge University Press, 1996), 12. On the location of the theatre and its implications, see Steven Mullaney, *The Place of the Stage: License, Play, and Power in Renaissance England* (Chicago: University of Chicago Press, 1988).
13. Meredith Anne Skura, *Shakespeare the Actor and the Purposes of Playing* (Chicago: University of Chicago Press, 1993).
14. The idea of disability as an identity category marking membership in a group became visible in the US with activism about civil rights for the

disabled in the 1970s. See *The Disability Studies Reader*, ed. Lennard J. Davis (New York: Routledge, 1997).
15. I follow here John Jowett's dating of the versions of *Sir Thomas More* in his Arden edition (2011).
16. Margaret Tudeau-Clayton, 'This is the Strangers' case': the utopic dissonance of Shakespeare's contribution to *Sir Thomas More*', *Shakespeare Survey* Vol. 65 (2012), 239–54.
17. Cressida and Lady Falconbridge are some exceptions. Goneril is also unfaithful, but this isn't presented as a vindication of her husband's suspicion of her.
18. Richard Strier, *Resistant Structures: Particularity, Radicalism, and Renaissance Texts* (Berkeley: University of California Press, 1995), 118–64; Thomas Cartelli, 'Shakespeare's *Merchant*, Marlowe's *Jew*: The Problem of Cultural Difference', *Shakespeare Studies* 20, ed. Leeds Barroll (New York: Burt Franklin, 1988), 259.
19. Geoffrey Bullough, ed., *Narrative and Dramatic Sources of Shakespeare* (London: Routledge and Kegan Paul, 1957), I, 450–1, 476–82.
20. Joel Altman, *The Tudor Play of Mind: Rhetorical Inquiry and the Development of Elizabethan Drama* (Berkeley: University of California Press, 1978).
21. A. J. Hoenselaars, *Images of Englishmen and Foreigners in the Drama of Shakespeare and His Contemporaries* (Rutherford, N. J.: Fairleigh Dickinson University Press, 1992), 21.
22. There are a few exceptions, such as Sophocles' Oedipus, who goes into exile.
23. Jean-Pierre Guépin, *The Tragic Paradox: Myth and Ritual in Greek Tragedy* (Amsterdam: Hakkert, 1968), summarized by Linda Woodbridge, in *The Scythe of Saturn*, 87.
24. René Girard, *A Theater of Envy* (New York: Oxford, 1991), 249, argues that for one group of spectators the play would work as a scapegoat ritual, while that for others, those who sympathize with Shylock, the play would be about scapegoating.
25. Northrop Frye, *A Natural Perspective: The Development of Shakespearean Comedy and Romance* (New York: Columbia University Press, 1965), 93, gives the Greek word '*idiotes*' to the character who is 'isolated from the action by being the focus of the anticomic mood, and so may be the technical villain, like Don John, or the butt, like Malvolio and Falstaff, or simply opposed by temperament to festivity, like Jaques.' ('*Idiotes*' in Greek refers to a private person, as opposed to someone who is involved in public issues.) He discusses the fool or clown as another kind of isolated character and notes that there is frequently an opposition

between the fool and the *idiotes*. C. L. Barber, *Shakespeare's Festive Comedy* (1959; rpt. New York: Meridian, 1963), has detailed discussions of the complex dramatic treatment of Shylock, Malvolio, and the Falstaff of the history plays.
26. Alan Bray, 'Homosexuality and the Signs of Male Friendship', in *Queering the Renaissance*, ed. Jonathan Goldberg (Durham: Duke University Press, 1994), 40–61.
27. Paroles is lower in class than Bertram and calls him 'boy' and 'my boy' (2.1.29, 2.3.262, 4.3.203, 4.3.280), so he seems older; he is a lesser version of Falstaff.
28. Frye says, *Natural Perspective*, 98, 'In tragedy, of course, the hero is always something of an *idiotes*, isolated from the society in which he has his being.'
29. Paul Hammond, *The Strangeness of Tragedy* (Oxford: Oxford University Press, 2009), 4.
30. René Girard; John Holloway, *The Story of the Night* (1961: rpt. Lincoln: University of Nebraska Press, 1963); Linda Woodbridge, 'Magical Politics: Shakespeare and the Scapegoat', in *Scythe of Saturn*; Naomi Conn Liebler, *Shakespeare's Festive Tragedy: The Ritual Foundations of Genre* (London: Routledge, 1995); Thomas Cartelli, *Marlowe, Shakespeare, and the Economy of Theatrical Experience* (Philadelphia: University of Pennsylvania Press, 1991).
31. See Meredith Anne Skura, *The Literary Use of the Psychoanalytic Process* (New Haven: Yale University Press, 1981), 226–8.

CHAPTER I

1. René Girard, *A Theater of Envy* (New York: Oxford University Press, 1991), 248–50.
2. Diarmaid MacCulloch, *Reformation: Europe's House Divided* (New York: Allen Lane, 2003), 285, 392.
3. See for example A. O. Scott, 'Putting a Still-Vexed Play in a Historical Context', *New York Times*, December 20, 2004, B1, B7. For a more scholarly example, see James Bulman, *The Merchant of Venice: Shakespeare in Performance* (New York: Manchester University Press, 1991), 17; on the other hand, see the critique of this assumption in Charles Edelman, 'Introduction', in *The Merchant of Venice: Shakespeare in Production*, ed. Edelman (New York: Cambridge University Press, 2002), 2–5.
4. Lindsay Kaplan, ed., *The Merchant of Venice: Texts and Contexts* (New York: Bedford, 2002), 243. Kaplan provides useful selections from English

travellers' descriptions of Jewish life in Venice. Historically, as in *MV*, the ghetto did not prohibit peaceful interactions between Jews and Christians. See Benjamin Kaplan, *Divided by Faith* (Cambridge: Harvard University Press, 2007), 294–300, and Robert Bonfil, *Jewish Life in Renaissance Italy* (Berkeley, 1994).

5. E. A. J. Honigmann, *Shakespeare: The 'lost years'*, 2nd ed., (Manchester: Manchester University Press, 1998), 116–17.

6. On the difficulty of categorizing Shakespeare's religion, discussed from a historicized standpoint rather than simply in terms of his 'negative capability', see Dympna Callaghan, 'Shakespeare and Religion', *Textual Practice*, 15 (2001), 1–4, and Jeffrey Knapp, *Shakespeare's Tribe: Church, Nation, and Theater in Renaissance England* (Chicago: University of Chicago Press, 2002), esp. 49–57. Worrying the question of Shylock as an outsider from a different perspective than mine, Stephen Orgel points out that his surname is an English one and that he could have been seen as an allusion to the familiar puritan moneylenders of Shakespeare's day—or alternatively to the threatening Catholic Spaniard; see 'Shylock's Tribe', *Shakespeare and the Mediterranean*, ed. Tom Clayton, Susan Brock, Vicente Fores (Newark: University of Delaware Press, 2004), 38–53.

7. The strength of this belief is important in noting, as Ania Loomba puts it in *Shakespeare, Race, and Colonialism* (New York: Oxford University Press, 2002), 149, that 'religion and race are so tightly woven together.' Continuing anxiety among some Christians about Jews who had converted shows that the prejudice was not simply theological: see Jerome Friedman, 'Jewish Conversion: The Spanish Pure Blood Laws and Reformation', *Sixteenth Century Journal*, 18:1 (Spring 1987), 3–29. Jews who converted to Christianity were hostilely known as Marranos. Some of them came to England because the prejudice against them in Spain and Portugal (both countries in 1492 required them to either convert or leave) was so strong. The *Othello* chapter will show ambiguity in the sources of hostility to the hero (race or presumed religion); the ambiguity is similar here (ethnicity or presumed religion) and therefore I use the more familiar and more inclusive term 'anti-Semitism' rather than 'anti-Judaism'. In Venice at this point there were many openly Jewish residents, because Venice needed them as a centre of international trade, but even in Venice they 'were required to wear a cap distinguishing them from others, to pay higher taxes, and to be confined to the ghetto', Loomba, *Shakespeare, Race*, 142.

8. Michael Wood, *Shakespeare* (New York: Basic Books, 2003), 124; James Shapiro, *Shakespeare and the Jews* (New York: Columbia University Press, 1996), 69–76.

9. Alexandra Walsham, *Charitable Hatred: Tolerance and Intolerance in England, 1500–1700* (Manchester: Manchester University Press, 2006), 12. Walsham finds the recent work of social historians on grassroots interactions among people of different religions more important than tolerationist statements by famous writers.
10. Paula Blank, *Shakespeare and the Mismeasure of Renaissance Man* (New York: Cornell University Press, 2006), 84–90. Blank sees Shylock's speech as grounded in commonplace sixteenth-century notions of a human 'equality by nature', though she argues that the play does not really present Shylock and Antonio as equal.
11. See Richard Strier, *Resistant Structures: Particularity, Radicalism, and Renaissance Texts* (Berkeley: University of California Press, 1995), 118–64.
12. Foxe, *Acts and Monuments*, Allen, *A True, Sincere, and Modest Defense of English Catholics*, and Allen, *A Brief Discourse containing Certain Reasons why Catholics Refuse to Go to Church*, are excerpted in Kaplan, *MV*, 250–5, 255–8, and 259–62, respectively; Michael Questier, *Conversion, Politics and Religion in England, 1580–1625* (Cambridge: Cambridge University Press, 1996), 161.
13. V. Norshov Olsen, *John Foxe and the Elizabethan Church* (Berkeley: University of California Press, 1973), 61, 199, 212. Thanks to Marcia Robinson for information about Foxe.
14. Strier, *Resistant Structures*, 152–3; Malcolm C. Smith, *Montaigne and Religious Freedom: The Dawn of Pluralism* (Geneve: Droz, 1991), 19–20; Perez Zagorin, *How the Idea of Religious Toleration Came to the West* (Princeton: Princeton University Press, 2003), 93–144; Strier, *Resistant Structures*, 143.
15. Smith, *Montaigne*, 20. Knapp, *Shakespeare's Tribe*, has recently emphasized the depth of Erasmus' influence on English Protestantism, the theatre, and Shakespeare.
16. Smith, *Montaigne*, 88. Though the Florio translation was not published until 1603, Shakespeare knew French, and it has been suggested that some English versions of Montaigne were circulated earlier. Since Florio was tutor to Shakespeare's patron Southampton, Shakespeare was more likely than most to see that translation before its publication. See Richard Wilson, *Secret Shakespeare: Studies in Theatre, Religion and Resistance* (Manchester: Manchester University Press, 2004), 28–9. Wilson argues that Shakespeare's views on religion were close to Montaigne's.
17. Nevill Coghill, 'The Theme of *The Merchant of Venice*', in *Twentieth Century Interpretations of The Merchant of Venice*, ed. Sylvan Barnet (Englewood Cliffs, N. J.: Prentice-Hall, 1970), 112.

18. James I, *Political Works*, ed. Charles Howard McIllwain (Cambridge: Harvard University Press, 1918), 322; Thomas Helwys, *A Short Declaration of the Mystery of Iniquity* (1612), ed. and introd. Richard Groves (Macon, Georgia: Mercer University Press, 1998). See also John Coffey, *Persecution and Toleration in Protestant England, 1558–1689* (London: Longman, 2000), 55.
19. Coffey, *Persecution*, 30.
20. Benjamin J. Kaplan, *Divided by Faith*, 26; William Covell, *A Modest and Reasonable Examination* (London: 1604), 200. I owe this reference to Kenneth Graham.
21. Much other evidence for this is presented by Stephen Greenblatt, *Will in the World* (New York: Norton, 2004), as well as Wilson, *Secret Shakespeare*.
22. See Thomas Cartelli, 'Shakespeare's *Merchant*, Marlowe's *Jew*: The Problem of Cultural Difference', *Shakespeare Studies* 20, ed. Leeds Barroll (New York: Burt Franklin, 1988), 259; Geoffrey Bullough, ed., *Narrative and Dramatic Sources of Shakespeare* (London: Routledge and Kegan Paul, 1957), I, 450–1, 476–82.
23. Zagorin, *Idea of Religious Toleration*, gives this title to his second chapter.
24. James Carroll, *Constantine's Sword: The Church and the Jews: A History* (New York: Mariner, 2001), 347, 373. Paul declared that charges of Jewish ritual murder came from 'the enemies of the Jews, blinded by hate and envy or, even more plausibly, by greed.' See Riccardo Calimani, *The Ghetto of Venice*, trans. Katherine Silverblatt Wolfthal (New York: M. Evans, 1987), 24–5.
25. Linda Woodbridge, *English Revenge Drama: Money, Resistance, Equality* (Cambridge: Cambridge University Press, 2010), 99–102.
26. Shapiro, *Shakespeare and the Jews*, discusses cannibalism fantasies on 104–5 and 109–11.
27. Bullough, ed. *Narrative and Dramatic Sources of Shakespeare*, I, 474; Shapiro, *Shakespeare*, 131.
28. Shylock's relationship with his daughter Jessica, who converts to Christianity because of dislike of her father's manners and love of the Christian Lorenzo, in some ways humanizes him, while Barabas' relationship with his daughter Abigail, whom he ultimately kills, mostly contributes to his demonization.
29. *Play of the Sacrament*, in Greg Walker, ed., *Medieval Drama: An Anthology* (Oxford: Blackwell, 2000), 213–33.
30. However, at the end he and the other Jews 'pledge a wandering exile... will remain perpetual foreigners on a penitential "voyage"': see Lisa Lampert, *Gender and Jewish Difference from Paul to Shakespeare*

(Philadelphia: University of Pennsylvania Press, 2004), 115. Lampert argues, 109–11, that the Spanish setting of this play contextualizes it with the 'pure blood' laws developed under the Inquisition. She also notes that the very rich merchant who sells him the host has a 'conversion' and hints at how this juxtaposition foreshadows that of Shylock and Antonio.

31. See for example Barbara Lewalski, 'Biblical Allusion and Allegory in *The Merchant of Venice*', *Shakespeare Quarterly* 13 (1962), rpt. in *Merchant of Venice*, ed. Leah Marcus (New York: Norton, 2006), 185–6.

32. Daniel Vitkus, ed., *Three Turk Plays from Early Modern England* (New York: Columbia University Press, 2000), 148–239. The salience of Ward's echoes of *MV* here may be increased by Michael Neill's evidence that Ward also echoes Othello. See '"His Master's Ass": Slavery, Service and Subordination in *Othello*', in *Shakespeare and the Mediterranean*, 228, n. 20.

33. Diarmaid MacCulloch, *Thomas Cranmer: A Life* (New Haven: Yale University Press, 1996), 589; Thomas Cranmer, *Miscellaneous Writings*, ed. John Edmond Cox, for the Parker Society (Cambridge: Cambridge University Press, 1946), 563.

34. MacCulloch, *Cranmer*, 603.

35. MacCulloch, *Cranmer*, 607.

36. 'The Burning Hand: Poetry and Reformation in Shakespeare's *Richard II*', *Religion and Literature* 32:2 (Summer 2000), 29–47; Knapp, *Shakespeare's Tribe*, 51.

37. Walter Cohen, 'Introduction', *Henry VIII (All is True)*, *The Norton Shakespeare*, 2nd ed., 3123.

38. I owe this point to Marsha Robinson.

39. This is the reading in the 1570 edition, rpt. 1857, rpt. in Kaplan, *MV*, 293. The 1583 version (London: John Day), 1884, consulted on microfilm at the Folger, has a side note at this point: 'The Archb. contented to recant.'

40. Marion Wynne-Davies, 'Rubbing at Whitewash: Intolerance in *The Merchant of Venice*,' in *A Companion to Shakespeare's Works, Vol. III: The Comedies*, edited by Richard Dutton and Jean Howard (Maldon, MA: Blackwell, 2003), 358–75, comes to a similar conclusion, beginning with Shakespeare's father's involvement in the required whitewashing over the images of saints in the Stratford Guild Chapel, four years after Elizabeth's accession, and the anti-Semitic story of St. Helena depicted there.

41. J. A., 'Archbishop Cranmer's death related by a By-stander', B. L. Harleian MS. 422, ff. 48. Brighton, Sussex: Harvester Press Microfilm Collection. Thanks to Susannah Monta for knowledge of this text and John McDiarmid for transcription of it.

42. MacCulloch, *Cranmer*, 577.

43. Sigurd Burckhardt, *Shakespearean Meanings* (Princeton: Princeton University Press, 1968), 221.
44. Leah Marcus, ed., *Merchant of Venice* (New York: Norton, 2006), xii, 55–62.
45. Judaism was, similarly, associated with justice, and many speeches in this scene play on the alliteration of 'justice' and 'Jew'. These associations come from early Christianity's attempt to distinguish itself, as allied with mercy, from Judaism; recent scholars of religion see them as more polemical than accurate, given the emphasis on mercy in Jewish tradition.
46. See Janet Adelman, 'Her Father's Blood: Race, Conversion, and Nation in *The Merchant of Venice*', *Representations* 81 (Winter 2003): 4–30.
47. Perez Zagorin, *Ways of Lying: Dissimulation, Persecution, and Conformity in Early Modern Europe* (Cambridge: Harvard University Press, 1990), discusses the rationales given for dissimulation of belief among Marranos, and compares them to 'persecuted Christians, both Protestant and Catholic', p. 61. Camille Wells Slights' view of this aspect of the play is similar to mine: 'Forcible conversion is unlikely to have struck Elizabethan audiences as a probable path to salvation.... the violence inherent in forcing people's consciences was becoming increasingly evident in the 1590s': *Shakespeare's Comic Commonwealths* (Toronto: University of Toronto Press, 1993), 146–7. Scholars used to assume that after he was converted he would no longer be able to lend money, but there were Christian money-lenders in both Italy and England; a significant example will be mentioned shortly.
48. Knapp, *Shakespeare's Tribe*, 50–1.
49. Ernst Honigmann, 'Shakespeare's Life', in *The Cambridge Companion to Shakespeare*, ed. Margreta de Grazia and Stanley Wells (Cambridge: Cambridge University Press, 2001), 7.
50. London: Bradocke, 1581; rpt. London: Malone Society Reprints, Oxford, 1952. This play exists in two versions; in the first, as the title page indicates based on the case of Francis Spera, the final messenger's speech says the main character hangs himself in despair; in the other one he finally repents. As Alan Dessen pointed out in commenting on this paper, financial motivation is important in his pressured conversion as well as that considered in *Three Ladies of London* and enacted in *Merchant of Venice*, and also in *A Christian Turned Turk*.
51. Even Derek Cohen, who calls *MV* 'a profoundly and crudely anti-Semitic play', believes that the audience has sympathy for him because of his humanity at the end. See his 'Shylock and the Idea of the Jew', excerpted from *Shakespearean Motives* (London: Macmillan, 1988), in *Merchant*, ed. Marcus, 201–6.

52. Quoted by Gail Kern Paster, *Humoring the Body* (Chicago: University of Chicago Press, 2004), 148.
53. Girard, *A Theater of Envy*, 249.
54. Leslie Fiedler, *The Stranger in Shakespeare* (1972: Frogmore: Paladin, 1974), 15–16. Fiedler nevertheless discusses Antonio frequently during the book.
55. Alan Bray, 'Homosexuality and the Signs of Male Friendship in Elizabeth England', in Jonathan Goldberg, ed., *Queering the Renaissance* (Durham: Duke University Press, 1994). 40–61. However, Bruce Smith, *Homosexual Desire in Shakespeare's England: A Cultural Poetics* (Chicago, 1991), shows literary traditions of 'cultural scenarios' for same-sex relations. Alan Sinfield argues, referring to Smith's evidence, that a homosexual identity may have been an emergent concept: 'There may have been, in early-modern Europe, especially in highly privileged circles, coteries where something like our concept of the homosexual individual occurred': *Cultural Politics: Queer Reading* (Philadelphia: University of Pennsylvania Press, 1994), 14. Mario DiGangi, *The Homoerotics of Early Modern Drama* (Cambridge: Cambridge University Press, 1997), discusses this controversy in his introductory chapter.
56. Lars Engle, *Shakespearean Pragmatism* (Chicago: University of Chicago Press, 1993), 85–6.
57. See Kenneth Borris, *Same-Sex Desire in the English Renaissance: A Sourcebook of Texts, 1470–1650* (New York: Routledge, 2004), 311–13; Paul Hammond, *Figuring Sex between Men from Shakespeare to Rochester* (Oxford: Clarendon Press, 2002), 90.
58. 'Il Pecorone', in Geoffrey Bullough, ed., *Narrative and Dramatic Sources of Shakespeare*, Vol. 1 (New York: Columbia University Press, 1957), 463–4.
59. Nothing in Shakespeare's text is explicit about the age difference, though Bassanio is called 'young' (2.9.87) and stage merchants were conventionally not young. Antonio does, however, say of himself 'The weakest kind of fruit | Drops earliest to the ground' (4.1.115–16) so he cannot be very old. By contrast to Antonio, Bassanio is sunny, talkative, and eager to please.
60. Hammond, *Figuring Sex*, 94. Hammond shows how Shakespeare increases the erotic possibilities of Shakespeare's source, and also how adaptations of *MV* from 1701 on attempt to remove these possibilities.
61. Alan Sinfield, 'How to Read *The Merchant of Venice* Without Being Heterosexist', in *Alternative Shakespeares*, v. 2, ed. Terence Hawkes (New York: Routledge, 1996), 137–8; Bruce Smith, *Homosexual Desire*, 65.
62. Cynthia Lewis, *Particular Saints* (Newark: University of Delaware Press, 1997), 31, says this title describes both Antonio and Ansaldo, his

prototype, but does not explicitly make a connection to the 'wether' line; Benjamin Kaplan, *Divided by Faith*, 28.
63. Laurie Shannon, *Sovereign Amity* (Chicago: University of Chicago Press, 2002), 113, notes that Emilia in *Two Noble Kinsmen*, who prefers women, makes an analogy between this preference and religion when she says to her sister Hippolyta, 'I am not | Against your faith, yet I continue mine' (1.3.96–7). But perhaps this resolution for Antonio recalls how the Church could use apparent contradictions of attitude; when the celibate Saint Anthony of Padua became the patron of lovers, on his feast day those without means to pay for a fancy wedding were married as a group. The same saint was also known as the Hammer of Heretics, a neat though perhaps coincidental parallel to Antonio's anti-Semitism and Shakespeare's allusion to Santiago Matamoros (St. James Moor-killler) when he gave a character identified in *Othello's* source only as 'Ensign', the name Iago. However, Cynthia Lewis, *Saints*, associates Antonio with Saint Anthony of Egypt, who was frequently linked with Saint Sebastian (Bassanio can be seen as a diminutive of Sebastian).
64. Sinfield, *Merchant*, 137.
65. Sinfield, *Merchant*, 135. Observations on their similarity have been made by W. H. Auden, 'Brothers and Others', in *The Dyer's Hand and Other Essays* (New York: Random House, 1962), 218–37, Girard, and many others.
66. *Il Pecorone*, excerpted in Bullough, 464.
67. Stanley Chojnacki, *Women and Men in Renaissance Venice* (Baltimore: Johns Hopkins, 2000), 249.
68. Guido Ruggiero, *The Boundaries of Eros* (New York: Oxford University Press, 1985), 121, 125.
69. Michael Rocke, *Forbidden Friendships: Homosexuality and Male Culture in Renaissance Florence* (New York: Oxford, 1996), 5, 121; Chojnacki, 266n, drawing on Nicholas Davidson, 'Theology, Nature, and the Law: Sexual Sin and Sexual Crime in Italy from the Fourteenth to the Seventeenth Centuries', in Trevor Dean and K. J. P. Lowe, eds, *Crime, Society, and the Law in Renaissance Florence* (Cambridge, 1994), 94–6.
70. Smith, *Homosexual Desire*, 48. Sex between women was not yet defined as a crime, and only anal sex was so defined for men, according to Borris, ed., *Same-Sex Desire*, 79.
71. Alan Bray, *Homosexuality in Renaissance England* (1982: London: GMP Publishers Ltd, 1988), 58–80; Borris, ed., *Same-Sex Desire in the English Renaissance*, 82–3.
72. The song is the Eishes Chayil, the praise of the 'woman of worth' from *Proverbs* 31, a traditional Sabbath song usually sung by a man (presumably

in praise of his wife). In a parallel move, at the end of the 2004 film by Michael Radford, the last shot is of Jessica, having run out of the mansion of Belmont, stroking Shylock's turquoise ring, which she actually has never sold.
73. C.L. Barber, *Shakespeare's Festive Comedy* (1959: Cleveland: Meridian Books, 1963).
74. Katherine E. Maus, Introduction to *MV*, *Norton Shakespeare*, 2nd ed., 1116–17.
75. Karen Newman, 'Portia's Ring: Unruly Women and Structures of Exchange in *The Merchant of Venice*', *Shakespeare Quarterly*, 38: 1(1987): 19–33.
76. Lars Engle, *Shakespearean Pragmatism*, 97, notes this.
77. Burckhardt, *Shakespearean Meanings*, 234–5.
78. Marc Shell, *Money, Language, and Thought* (Berkeley: University of California Press, 1982), 75n.
79. Girard, *A Theater of Envy*.
80. Kiernan Ryan, *Shakespeare's Comedies* (New York: Palgrave Macmillan, 2009), 119.

CHAPTER 2

1. Leonard Digges, quoted from E. K. Chambers, *William Shakespeare: A Study of Facts and Problems*, vol. 2 (Oxford: Oxford University Press, 1951), 233, in Carol Thomas Neely, *Distracted Subjects: Madness and Gender in Shakespeare and Early Modern Culture* (Ithaca: Cornell University Press, 2004), 158. Neely shows that even recent editions often choose more illustrations of stage presentations of Malvolio than of any other character. *TN* was sometimes referred to as *Malvolio*: see Keir Elam, Introduction, *Twelfth Night*, ed. Keir Elam (London: Arden, 2008), 4–5.
2. See Northrop Frye, *A Natural Perspective: The Development of Shakespearean Comedy and Romance* (New York: Columbia University Press, 1965), 93; C. L. Barber, *Shakespeare's Festive Comedy: A Study of Dramatic Form and its Relation to Social Custom* (Princeton: Princeton University Press, 1959), p. 256; and Leslie Fiedler, *The Stranger in Shakespeare* (1972; Frogmore: Paladin, 1974), 16. Festivals in England at the time often involved identifying someone as a 'churl', another name for this role: see Bruce Smith, Introduction, in Bruce Smith, ed., *Twelfth Night: Texts and Contexts* (New York: Bedford/St. Martin's, 2001), 4.
3. Smith, *TN*, 336–7, writes, 'the principles of [puritan] righteousness happened to be good for business', and notes the relevance to the play of the influential puritan advice book Robert Cleaver and John Dod's *Godly Form of Household Government*, which emphasizes the importance of laboring at one's vocation, a concept meaningless to Toby and Andrew.

4. Cristina Malcolmson, '"What You Will": Social Mobility and Gender in *Twelfth Night*' in *The Matter of Difference*, ed. Valerie Wayne (Ithaca: Cornell University Press, 1991), 38. Gentlemen, also known as 'gentry', were either 'descendants of the aristocracy whose holdings were smaller' than aristocrats or 'persons who through commercial enterprise...had managed to amass property and prestige': see Russ McDonald, *The Bedford Companion to Shakespeare: An Introduction with Documents*, 2nd edition (Boston: Bedford/St. Martin's, 2001), 274.
5. David Schalkwyk, *Shakespeare, Love and Service* (Cambridge: Cambridge University Press, 2008), 124n; Penny Gay, 'Introduction', in *Twelfth Night*, Updated Edition, ed. Elizabeth Story Donno (Cambridge: Cambridge University Press, 2004), 11. Malcolmson, 'Social Mobility', 34–5, summarizes the views of both early modern and contemporary commentators that social mobility was increasing at this time: early moderns had varying views of its benefits. Since Malvolio turns out to be a gentleman, his aspiration to marry Olivia crosses a smaller gap than may have first appeared, but nevertheless as a countess she would still be considered above him.
6. Although the play is nominally set in Illyria, and includes some allusions to such distant worlds as the Ottoman Empire, the context is basically English. See Elam, *TN*, 71–5. On 20 he also suggests the relevance of 'cakes and ale' to English 'church-ales' (parish festivals) and 'Twelfth Night cakes'.
7. Kristin Poole, *Radical Religion from Shakespeare to Milton* (Cambridge: Cambridge University Press, 2000), 3–4; Manningham quoted in Neely, *Distracted Subjects*, 156.
8. Andrew's fantasy of beating Malvolio continues, but later it is focused more on his pretensions rather than his religion. During the eavesdropping scene, he exclaims, "Slight, I could so beat the rogue!' (2.5.28) and 'Pistol him, pistol him' (32). Toby wishes for 'a stone-bow, to hit him in the eye' (41), and when Malvolio appears in his yellow stockings, Maria says, 'I can hardly forbear hurling things at him. I know my lady will strike him' (3.2.69–70). No one else in the play is the target of fantasies of violence, although Toby and Andrew both get wounded in fights with Antonio and Sebastian.
9. John Bate, *The Portraiture of Hypocrisie, Lively and Pithilie Pictured in her Colours* (London: 1589), quoted in Christopher Haigh, 'The Character of an Antipuritan', *Sixteenth Century Journal* 35:3 (2004): 673. Since Shylock also doesn't like festivity, and some antipuritans compared puritans to Jews, a few critics have argued that *MV* would also have been received as dealing with puritans.

10. Smith, Introduction to excerpt from Richard Bancroft, 'A Survey of the Pretended Holy Discipline', in *TN*, ed. Smith, 334.
11. Poole, *Radical Religion*.
12. Haigh, 'Anti-Puritan', 672, 685.
13. Feste swears 'By'r Lady' (2.3.56), 'Beshrew me' (2.3.72), 'By Saint Anne' (2.3.105), 'Marry' (5.1.15, 40); Sir Toby, 'Marry, hang thee' (2.5.93), 'Marry' (3.4.258, 264); Maria, 'Marry' (3.4.95). The 'Marry' oaths all mean 'By Mary', and were, like 'By Saint Anne', particularly objectionable to puritans, who didn't like mention of such saints, but they also suggest Shakespeare's punning anticipation of the final marriages.
14. Patrick Collinson, *The Religion of Protestants: The Church in English Society, 1559–1625* (Oxford: Clarendon Press, 1982), 47.
15. Neely, *Distracted Subjects*, 139, discusses the vigorous debate in print about exorcism in the late 1590s and at the turn of the century, close to the time when *TN* was written. A puritan exorcist, John Darrell, was accused of teaching people how to pretend they were possessed.
16. Neely, *Distracted Subjects*, 139. In Shakespeare's early *Comedy of Errors*, a foreigner confused by constantly being mistaken for his identical twin is called mad and also confined in a dark room, and Rosalind in *AYLI* speaks of a dark house as a punishment and cure for madness (3.2.358–60). However, Neely has shown in *Distracted Subjects*, 158–63, according to the notebooks of the early modern physician Napier, such treatment of the mad was actually rare at this time in England.
17. Malcolmson, 'Social Mobility', 38.
18. Camille Wells Slights, *Shakespeare's Comic Commonwealths* (Toronto: University of Toronto Press, 1993), 226.
19. Trevor Nunn, director, *Twelfth Night*, UK, 1996. Nigel Hawthorne plays Malvolio.
20. Meredith Skura, *Shakespeare the Actor and the Purposes of Playing* (Chicago: University of Chicago Press, 1993), 206–7. See also Elam, *TN*, 'Introduction', 8–9.
21. Neely, *Distracted Subjects*, 163–5, argues that 'stage attitudes toward Malvolio's madness came to influence attitudes toward patients in Bethlem Hospital', dehumanizing them. She compares the 1709 Rowe engraving of Malvolio's confinement with a 1710 engraving of Bedlam by Bernard Lens and John Sturt in the fifth edition of Jonathan Swift's *Tale of a Tub*. Roger Warren and Stanley Wells, 'Introduction', in *Twelfth Night*, ed. Warren and Wells (Oxford: Clarendon Press, 1994), 43, speculate that the tendency of actors and critics to find pathos in Malvolio began in 1741 with Macklin's performance.

22. Skura, *Shakespeare the Actor*, 207, argues that at the end the audience might feel guilty about their enjoyment of Malvolio's baiting, and also refers to Keith Thomas, *Man in the Natural World: A History of the Modern Sensibility* (New York: Pantheon, 1983), 157, 159, on generally increased sympathy for baited bears at this time, 307n.
23. Jeffrey Knapp, *Shakespeare's Tribe: Church, Nation, and Theater in Renaissance England* (Chicago: University of Chicago Press, 2002), 50.
24. See Sherman Hawkins, 'The Two Worlds of Shakespearean Comedy', *Shakespeare Studies* 3 (1967): 62–80.
25. See the discussion in the *MV* chapter for more on early modern same-sex love and sexuality, and on the tradition of valuing male friendship more than heterosexual marriage.
26. Su Fang Ng, 'The Frontiers of *Twelfth Night*' in *Early Modern England and Islamic Worlds*, ed. Bernadette Andrea and Linda McJannet (Palgrave Macmillan, 2011), 186–7.
27. Roger Warren and Stanley Wells, Introduction, *Twelfth Night*, ed. Warren and Wells (Oxford: Clarendon Press, 1994), 41. They also suggest that his ship, 'for shallow draught and bulk unprizable' (5.1.49), was typical of pirate ships, but question whether the Elizabethan audience would have realized this, 202n.
28. Ng, 'Frontiers', 188–9. She does not see Raleigh and Drake as unique, but points out, referring to C. M. Senior, *A Nation of Pirates* (New York: Crane, Russak and Co., 1976), that English merchants of this time frequently 'would switch between trade and piracy, depending on opportunity', 188. This possibility links Antonio in another way to the Antonio who is the titular *Merchant of Venice*.
29. Bruce Smith, *Homosexual Desire in Shakespeare's England* (Chicago: University of Chicago Press, 1991), 121. See also B.R. Burg, *Sodomy and the Pirate Tradition: English Sea Rovers in the Seventeenth-Century Caribbean* (New York: New York University Press, 1984), 1–42. Illyria was close to the Ottoman Empire, and the English also associated Turks, to whom *TN* has a number of references, with sodomy. However, as Keir Elam has pointed out, this region also had a tradition of religious ceremonies of same-sex union: see Elam, Introduction, *TN*, ed. Keir Elam, 73.
30. Valerie Traub, *Desire and Anxiety: Circulations of Sexuality in Shakespearean Drama* (New York: Routledge, 1992), 132. She writes, 'By "homoerotic" I refer to erotic bonds animated by specifically erotic desire, though that desire may not be fully conscious to or accepted by the desiring subject' (22). As Alan Bray has shown, in England, demonstrative love between men was not necessarily suspected of implying sodomy if both were of the same class, nation, and politics: see 'Homosexuality and the Signs of Male

Friendship in Elizabethan England', in *Queering the Renaissance*, ed. Jonathan Goldberg (Durham, N.C.: Duke University Press, 1994), pp. 40–61. The shadow of piracy might make the shadow of sodomy more likely, but Antonio's captors never make this accusation.
31. Traub, *Desire*, 133–4.
32. David Schalkwyk, *Shakespeare, Love and Service*, 128. Schalkwyk has much of interest to say about the relation between love and service in both Antonio and Viola, as well as its parody in Malvolio.
33. Joseph Pequigney, 'The Two Antonios and Same-Sex Love in *Twelfth Night* and *The Merchant of Venice*', *ELR* 22 (1992): 201–21.
34. Traub, *Desire*, 138–9. In the filmed version of *TN* directed by Kenneth Branagh (Renaissance Theatre Company, 1988, Thames Television/Films Media Group), Antonio (Tim Barker) has a large birthmark on his face, no doubt suggested by this line.
35. Plato, *Dialogues*, trans. Benjamin Jowett, 3d ed. rev., 2 vols. (1892; rpt. New York: Random, 1937), 1: 317. Ficino describes unrequited love as death and requited love as resurrection in his *Commentary on Plato's Symposium*, trans. Sears Jayne, University of Missouri Studies 19 (Columbia: University of Missouri Press, 1944), 144–6. His examples are often homoerotic.
36. Roger Warren and Stanley Wells, *TN*, 69.
37. J. M. Lothian and T. W. Craik, 'Introduction', in *Twelfth Night*, ed. J. M. Lothian and T. W. Craik (1975; rpt. Thomson, 2001), lxxxii. Laurie Osborne, *The Trick of Singularity: Twelfth Night and the Performance Editions* (Iowa City: University of Iowa Press, 1996), notes that the changes made by Kemble and others in the nineteenth century reinterpret 'Antonio's defence of his beloved Sebastian as the more acceptable defence of a maiden', 85.
38. Alan Sinfield, *Faultlines: Cultural Materialism and the Politics of Dissident Reading* (Berkeley: University of California Press, 1992), 73. See also Neely, *Distracted Subjects*, 119.
39. In *Twelfth Night: Shakespeare in Performance*, ed. Elizabeth Schafer (Cambridge: Cambridge University Press, 2009), 216n., 222n., the only twentieth century performances noted in which Sebastian and Antonio are linked at the end—Sebastian invites Antonio into the group or to his side—occurred in 1912 (Granville Barker) and 1943 (Rosmer, in Stratford-upon-Avon). The Kemble addition noted earlier was still being used occasionally in 1893.
40. Warren and Wells, *TN*, 69.
41. Elam, *TN*, 112.
42. Traub, *Desire*, 123. Since this Antonio is so close both to the Antonio of *MV* and to the persona of the sonnets, the ambiguity looks much more like deliberate openness than lack of interest on Shakespeare's part.

43. See Elam, *TN*, Introduction, 89.
44. Jean Howard, *The Stage and Social Struggle in Early Modern England* (New York: Routledge, 1994), 114.
45. Diana Henderson, 'The Theater and Domestic Culture', in *A New History of Early English Drama*, ed. John D. Cox and David Scott Kastan (New York: Columbia University Press, 1997), 194; Amy Louise Erickson, *Women and Property in Early Modern England* (New York: Routledge, 1993), 8–9; both quoted by Phyllis Rackin, *Shakespeare and Women* (Oxford: Oxford University Press, 2005), 19.
46. Rackin, *Shakespeare*, 7.
47. John Manningham, *The Diary of John Manningham of the Middle Temple 1602–1603*, ed. Robert Parker Sorlien (Hanover, NH: University of New England Press, 1976), quoted by Smith, Introduction, in *TN*, 2–3: see also Neely, *Distracted Subjects*, 155–8.
48. When the play presents Antonio as left behind, the replacement of Andrew by Maria parodies the other plot. According to Schafer, *Performance*, 223n., in Branagh's 1987 Renaissance Theatre production, Antonio and Andrew were each alone on the side of the stage as the happy couples departed.
49. The Oxford and Norton texts modernize to 'distraught', but the Folio and Quarto read 'distract'.
50. Ng, 'Frontiers', 189–90.
51. Lois Potter, *Twelfth Night: Text and Performance* (New York: Macmillan, 1985), 31, says that Andrew's response to Toby's scorn could be 'anything from an inane giggle to a silent, deeply wounded departure by a different door from Toby's'; Warren and Wells, *TN*, 63; Schafer, *Performance*, 49. They usually exit separately.
52. Some later critics have quoted Barber, 'in the long run, in the 1640s, Malvolio was revenged on the whole pack of them,' *Festive Comedy*, 257, without noticing that he qualifies this comment by preceding it with 'One could moralize the spectacle by observing that'. Another irony in considering Malvolio as a role is noted by Stephen Greenblatt in *Will in the World* (New York: Norton, 2004), 75–84: Malvolio 'practising behaviour to his own shadow' is like an actor learning a part, and Malvolio's desire to rise socially is like Shakespeare's own; a few years before writing *Twelfth Night* Shakespeare had applied to a coat of arms to secure the status of gentleman for his father and therefore himself.
53. Linda Woodbridge, *The Scythe of Saturn: Shakespeare and Magical Thinking* (Urbana: University of Illinois Press, 1994), 97, referring to René Girard, Sam Keen, Jacques Derrida. On 121 she considers Malvolio as a

scapegoat particularly in relation to Olivia's need to enforce household laws while avoiding hostility directed against herself.
54. The most thorough documentation of this is in Schafer, *Performance*.
55. The concept that everyone had a sexual identity was not part of the dominant ideology in Shakespeare's time; Valerie Traub argues that in Shakespeare's time marriage and friendship were mostly expected to fulfill different needs, but when the idea of companionate marriage, including friendship in itself, later became more widespread, marriage and same-sex friendship began to seem more threatening to each other. See her *The Renaissance of Lesbianism in Early Modern England* (Cambridge: Cambridge University Press, 2002).
56. Frye, *Natural Perspective*, 46. Speaking of the power of Shylock's 'Hath not a Jew' speech, he says that it makes us 'participate in what we have been conditioned to think of as removed from us and our sympathies' (161).

CHAPTER 3

1. Singling out any one play to represent Shakespeare's treatment of women would be inadequate; however, there are patterns that repeat in several plays, which I discuss here.
2. Leslie Fiedler, *The Stranger in Shakespeare* (1972; Frogmore: Paladin, 1974).
3. Simone de Beauvoir, *The Second Sex*, trans. H. M. Parshley (1952; rpt. New York: Vintage, 1974), xxii. More recently, Dympna Callaghan has referred to early modern women as 'excluded participants', in her 'Introduction' to *The Impact of Feminism in English Renaissance Studies*, ed. Dympna Callaghan (New York: Palgrave, 2007), 7.
4. Fiedler, *Stranger*, 37.
5. I am thinking in particular of discussions of how simultaneous membership in many different groups means that people are not only either outsiders or insiders, and of the situation of the outsider who joins a group of insiders in Patricia Hill Collins, 'Learning From the Outsider Within,' *Social Problems*, 33 (1986) as well as in Robert Merton, 'Insiders and Outsiders', *American Journal of Sociology* 78 (1972): 9–47.
6. Elizabeth I, 'Speech to the Troops at Tilbury', *The Female Spectator: English Women Writers Before 1800*, ed. Mary R. Mahl and Helene Koon (Bloomington: Indiana University Press, 1977), 48.
7. Phyllis Rackin, *Shakespeare and Women* (New York: Oxford University Press, 2005), 7.

8. Sara Mendelson and Patricia Crawford, *Women in Early Modern England, 1550–1720* (Oxford: Clarendon Press, 1998), 205.
9. Prescriptive literature for women is discussed in Suzanne Hull, *Chaste, Silent, and Obedient: English Books for Women 1475–1640*, rev. ed (Huntington, CA: Huntington Library Press, 1988). However, when women are repeatedly told not to do something, it may be presumed that many are doing it.
10. Fiona McNeill, *Poor Women in Shakespeare* (Cambridge: Cambridge University Press, 2007), 56.
11. This is not just because women were played by boy actors, though I will discuss that connection later: characters in ethnic/religious/national outsider groups were also usually if not always played by actors outside those groups. A sentence that sounds as if it might parallel Rosalind's but does not is Iago's 'Were I the Moor, I would not be Iago' (1.1.57). It is either tautological or obscure, or else it ought to read 'Moor's': Neill, ed., *Othello* (Oxford, 2006), 200n.
12. Linda Woodbridge, *Women and the English Renaissance: Literature and the Nature of Womankind, 1540–1620* (Urbana: University of Illinois Press, 1984), discusses and quotes extensively from Agrippa (esp. on 38–45) and Castiglione (esp. on 52–8) as well as many other defenders (and attackers) of women.
13. Edmund Tilney, *The Flower of Friendship*, ed, and introd, Valerie Wayne (Ithaca: Cornell University Press, 1992), 133. Isabella, who takes this position, is associated by Wayne with Queen Elizabeth, because of her singleness as well as because of her name (the Spanish equivalent of Elizabeth), and because the book is dedicated to Elizabeth and presented in the text as having been written up at Isabella's request. However, in the text Isabella is not presented as a queen or princess.
14. Jane Anger, 'Her Protection for Women', in *Half Humankind: Contexts and Texts of the Controversy about Women in England, 1540–1640*, ed. Katherine Usher Henderson and Barbara F. McManus (Urbana: University of Illinois, 1985), 172–88.
15. Moderata Fonte, *The Worth of Women*, ed. and trans. Virginia Cox (Chicago: University of Chicago Press, 1997), 190.
16. Aemilia Lanyer, *Poems: Salve Deus Rex Judaeorum*, ed. Susanne Woods (New York: Oxford University Press, 1993).
17. Esther Souernam, 'Esther Hath Hanged Haman', in *Half Humankind*, ed. Henderson and McManus, 217–43; 'Haec Vir', in *Half Humankind*, 277–89; quote is from 284.
18. Isabella and Paulina play similar roles of outsiders with insight without going into disguise.

19. Stephen Orgel, *Impersonations: The Performance of Gender in Shakespeare's England* (New York: Cambridge University Press, 1996), 51–2.
20. I follow the Oxford editors in judging that *Taming of the Shrew* was the source for *Taming of a Shrew*, which also includes a father.
21. Rackin, *Shakespeare*, 20.
22. Amy M. Froide, *Never Married* (New York: Oxford University Press, 2005), gives 30.2 percent as the average figure in England between 1574 and 1821, and finds that in the late seventeenth century 34 percent of women were single in Southampton and 54.5 percent in London.
23. Camille Wells Slights, *Shakespeare's Comic Commonwealths* (Toronto: University of Toronto Press, 1993), 241.
24. Carolyn Heilbrun, 'Sex and the Female Tragic Hero', in *The Female Tragic Hero in English Renaissance Drama,* ed. Naomi Conn Liebler (New York: Palgrave, 2002), 206, notes her silence at the end and believes that she 'has no words to express her grief', and this would be the more human Volumnia, but earlier she has said, 'Had I a dozen sons...I had rather had eleven die nobly for their country than one voluptuously surfeit out of action' (1.3.18–21). She does not know that the Volscians will kill Coriolanus because of his own pride as well as because of the mercy he has shown to Rome.
25. Adrienne Rich, 'Compulsory Heterosexuality and Lesbian Existence', in Rich, *Blood, Bread, and Poetry: Selected Prose 1979–1985* (New York: Norton, 1986), 23–75.
26. Nor does Paulina have a scripted response to Leontes' match of her with Camillo, but stage and critical history has not been much bothered by this. However see J. C. Meagher, 'Economy and Recognition: Thirteen Shakespearean Puzzles', *Shakespeare Quarterly* (1984), 7–21.
27. Ania Loomba, *Gender, Race, Renaissance Drama* (Manchester: Manchester University Press, 1989), 55, discusses these lines as showing Desdemona's projection of her fantasies onto Othello, which is in itself a kind of identification.

CHAPTER 4

1. Ania Loomba, *Shakespeare, Race, and Colonialism* (Oxford: Oxford University Press, 2002), 100.
2. Emily Bartels, *Speaking of the Moor: From Alcazar to Othello* (Philadelphia: University of Pennsylvania Press, 2008), 156. Discussing *MV*, I stress the relevance of the portrayal of Jews to Shakespeare's England, here I look primarily at the context in the historical Venice and in what England knew of Venice. However, early audiences' reactions to Othello

might also have been affected by the fact that there were black servants, entertainers, and seamen in London, as noted by Peter Fryer, *Staying Power* (London: Pluto, 1984), 8; see also Nabil Matar's *Turks, Moors, Englishmen in the Age of Discovery* (New York: Columbia University Press, 2000).
3. Such positive images have been most stressed recently by Bartels in *Speaking of the Moor* (Pennsylvania, 2008), 176.
4. See Edward Pechter, *Othello and Interpretive Traditions* (Iowa City: University of Iowa Press, 1999), 38–49.
5. Emrys Jones, *The Origins of Shakespeare* (New York: Oxford 1977), 76–7. A link that may reinforce this association is that St. Maurice, a late third century military saint who was portrayed as black (perhaps because his name suggested 'Moor'), was known for accepting martyrdom by saying, 'I have kept the commandment the Lord gave Peter: "Put your sword into its sheath!"'; see Andrew Moran, 'From Maurice to Mohammed: Othello, Islam, and Baptism', in *Early Modern England and Islamic Worlds*, ed. Bernadette Andrea and Linda McJannet (New York: Palgrave Macmillan, 2011), 24.
6. Ian Smith, *Race and Rhetoric in the Renaissance* (New York: Palgrave Macmillan, 2009), 1–3, 139; Bruce Smith, *Shakespeare and Masculinity* (Oxford, 2000), 117.
7. Ania Loomba, 'Shakespeare and Cultural Difference', in *Alternative Shakespeares*, vol. 2, ed. Terence Hawkes (New York: Routledge, 1996), 174–6, 256n. On gender implications of 'Asiatic style', see Patricia Parker, 'Virile Style', in *Premodern Sexualities*, ed. Louise Fradenburg and Carla Freccero (New York: Routledge, 1996), 199–222.
8. Robert Watson, 'Shakespeare's New Words,' *Shakespeare Survey*, Vol. 65 (2012), 368. Watson finds Othello's language responding to 'a double-bind often lamented by racial-ethnic minorities, who find themselves required to stand out and yet to assimilate, at once to exemplify and reject the stereotyped expectations of the majority', and puts this all in the context of the Elizabethan audience's interest in learning new words. He also relates the language doubling to the fact that Othello's very name begins with an echo of 'Othman', the founder of the Ottoman (Turkish) empire, and ends Italian-style with 'ello' (as in the writer Bandello), drawing on David Schalkwyk, *Speech and Performance in Shakespeare's Sonnets and Plays* (Cambridge, 2002), 180–3.
9. Pechter, *Traditions*, 140, 40.
10. On the traveller's perspective, see Joel Altman, *The Improbability of Othello* (Chicago: University of Chicago Press, 2010), 324; both Orlando and Othello introduce themselves with reference to royal ancestry, and

say they dislike boasting; see Meredith Skura, 'Reading Othello's Skin: Contexts and Pretexts', *Philological Quarterly* 87 (Summer–Fall 3–4, 2008), 299–334; Jason Lawrence, '"The story is extant, and written in very choice Italian": Shakespeare's dramatization of Cinthio', in *Shakespeare, Italy, and Intertextuality*, ed. Michele Marrapodi (Manchester: Manchester University Press, 2004), 98–9.

11. Tayeb Salih, *Season of Migration to the North* (1969; rpt. Boulder, CO: Lynne Rienner, 1997), 38.
12. Michael Neill, Introduction, in *Othello*, ed. Michael Neill (New York: Oxford, 2006), 115.
13. Julia Reinhard Lupton, *Citizen-Saints: Shakespeare and Political Theology* (Chicago, 2005), 105–23; on other ambiguities, see Bartels, *Moor*, 168–70.
14. Pechter, *Traditions*, 35. Altman, *Improbability*, 294, makes a similar point about mixing of categories in *Othello*.
15. Ania Loomba and Jonathan Burton, eds. *Race in Early Modern England: A Documentary Companion* (New York: Macmillan Palgrave, 2007), 18; Caroline Spurgeon, *Shakespeare's Imagery* (Cambridge: Cambridge University Press, 1935), 335–6.
16. Loomba and Burton, eds., *Race*, 3–4.
17. Carol Thomas Neely, 'Circumscriptions and Unhousedness: Othello in the Borderlands', in Deborah Barker and Ivo Kamps, ed., *Shakespeare and Gender: A History* (London: Verso, 1995), 303–4; Neill, Introduction, 125; Loomba, *Shakespeare, Race*, 22–3, 35–6. 'Race' could also refer to national or class groups, or even to women as a distinct group, 24–35.
18. Mary Floyd-Wilson, *English Ethnicity and Race in Early Modern Drama* (Cambridge University Press, 2003).
19. Anthony Barthelemy, *Black Face, Maligned Face* (Baton Rouge: LSU Press, 1987), 48–9; Lupton, *Citizen-Saints*, 110, finds a similar figure, though not celebrating Elizabeth, in Thomas Middleton's 1613 masque *The Triumph of Truth*. G. K. Hunter mentions Moors in pageants of 10 other years between 1519 and 1624 but claims they are 'bogey-man figures', 'Othello and Colour Prejudice', in *Othello*, ed. Edward Pechter (Norton, 2004), 251. See also references to the biblical eunuch baptized by the Apostle Philip, the Queen of Sheba, and Saint Maurice in *Othello: Texts and Contexts*, ed. Kim Hall (Bedford:St. Martin's, 2007), 172.
20. Lupton, *Citizen-Saints*, 108; David Bindman, Henry Louis Gates, Jr., and Karen C. C. Dalton, eds., *The Image of the Black in Western Art*, Volume III: *From the 'Age of Discovery' to the Age of Abolition*, (Cambridge, MA: Harvard/Belknap, 2010); see also Karen C. C. Dalton, 'Art for the Sake of Dynasty: The Black Emperor in the Drake Jewel and Elizabethan Imperial Imagery', in *Early Modern Visual Culture:*

Representation, Race, and Empire in Renaissance England, ed. Peter Erickson and Clarke Hulse (University of Pennsylvania Press, 2000), 213–14.
21. *Purchas his Pilgrimage or relations of the World* (London: William Stansby, 1626). In *HAKLUYTUS POSTHUMUS, or Purchas his Pilgrimage*, v. 5 of 20. Rpt. Glasgow. James MacLehose, 1905: *Book Six, written c. 1526: Observations of Africa, taken out of John Leo his nine books, translated by Master Pory, and the most remarkable things hither transcribed*, 355–6. For further discussion of Africanus, at birth named al-Hasan al-Wazzan, see Natalie Zemon Davis, *Trickster Travels* (New York: Hill & Wang, 2006), and Bartels, *Moor*, 138–54. Pory's English version first appeared in 1600.
22. Kim Hall challenges this tradition, claiming it turns aside racial issues to consider aesthetics. But clearly the two are connected. See *Things of Darkness: Economies of Race and Gender in Early Modern England* (Ithaca: Cornell University Press, 1995), 69–71.
23. Lewis Lewkenor, *The Commonwealth and Government of Venice*, by Cardinall Gasper Contareno (London: 1599), Sig.S2v.EEBO. Bartels, *Moor*, 158, also cites evidence for this practice in the 1549 *History of Italy*, by William Thomas.
24. David McPherson, *Shakespeare, Jonson, and the Myth of Venice* (Newark: University of Delaware Press, 1990), 73. He also notes, on 36, Venice's self-concept, found in Contarini, of its impartiality and fairness toward outsiders; Sharon Kinoshita, conversation after a Pittsburgh lecture, 2011.
25. M. E. Hallett and J. R. Hale, *The Military Organization of a Renaissance State: Venice c. 1400 to 1617* (Cambridge: Cambridge University Press, 1984), 315–26.
26. Cinthio, 'From Gli Hecatommithi', in Hall, ed., *Othello*, 33.
27. Floyd-Wilson, *Ethnicity*, 1–2.
28. Michael Neill, ed., *Othello*, 310n, 270, see also Michael Neill, '"Mulattos," "Blacks," and "Indian Moors;"*Othello* and Early Modern Constructions of Human Difference,' *Shakespeare Quarterly* 49 (Winter 1998), 361–74.
29. Leah Marcus, 'The Two Texts of *Othello* and Early Modern Constructions of Race', in *Textual Performances*, ed. Lukas Erne and Margaret Jane Kidnie (Cambridge, 2004), 30.
30. Altman, *Improbability*, 334; Ian Smith, *Race*, 2, 232.
31. Marcus, 'Two Texts', 21–36; quote is from 32; she argues that the Folio text is more sexually explicit and has a 'strikingly concrete representation of the dangers of racial difference', and finds this unsettling to contemplate, whichever text came first.
32. Neill, *Othello*, 464, notes evidence that Indians were frequently associated with ignorance about the value of precious stones, and also often

conflated with Moors. Balthasar, the black one of the Three Kings or Magi, is supposed to have been the giver of myrrh, according to Moran, 'Maurice', 24.

33. B. J. Sokol, *Shakespeare and Tolerance* (Cambridge: Cambridge University Press, 2008), 140.
34. Michael Neill, *Putting History to the Question: Power, Politics, and Society in English Renaissance Drama* (New York: Columbia University Press, 2000), 249. This argument appeared earlier in '"Unproper Beds": Race, Adultery and the Hideous in *Othello*', *Shakespeare Quarterly* 40 (1989), 383–412. Pechter, *Traditions*, makes a similar point, 72–3 and elsewhere, and also emphasizes the way the play arouses opposed emotional states, 29.
35. Ian Maynard Begg et al., 'Dissociation of Processes in Belief: Source Recollection, Statement Familiarity, and the Illusion of Truth', *Journal of Experimental Psychology: General* 121: 4 (1992): 446–5. Thanks to Bruce Goldstein for this reference. See also www.understandingprejudice.org
36. Neill, Introduction, 37, says that his killing of Desdemona was the scene most likely to be illustrated up to the twentieth century, but that more recently the temptation scene is more frequently chosen.
37. Daniel Vitkus, *Turning Turk: English Theater and the Multicultural Mediterranean 1570–1630*, (New York: Palgrave, 2003), 104.
38. Virginia Mason Vaughan, 'Teaching Richard Burbage's Othello', in *Approaches to Teaching Shakespeare's Othello*, ed. Peter Erickson and Maurice Hunt (MLA, 2005), 149; Neill, Introduction, in *Othello*, ed. Neill, 1–2. In the First Folio, Othello's speech descriptions always call him Othello, never Moor (unlike the way Shylock sometimes becomes 'Jew' and Edmund is usually 'Bastard').
39. Loomba, *Shakespeare, Race*, 47. Excerpts from Rymer and Gildon appear in *Othello*, ed Pechter. Gildon (1694) attributes to Othello 'extraordinary merit and virtues' and attacks the 'customary barbarity of confining nations, without regard to their virtue and merit, to slavery and contempt for the mere accident of their complexion' (213).
40. Payne, B. K., 'Prejudice and perception: The role of automatic and controlled processes in misperceiving a weapon', *Journal of Personality and Social Psychology* 81 (2001): 181–92. Thanks to Edouard Machery for this reference. See also www.implicit.harvard.edu.
41. And *Guess Who* can also be criticized for its image of the one exceptional black man.
42. Carol Chillington Rutter notes some of this ambiguity in *Enter the Body: Women and Representation on Shakespeare's Stage* (London: Routledge,

2001), 145: 'the very tropes that confine women "indoors" in *Othello* simultaneously undo confinement'.
43. Neill notes that the 1989 Trevor Nunn production, later filmed by the BBC, puts special emphasis on 'the general predicament of women in a claustrophobically male-dominated world from which they were for most practical purposes excluded' (Introduction, 106).
44. Neely, *Broken Nuptials in Shakespeare's Plays* (New Haven: Yale University, 1985), 109.
45. Neely, in 'Circumscribed', 305, writes, 'Othello is an outsider who chooses to move inside.... she is an insider who chooses... to break out of her house, her milieu, and her country.'
46. Loomba, *Gender, Race, Renaissance Drama* (Manchester: Manchester University Press, 1989).
47. Bartels, *Moor*, 184.
48. Penny Gay, 'Listening to Emilia: *Othello* 4.3 in Recent Performance', Paper delivered at the International Shakespeare Congress, Prague, July 2011.
49. Neely, 'Women and Men in Othello: 'What should such a fool do with so good a woman?' *Shakespeare Studies* 10 (1977): 133–58, rpt. with revisions in *Broken Nuptials*; Loomba, *Gender, Race*; Paula Vogel, *Desdemona: A Play about a Handkerchief* (New York: Dramatists' Play Service, 1994; Djanet Sears, *Harlem Duet* (Winnipeg: Scirocco Drama, 1998).
50. Rutter, *Body*, 166, analyzes this in Zoe Wanamaker's performance in the Trevor Nunn film.
51. Ann Rosalind Jones, *The Currency of Eros: Women's Love Lyric in Europe, 1540–1620* (Bloomington: Indiana University Press, 1990), 178. The term '*meretrix honesta*', the equivalent word in Latin, is described as 'one who distinguished herself from the common prostitute by her good manners and refined education', in Federica Ambrosini, 'Toward a Social History of Women in Venice: From the Renaissance to the Enlightenment', in *Venice Reconsidered*, ed. John Martin and Dennis Romano (Baltimore: Johns Hopkins University, 2000), 436. On 429 and 438, this article refers to a Venetian noblewoman, Bianca Cappello di Bartolomeo, who eloped with and married a young Florentine clerk in 1563, then became the mistress of a Medici and eventually married him and became the Grand Duchess of Tuscany—she was famous enough that her portrait adorned many Venetian homes. Was there an allusion to her in the play appreciated by those who had travelled to Italy?
52. Pechter, *Traditions*, 132–40 and notes, discusses the assumptions that editors and critics have made about Bianca, and the lack of evidence

for them except Iago's description of her, which is unreliable though influential.
53. Neill, Introduction, 177.
54. Vogel's play *Desdemona: The Story of a Handkerchief* emphasizes the class hostility between Emilia and Bianca and makes Emilia similarly resentful of her snooty and promiscuous Desdemona.
55. Neill, Introduction, 176–7.
56. Keith Thomas, 'The Double Standard', *Journal of the History of Ideas*, 20:2 (April, 1959): 195–216.
57. McPherson, *Myth of Venice*, 88.
58. Neill, *Othello*, Appendix B, 421–2; Scott McMillin, *The First Quarto of Othello* (Cambridge: Cambridge University Press, 2001).
59. Woodbridge discusses these speeches as well as Edmund's in *English Revenge Drama*, 263–70.
60. Woodbridge, *English Revenge Drama*, 242–6. She draws especially on Jonathan Hope, 'Shakespeare's "Native English"', in *A Companion to Shakespeare*, ed. David Scott Kastan (Oxford: Basil Blackwell, 1999), 239–55. See also Pechter, *Traditions*, 61.
61. Neill, Introduction, 163.
62. Iago also loathes Cassio, disliking his bookish rather than experiential approach, as well as resenting Othello's choice of Cassio as lieutenant, but later he gives a different reason, which I will quote shortly. The phrase 'ancient grudge' appears in the prologue to *R & J* referring to the hatred between the Capulets and the Montagues, and is used by Shylock in *MV* 1.3.2 to describe his attitude to Antonio.
63. Loomba, *Shakespeare, Race*, 30, 32.
64. *Hic Mulier* in *Half Humankind*, ed. Katherine Usher Henderson & Barbara F. McManus (Urbana: University of Illinois Press, 1985), 269; the quote from *Haec Vir* is on 284.
65. Constance Jordan, *Renaissance Feminism: Literary Texts and Political Models* (Ithaca: Cornell University Press, 1990).
66. Maynard Mack, 'The Jacobean Shakespeare: Some Observations on the Construction of the Tragedies', in *Othello*, ed. Alvin Kernan (New York: Signet Classic, 1963), 198; Altman, *Impossibility*, 107.
67. Werner Sollors, 'Ethnicity', in *Critical Terms for Literary Study*, ed. Frank Lentriccia and Thomas McLaughlin (Chicago: University of Chicago Press, 1990), 288, quoted in Pechter, *Traditions*, 66.
68. Altman, *Impossibility*, 141–5.
69. Loomba, *Gender, Race*, 51; Neill, Introduction, 78, traces the 'sublimated homosexual' interpretation of Iago to the Freudian Ernest Jones and Olivier's 1938 performance.

70. See William Hazlitt, '[Iago, Heroic Tragedy, and Othello]', in *Othello*, ed. Pechter, 222–3.
71. Pechter, *Traditions*, 104, 135; scapegoat question, 162.
72. Pechter, *Traditions*, criticism 28, 52, 72; stage 27; Neill, Introduction, stage 86–100; criticism 146.
73. Marcus, 'Two Texts', 27; Patricia Parker, '*Othello* and *Hamlet*: Dilation, Spying, and the "Secret Place" of Woman', in *Othello*, ed. Pechter; Neill, Introduction, 130–46.
74. Neely, *Broken Nuptials*, 132. Lynda Boose, 'The getting of a lawful race: racial discourse in Early Modern England and the unrepresentable black woman', in *Women, 'Race', and Writing in the Early Modern Period*, ed. Margo Hendricks and Patricia Parker (London: Routledge, 1994), 41–2, argues that in the early modern period and earlier 'the black male-white female union is...most frequently depicted as the ultimate romantic-transgressive model of erotic love.' Black-white love was not seen as lustful in the Middle Ages, Ania Loomba shows, *Shakespeare, Race*, 47. Sokol, *Shakespeare and Tolerance*, 122, gives evidence of some early modern acceptance of transracial marriage outside literature.
75. Some research suggests that reading fiction can make people more empathetic in real life; it is even more likely that experience in reading would lead to more empathy in fiction, unless the experience is in a literary methodology that emphasizes other dimensions of reading or limits the kind of character with whom the reader empathizes. See Annie Murphy Paul, 'Your Brain on Fiction', *New York Times*, Sunday, 18 March 2012, citing research from Keith Oatley and Raymond Mar in 2006 and 2009.
76. Loomba, *Gender, Race*, 55, sees Desdemona as projecting her fantasies of freedom onto 'the outsider', Othello. For further development of the idea of 'Desdemona's Blackness', see Lara Bovilsky, *Barbarous Play* (Minneapolis: University of Minnesota Press, 2008), 37–65, and compare Karen Newman, '"And wash the Ethiop white": femininity and the monstrous in *Othello*', in *Shakespeare Reproduced: The Text in History and Ideology*, ed. Jean E. Howard and Marion F. O'Connor (New York: Methuen, 1987), 141–62.
77. Mary Beth Rose, *The Expense of Spirit: Love and Sexuality in English Renaissance Drama* (Ithaca: Cornell University Press, 1988), 116–55, which includes an analysis of *Othello* in these terms.
78. Naomi Conn Liebler, *Shakespeare's Festive Tragedy: The Ritual Foundations of Genre* (New York: Routledge, 1995).

CHAPTER 5

1. Meredith Skura, 'Dragon Fathers and Unnatural Children: Warring Generations in *King Lear* and its Sources', *Comparative Drama*, 44:2 (Summer 2008): 121. Skura shows that the complications of sympathy result from Shakespeare's changes to a simpler good vs. evil moral clarity in his main source, *King Leir*.
2. See Linda Woodbridge, *Vagrancy, Homelessness, and English Renaissance Literature* (Urbana: University of Illinois Press, 2001), 215–18, for the availability of radical political ideas promoting redistribution of wealth at the time.
3. Jane Kingsley-Smith, *Shakespeare's Drama of Exile* (New York: Palgrave Macmillan, 2003), 124.
4. Robert Miola, *Shakespeare and Classical Comedy* (New York: Oxford University Press, 1995), 194. Instead, Ragan sends a messenger to murder him (Leir persuades him not to).
5. Kathleen McLuskie, 'The patriarchal bard: feminist criticism and Shakespeare: *King Lear* and *Measure for Measure*', in *Political Shakespeare*, ed. Jonathan Dollimore and Alan Sinfield (Ithaca: Cornell University Press, 1985), 88–108; quotation is from 98.
6. McLuskie, 'Patriarchal', 99, 103.
7. Keith Thomas, *Age and Authority in Early Modern England* (London: British Academy, 1976), 10; rpt. from his article of the same name in *Proceedings of the British Academy* 62 (1976): 205–48; see also Lawrence Stone, 'Walking Over Grandma', *New York Review of Books*, May 12, 1977, pp. 10–16.
8. Philip Collington, 'Sans Wife: Sexual Anxiety and the Old Man in Shakespeare', in *Growing Old in Early Modern Europe*, ed. Erin Campbell (Aldershot: Ashgate, 2006), 185–209; quotation from 190.
9. Collington, 'Sans Wife', 200–4, quoting statistics from Peter Laslett, 'The Traditional English Family and the Aged in our Society', in *Aging, Death, and the Completeness of Being*, ed. David D. Van Tassel (Philadelphia: University of Pennsylvania Press, 1979), 97–113, esp. 105.
10. Nina Taunton, *Fictions of Old Age in Early Modern Literature and Culture* (New York: Routledge, 2007), 61.
11. Taunton, *Fictions*, 51.
12. Taunton, 52. Historically it has usually devolved on women even when there are sons as well as daughters.
13. Linda Woodbridge, *The Scythe of Saturn* (Urbana: University of Illinois Press, 1994), gives a thorough picture of generational conflict in historical early modern England and Shakespeare's plays in her chapter 'Shakespeare and the Carnival of Time', 265–325.

14. William Carroll, *Fat King, Lean Beggar: Representations of Poverty in the Age of Shakespeare* (Ithaca: Cornell University Press, 1996), 23.
15. Michael Neill, '"In Everything Illegitimate": Imagining the Bastard in English Renaissance Drama', in Neill, *Putting History to the Question* (New York: Columbia University Press, 2000), 127–49, and Alison Findlay, *Illegitimate Power: Bastards in Renaissance Drama* (Manchester: Manchester University Press, 1994). Edmund's emphasis on his physical superiority resembles the insistence of the bastard in *King John* on how much more handsome he is than his legitimate brother.
16. Marilyn Williamson, *The Patriarchy of Shakespeare's Comedies* (Detroit: Wayne State University Press), 81–4.
17. Findlay, *Illegitimate*, 41; Neill, 'Illegitimate', n. 442. They were also excluded from membership of guilds and societies.
18. Although he is a skeptical and even cynical commentator on events, this character, unlike Shakespeare's other bastards, is not associated with plotting but with military heroism and patriotism.
19. In the Folio, while stage directions almost always call him 'John the bastard', the one scene in which his speech prefix is simply Bastard is Act 3 Scene 2, the one in which he tells Claudio that Hero is unfaithful.
20. In *Troilus and Cressida*, the Greek Thersites reveals himself as a bastard in Act 5, when he refuses to fight with a Trojan who identifies himself as a bastard son of Priam. His bastardy is Shakespeare's addition to the character in Homer's *Iliad*, who like Shakespeare's is critical of the war and is repeatedly described as ugly. Thersites' pacifism contrasts markedly to the military ambitions of the bastards of *King John*, *Much Ado*, and *Lear*, and to the bastard warrior Don John of Austria, still well known in Shakespeare's time for having defeated the Turks at Lepanto in 1573.
21. This is analogous to his framing Katherine in *Taming of the Shrew* by giving her a father and showing negotiations over her marriage: no other 'shrew' in Elizabethan drama is imagined in such a context.
22. It may suggest this sympathy that, in the Folio, this is the only scene in which his speech prefix is his name and not 'Bastard'.
23. Findlay, *Illegitimate*, 41, finds similar texts on the strength of bastards in Cardan (1580) and da Vinci. See also Neill, 'Illegitimate', 132. These three speeches are compared in Linda Woodbridge, *English Revenge Drama: Money, Resistance, Equality* (Cambridge: Cambridge University Press, 2010), 263–70.
24. Jonathan Dollimore, *Radical Tragedy*, 3d edition (Durham: Duke University Press, 2004), 201.
25. Joan Thirsk, 'Younger Sons in the Seventeenth Century', *History* 54: 182 (October 1969): 358–77. Attacks on primogeniture, like Edmund's speech,

also attacked 'custom'. Louis Montrose, '"The Place of a Brother" in *As You Like It*: Social Process and Comic Form', *Shakespeare Quarterly* 32 (1981): 38.
26. Neill, 'Illegitimate', 132; on gavelkind, n. 443.
27. Lars Engle, 'Sovereign Cruelty in Montaigne and *King Lear*', in *Shakespeare International Yearbook* Special Section, Shakespeare and Montaigne Revisited, guest ed. Peter Holbrook, (Ashgate, 2006), 130.
28. Woodbridge, *Vagrancy*; 219; Engle, 'Cruelty', 129.
29. The Quarto has 'recreant', which means the same thing.
30. Othello is most clearly alone; Shylock has Jessica at the beginning and Tubal in one scene. History plays might have several characters from France, for example, who are all outsiders in England.
31. Woodbridge, *Vagrancy*.
32. As David Schalkwyk writes in *Shakespeare, Love, and Service* (Cambridge: Cambridge University Press, 2008), 236, the services these characters give Lear 'gain considerably weight and humanity precisely because they have been stripped of their usual informing power relations'.
33. Carol Thomas Neely, *Distracted Subjects: Madness and Gender in Shakespeare and Early Modern Culture* (Ithaca: Cornell University Press, 2004), 63, shows how 'his alienation is rendered on a continuum with his normalcy, from which it gradually emerges', and analyses how his language while mad involves 'fragmentation, formula, depersonalization, the intersection by communal voices, and secularized ritual'.
34. Herman Melville, 'Hawthorne and His Mosses', in *The Piazza Tales and other Prose Pieces 1839–1860* (Evanston: Northwestern University Press, 1987), 244.
35. See Janet Adelman, *Suffocating Mothers*, on how the play evokes 'the betrayal inherent in individuation itself' (New York: Routledge, 1992), 214–25.
36. See William Carroll, *Fat King*, 193–4. Carroll, Woodbridge, *Vagrancy*, and Neely have detailed analyses of Edgar's disguise in its social context.
37. Woodbridge, *Vagrancy*, 223–4.
38. This phrase is used (with capital letters) by Virginia Woolf in *Three Guineas* (New York: Harcourt, Brace, 1938), 113. She was not consciously thinking of *Lear*, but of the 'daughters of educated men' (13), but she knew the play well, and the book is concerned with issues such as oppressive father–daughter relationships, intellectual freedom, and the bad effects of hierarchy and privilege, which are all found in *Lear*.
39. Woodbridge, *Vagrancy*, 214.
40. Janet Adelman discusses Edgar's spectatorial role in her Introduction to *Twentieth Century Interpretations of King Lear* (Englewood Cliffs, N.J.:

Prentice-Hall, 1978), 3–4. The introduction contains much other acute analysis of Edgar as well.
41. R. A. Foakes, Introduction, 143, in *King Lear*, ed. Foakes, Arden Shakespeare (London: Thomas Nelson, 1997), points out that F also removes similar speeches from Kent and Albany.
42. On the issue of sympathy and distance, see Sandra Lee Bartky, '*Sympathy and Solidarity' and Other Essays* (Lanham, Maryland: Rowman & Littlefield, 2002), 81.
43. Adelman, Introduction, 1–21; Stanley Cavell, 'The Avoidance of Love: A Reading of *King Lear*', in *Must We Mean What We Say?* (New York: Charles Scribner's Sons, 1969), 310–53.
44. Skura, 'Dragon Fathers'.
45. *The Boke Named the Governour*, ed. Ernest Rhys (London n.d.8), quoted by F. T. Flahiff in 'Edgar: Once and Future King', in *Some Facets of King Lear: Essays in Prismatic Criticism*, ed. Rosalie L. Colie and F. T. Flahiff (Toronto: University of Toronto Press, 1974), 230. Foakes, in his introduction to Arden edition 107–8, gives other information about this Edgar and shows that he is recalled in the Lord Mayor's pageant of 1605 and that another heroic Edgar figures in Holinshed's *Chronicles*.
46. In the Quarto edition, Albany speaks these lines. Albany is not as old as Lear, but since his own father doesn't appear in the play he is not clearly marked as young, unlike Edgar.
47. See Schalkwyk, *Shakespeare, Love and Service*, 240.
48. For a thorough, probing, and historically contextualized discussion of Kent's service to Lear and the poignancy of Lear's lack of acknowledgment, see Schalkwyk, *Shakespeare, Love and Service*, esp. 234–6.
49. Maynard Mack, *King Lear in Our Time* (Berkeley: University of California Press, 1965), 56–7; Foakes, ed., *King Lear*, 235n.
50. Leo Salingar, *Dramatic Form in Shakespeare and the Jacobeans* (Cambridge: Cambridge University Press, 1986), 95–6.
51. A. C. Bradley, *Shakespearean Tragedy: Hamlet, Othello, King Lear, Macbeth* (1904; Greenwich, Connecticut: Fawcett, 1966), 248.
52. Brook also directed a film version of this production, released in 1971. Lear's cruelty is also emphasized in the 1998 film directed by Richard Eyre.
53. *Lear's Daughters* is available in *Adaptations of Shakespeare*, ed. Daniel Fischlin and Mark Fortier (New York: Routledge, 2000).
54. Skura, 'Dragon Fathers', makes this point, also quoting the lines that follow.
55. *King Leir* in *Narrative and Dramatic Sources of Shakespeare*, VII, ed. Geoffrey Bullough, ed., 344. This is not enough for Leir, however; like his namesake, he disinherits her.

56. In the chronicle stories, however, after ruling some years Cordelia is challenged by her nephews (who resent seeing a woman ruling) and eventually kills herself; the orders that her death should be publicly presented as a suicide is the remnant of this narrative in Shakespeare's version.
57. R. A. Foakes, *Hamlet versus Lear* (Cambridge: Cambridge University Press, 1993), 2–4.
58. Adelman, *Suffocating Mothers*, 124–5.
59. See Meredith Skura, *Shakespeare the Actor and the Purposes of Playing* (Chicago: University of Chicago Press, 1993), 148. On sympathy as politically radical in Shakespeare, see William Hazlitt, 'A Letter to William Gifford, Esq.', in *Complete Works*, ed. P. P. Howe (1930; rpt. New York: AMS Press, 1967) 9:24n, and Jonathan Bate, *Shakespearean Constitutions* (Oxford: Clarendon Press, 1989), 159.
60. Woodbridge, *Vagrancy*, 224.
61. Richard Strier, *Resistant Structures: Particularity, Radicalism, and Renaissance Texts* (Berkeley: University of California Press, 1995), 165–202.

EPILOGUE

1. Virginia Vaughan and Alden Vaughan, *Shakespeare's Caliban: A Cultural History* (Cambridge: Cambridge University Press, 1991), xiv.
2. Peter Hulme, *Colonial Encounters: Europe and the Native Caribbean, 1492–1797* (London: Methuen, 1986), 89–134.
3. There are also analogies between Caliban's situation and that of the Irish ruled by England, discussed by Dympna Callaghan in *Shakespeare Without Women: Representing Gender and Race on the Renaissance Stage* (London: Routledge, 2000), 97–138.
4. Vaughan and Vaughan, *Caliban*, 14.
5. Meredith Skura, 'Discourse and the Individual: The Case of Colonialism in *The Tempest*', *Shakespeare Quarterly* 40 (1989), 42–69.
6. Skura, 'Discourse', 64, notes his childlike quality, which is unusual among the other characters to whom she compares him, who all become targets of anger of a detached authority figure—Falstaff, Shylock, Jaques, and Lucio (all of whom I discuss as outsiders, though the last two very briefly).
7. Vaughan and Vaughan, *Caliban*, 19.
8. W. H. Auden, *The Sea and the Mirror*, in *Collected Poems*, ed. Edward Mendelson (New York: Vintage, 1976, 1991), 410–22. A sample at the end of his opening poem: 'I am I, Antonio,/By choice myself alone', 412. In this section, labelled 'The Supporting Cast, Sotto Voce', he comments on

poems by each of the other characters, always ending by applying to himself the word 'alone'.
9. Stephen Orgel, Introduction, in Orgel, ed., *The Tempest* (New York: Oxford University Press, 1987), 54–5.
10. See for example those in *Cross-Cultural Performances: Differences in Women's Re-Visions of Shakespeare*, ed. Marianne Novy (Urbana: University of Illinois Press, 1993).
11. Orgel, *Tempest*, 204n.
12. Edward Pechter, *Othello and Interpretive Traditions* (Iowa City: University of Iowa Press, 1999), 153, speculates, 'Perhaps there are no really good scapegoats anywhere in Renaissance tragedy. The playwrights, not just Shakespeare, effectively detached themselves from ritual foundations, psychologizing and estheticizing their practices for spectators increasingly conscious of their own obligations to what they recognized as a fiction.'

Further Reading

Leslie Fiedler's *The Stranger in Shakespeare* (Frogmore: Paladin, 1974), has much provocative analysis on most of the topics discussed in this book, pursuing many of them through some of Shakespeare's other writings, though it is lacking in scholarly documentation and, written in 1972, is unreliable on gender and race. B. J. Sokol's *Shakespeare and Tolerance* (Cambridge, 2009) has more recently approached many of the topics of this book, though from another direction, and by contrast to Fiedler's is especially useful for its references to other more specialized scholarship. Another books relevant to this one's main concerns, Linda Woodbridge's *English Revenge Drama: Money, Resistance, Equality* (Cambridge: Cambridge University Press, 2010), analyzes the cultural use and meaning of revenge plots, which were very popular in Shakespeare's time. It has detailed analyses of the language of the outsiders Iago, Shylock, Emilia, and Edmund—for the last three discussing their speeches demanding their rights in terms of justification for revenge. It also discusses many other revenge plays. Julia Reinhard Lupton's *Citizen-Saints: Shakespeare and Political Theology* (Chicago: University of Chicago Press, 2005), is interested in how religious diversity can or cannot be included in citizenship: she discusses *Merchant of Venice*, *Othello*, and *Measure for Measure* along with non-Shakespearean works.

Two important books on Shakespeare's drama in relationship to the historical background of the theatre and acting practices in relation to the theatre's position on the margin and the actors' roles as outsiders are Steven Mullaney's *The Place of the Stage: License, Play, and Power in Renaissance England* (Chicago: University of Chicago Press, 1988), and Meredith Skura's *Shakespeare the Actor and the Purposes of Playing* (Chicago: University of Chicago Press, 1993). Joel Altman's *The Tudor Play of Mind: Rhetorical Inquiry and the Development of Elizabethan Drama* (Berkeley: University of California Press, 1978), provides good analysis of how the Tudor educational system prepared playwrights to argue on both sides of any question. Reliable historical overviews of England at the time are Keith Wrightson's *English Social History 1580–1680* (London: Hutchinson & Co., 1982) and Susan Amussen's *Gender and Class in Early Modern England* (New York: Columbia University Press, 1988). Laura Hunt Yungblut's *Strangers Settled Here Amongst Us: Policies, Perceptions, and the Presence of Aliens in Elizabethan England*

(London: Routledge, 1996), deals with immigrants from continental Europe and is a good context for *Sir Thomas More*, as is the introductory material in John Jowett's Arden edition (2011).

Two classic books from the mid-twentieth century, both influenced by anthropology, discuss Shakespeare's comedies, with many references to the role of the outsider (including the spoilsport): Northrop Frye's *A Natural Perspective: The Development of Shakespearean Comedy and Romance* (New York: Columbia University Press, 1965) and C. L. Barber's *Shakespeare's Festive Comedy* (1959; rpt. New York: Meridian, 1963). Barber is more interested in analyzing the patterns of individual plays, as well as relating them to festive rituals of England in Shakespeare's time. A third more recent book, Camille Wells Slights' *Shakespeare's Comic Commonwealths* (Toronto: University of Toronto Press, 1993), has much good discussion of the relation of outsiders to the communities of the comedies.

Several recent books that discuss the plays in relation to ritual and anthropology concentrate on tragedies, though some of them also discuss *The Merchant of Venice*. Linda Woodbridge's *The Scythe of Saturn: Shakespeare and Magical Thinking* (Urbana: University of Illinois Press, 1994) has a chapter critically analyzing the relevance of the scapegoat to Shakespeare's plays. That theme is also discussed in her co-authored introduction to *True Rites and Maimed Rites: Ritual and Anti-Ritual in Shakespeare and His Age* (Urbana: University of Illinois Press, 1992), which she co-edited with Edward Berry, and in Naomi Conn Liebler's *Shakespeare's Festive Tragedy: The Ritual Foundations of Genre* (London: Routledge, 1995). All these books relate their analysis to specific historical contexts in early modern England.

Ania Loomba has written several influential analyses which discuss Shakespeare's plays in relation to the history of racial and other categories. *Gender, Race, Renaissance Drama* (New York: Oxford, 1992; also published with the title *Race, Gender, Renaissance Drama*) considers *Othello* and *The Tempest* as well as plays by Middleton and Webster, and includes analyses of their role in the educational system of India. *Shakespeare, Race, and Colonialism* (New York: Oxford University Press, 2002) has readable and intensely historicized chapters on *Titus Andronicus*, *The Merchant of Venice*, *Othello*, *Antony and Cleopatra*, and *The Tempest*, as well as on the history of the construction of race and its relation to religion and many good suggestions for further reading. Her chapter 'Outsiders in Shakespeare's England' in *The Cambridge Companion to Shakespeare*, ed. Margreta DeGrazia and Stanley Wells (Cambridge: Cambridge University Press, 2001), also discusses the English attitude to other Europeans.

On Christianity in England in Shakespeare's time, Christopher Haigh's *English Reformations: Religion, Politics and Society Under the Tudors* (New

York: Oxford University Press, 1993) is a good presentation of fairly recent research. Diarmaid McCulloch's vast *Reformation* (London: Penguin, 2003) provides a larger canvas including continental Europe. Eamon Duffy's *Saints, Sacrifice and Sedition under the Tudors* (London: Bloomsbury, 2012) gives more of the Catholic point of view. Stephen Greenblatt's *Will in the World: How Shakespeare Became Shakespeare* (New York: Norton, 2004) provides among other things a popularized picture of the likely impact on Shakespeare and his generation of the religious changes, conflicts, and persecution in their England and that of their parents and grandparents.

Alan Bray's *Homosexuality in Renaissance England* (1982; rpt. New York: Columbia University Press, 1995) is the founding book for recent discussions of Shakespeare in relation to the history of sexuality. His article 'Homosexuality and the Signs of Male Friendship' in Jonathan Goldberg's *Queering the Renaissance* (Durham, N. C. : Duke University Press, 1994), 40–61, has also been very influential and is easily applied to *Merchant of Venice* and *Twelfth Night*. Bruce Smith's *Homosexual Desire in Shakespeare's England* (Chicago: University of Chicago Press, 1991), discusses many literary traditions and forms of the time that portray male same-sex desire: he considers *Merchant of Venice*, *Twelfth Night*, the sonnets, and other plays. Paul Hammond puts *Merchant of Venice* and the sonnets in the context of writings by authors earlier and later in *Figuring Sex between Men from Shakespeare to Shirley* (Oxford: Clarendon Press, 2002). Kenneth Borris's *Same-Sex Desire in the English Renaissance: A Sourcebook of Texts, 1470–1650* (New York: Routledge, 2004) includes material from law (and analyses which challenge Bray's view), medicine, theology, astrology, and physiognomics, as well as discussions of hermaphrodites, love and friendship, sexuality between women, and a few examples of erotica.

Sara Mendelson and Patricia Crawford co-authored *Women in Early Modern England* (Oxford: Clarendon, 1996) a thorough study with much interesting detailed research. Influential works by historians that document women's position as both insiders and outsiders include *Domestic Dangers: Women, Words, and Sex in Early Modern London* (New York: Oxford, 1996), *Common Bodies: Women, Touch, and Power in Seventeenth-Century England* (New Haven: Yale University Press, 2003), and *Gender Relations in Early Modern England* (Addison-Wesley, 2012), all by Laura Gowing, and Amy Louise Erickson, *Women and Property in Early Modern England* (London: Routledge, 1993). The first book of feminist Shakespeare criticism, Juliet Dusinberre's *Shakespeare and the Nature of Women* (1975; rpt. New York: Palgrave Macmillan, 2003), sees Shakespeare as empowering women and critiquing women's subordination. Lisa Jardine's *Still Harping on Daughters: Women and Drama in the Age of Shakespeare* (Brighton: Harvester, 1983) and

Peter Erickson's *Patriarchal Structures in Shakespeare's Drama* (Berkeley: University of California Press, 1985) stress how much that subordination continues in the plays. Carol Thomas Neely's *Broken Nuptials in Shakespeare's Plays* (New Haven: Yale University Press, 1985) and my *Love's Argument: Gender Relations in Shakespeare* (Chapel Hill: University of North Carolina Press, 1984), attempt to strike a balance, as does Phyllis Rackin, *Shakespeare and Women* (New York: Oxford, 2000), writing against a critical world in which the emphasis on past oppression dominates. *The Women's Part: Feminist Criticism of Shakespeare*, ed. Carolyn Ruth Swift Lenz, Gayle Greene, and Carol Thomas Neely (Urbana: University of Illinois Press, 1980), has a good introduction describing early developments in feminist Shakespeare criticism and includes a range of accessible essays. Still influential and drawing on a wider range of literature are Catherine Belsey, *The Subject of Tragedy: Identity and Difference in Renaissance Drama* (London: Methuen, 1985) and Linda Woodbridge, *Women and the English Renaissance: Literature and the Nature of Womankind, 1540–1620* (Urbana, Illinois: University of Illinois Press, 1985). Dympna Callaghan's anthology *A Feminist Companion to Shakespeare* (Oxford: Blackwell, 2000) shows many current approaches. Some other recent feminist analyses on more specific topics are Natasha Korda, *Shakespeare's Domestic Economies: Gender and Property in Early Modern England* (Philadelphia: University of Pennsylvania Press, 2002); Janet Adelman's accessible feminist psychoanalytic *Suffocating Mothers: Fantasies of Maternal Origin in Shakespeare's Plays, Hamlet to The Tempest* (New York: Routledge, 1992); Jean Howard and Phyllis Rackin, *Engendering a Nation: A Feminist Account of Shakespeare's Histories* (London: Routledge, 1997), Coppelia Kahn, *Roman Shakespeare: Warriors, Wounds, and Women* (London: Routledge, 1997), and Fiona McNeill, *Poor Women in Shakespeare* (Cambridge: Cambridge University Press, 2007), which explores much more of the literary and historical world than the title suggests. Stephen Orgel's *Impersonations: The Performance of Gender in Shakespeare's England* (Cambridge: Cambridge University Press, 1996) is an important book on the implications of the use of male actors to play women's roles in Shakespeare's theatre.

Books on other categories of outsiders that appear in several of the plays I discuss are Carol Thomas Neely's *Distracted Subjects: Gender and Madness in the Age of Shakespeare* (Ithaca: Cornell University Press, 2004), and David Schalkwyk's *Shakespeare, Love, and Service* (Cambridge: Cambridge University Press, 2008). Both of them are particularly useful in relation to *Twelfth Night* and *King Lear*.

James Shapiro's exhaustive *Shakespeare and the Jews* (New York: Columbia University Press, 1997) contextualizes *Merchant of Venice* in relation to the history of anti-Semitism in England, with most of the emphasis being on the contextualization and how the play resonates with it rather than on details of the play that might critique it. The Bedford edition of *Merchant of Venice*, edited by Lindsay Kaplan (2002), includes a good sampling of historical texts that suggest attitudes toward Jews as well as Jews' own viewpoints. Leah Marcus's Norton edition (2006) includes a range of recent criticism. James C. Bulman's The *Merchant of Venice* (Shakespeare in Performance: Manchester: Manchester University Press, 1991) and Charles Edelman's *The Merchant of Venice* (Shakespeare in Production: Cambridge: Cambridge University Press, 2003) are performance histories that show the range of interpretations possible.

Cristina Malcolmson's '"What You Will": Social Mobility and Gender in Twelfth Night' in *The Matter of Difference: Materialist Feminist Criticism of Shakespeare*, ed. Valerie Wayne (Ithaca: Cornell University Press, 1991), is especially good on class in *Twelfth Night*. Bruce Smith's edition *Twelfth Night: Texts and Contexts* (Boston: Bedford St. Martin's, 2001), includes useful readings relevant to many contexts of the play. The editions of Roger Warren and Stanley Wells (Oxford: Clarendon Press, 1994) and Keir Elam (Arden, 2008) both have very good introductions with much interesting performance history. Valerie Traub's *Desire and Anxiety: Circulations of Sexuality in Shakespeare's Drama* (New York: Routledge, 1992) has a ground-breaking discussion of same-sex desire (including that by female characters) in *Twelfth Night*: it is further extended and contextualized in *The Renaissance of Lesbianism in Early Modern England* (Cambridge: Cambridge University Press, 2002).

Anthony Barthelemy's *Black Face: Maligned Race: The Representation of Blacks in English Drama from Shakespeare to Southerne* (Baton Rouge, LA, 1987), contextualizes Othello with earlier and later dramatic traditions representing Africans. *Shakespeare and Race*, ed. Catherine M. S. Alexander and Stanley Wells (Cambridge, 2000), shows the historical development of the field. Emily Bartels' *Speaking of the Moor: From Alcazar to Othello* (Philadelphia: University of Pennsylvania Press, 2008) focuses specifically on the tradition of representing Moors, rather than blacks, shows the ambivalent set of relations that appear between the English and Moors in drama, diplomatic correspondence, and historiography, and emphasizes more than most earlier critics the admiration Othello receives in the play. Michael Neill's Oxford edition (2006) has a magisterial introduction of over 170 pages that deals thoroughly with the play's critical and performance history, with particular attention to changing constructions of race and of service. Neill's three important articles on *Othello*, as well as much else, are collected in his *Putting History to the Question: Power, Politics, and Society in English*

Renaissance Drama (New York: Columbia, 2000). Edward Pechter's *Othello and Interpretive Traditions* (Iowa City: University of Iowa Press, 1999), also surveys the history of critical response in relation to a close reader-response analysis of the play. His Norton edition (2004) presents a range of criticism, from seventeenth century through romantic, Victorian, and modernist examples, up to recent articles mainly dealing with gender and race issues. Kim Hall's *Othello: The Moor of Venice: Texts and Contexts* (Boston: Bedford St. Martin's, 2007) has a useful collection of contextual material, not just on race but also on marriage, the military world, and ideas of passion. Ian Smith's *Race and Rhetoric in the Renaissance: Barbarian Errors* (New York: Palgrave Macmillan, 2009), which discusses how descriptions of language could function as an early modern racial code, has a chapter mostly on *Othello*. Mary Floyd-Wilson uncovers unexpected complexity in early modern ideas of Africans (and the English) in *English Ethnicity and Race in Early Modern Drama* (Cambridge: Cambridge University Press, 2003). Historical contexts of different kinds appear in Nabil Matar's *Turks, Moors, Englishmen in the Age of Discovery* (New York: Columbia University Press, 2000) and in George M. Fredrickson's *Racism: A Short History* (Princeton: Princeton University Press, 2002). Virginia Vaughan's *Othello: A Contextual History* (Cambridge: Cambridge University Press, 1994) offers both a range of perspectives contemporary with *Othello* and also a study of how performances have changed over the centuries.

Keith Thomas's *Age and Authority in Early Modern England* (London: British Academy 1976), originally published in *Proceedings of the British Academy* 62 (1976): 205–48, began much of the social historical work on old age. Nina Taunton's *Fictions of Old Age in Early Modern Literature and Culture* (New York: Routledge, 2007) extends concern to representations, and Philip Collington's 'Sans Wife: Sexual Anxiety and the Old Man in Shakespeare' in *Growing Old in Early Modern Europe*, ed. Erin Campbell (Aldershot: Ashgate, 2006, 185–209), is particularly relevant to *Lear*. Two key articles on bastardy are included in Michael Neill's book *Putting History to the Question* and Alison Findlay has written a book on early modern English representations of bastardy on the stage, *Illegitimate Power: Bastards in Renaissance Drama* (1984: rpt. Manchester: Manchester University Press, 2009). *Lear*'s treatment of poverty and homelessness is compared to that of other writers of the time and earlier by William Carroll in *Fat King, Lean Beggar: Representations of Poverty in the Age of Shakespeare* (Ithaca: Cornell University Press, 1996) and by Linda Woodbridge in *Vagrancy, Homelessness, and English Renaissance Literature* (Urbana: University of Illinois Press, 2001). R. G. Foakes' Arden edition of *Lear* (1997) discusses the play's textual, critical, and performance history and sets changing attitudes to the play clearly in a context of large-scale historical change (e.g. mid-twentieth century skepticism resulting in part from the vast casualties of World War II) and he also develops this idea in *Hamlet versus Lear* (Cambridge: Cambridge University Press, 2004). Janet Adelman's *Twentieth Century Interpretations of King Lear* (Englewood Cliffs, N.J.: Prentice-Hall, 1978) includes two original analyses that begin with Edgar's failure to identify himself to his blind father, one in her introduction and one a reprint of Stanley Cavell's essay 'The Avoidance of Love' from his *Must We Mean What We Say?* (1969). *The Division of the Kingdoms: Shakespeare's Two Versions of King Lear*, ed. Gary Taylor and Michael Warren (Oxford: Clarendon Press, 1983), offers a variety of views on the implications of the differences between the Quarto and the Folio versions.

Peter Hulme, *Colonial Encounters: Europe and the Native Caribbean 1492–1797* (London: Methuen, 1986), includes a fascinating treatment of the relation of *The Tempest* to texts about early American settlers and their contact with Native Americans. Meredith Ann Skura, 'Discourse and the Individual: The Case of Colonialism in *The Tempest*', *Shakespeare Quarterly* 40 (1989): 42–69, provides historical arguments against some analyses of postcolonial critics and relates Caliban and Prospero to earlier Shakespearean characters. Stephen Orgel's Oxford (1998) edition includes an introduction which gives a thorough picture of the intellectual context and performance history. Virginia and Alden Vaughan trace the prehistory and later permutations of Caliban in their book *Shakespeare's Caliban: A Cultural History* (Cambridge: Cambridge University Press, 1991), and in their recent revised Arden edition (2011), which adds a useful survey of very recent performance history to the extensive introduction.

For discussions of later appropriations of Shakespeare's outsiders, see Thomas Cartelli, *Repositioning Shakespeare: National Formations, Postcolonial Appropriations* (New York: Routledge, 1999), Peter Erickson's *Rewriting Shakespeare, Rewriting Ourselves* (California, 1991) and *Citing Shakespeare: The Reinterpretation of Race in Contemporary Literature and Art* (New York: Palgrave Macmillan, 2007), my collections *Women's Re-Visions of Shakespeare* (1990) and *Cross-Cultural Performances* (1993), both from University of Illinois Press, and *Transforming Shakespeare* (New York: St. Martin's, 1999) and my *Engaging with Shakespeare: On Responses of George Eliot and Other Women Novelists* (1994; rpt. University of Iowa Press, 1996) and Jonathan Goldberg, *Tempest in the Caribbean* (Minneapolis, 2004). On adaptations and appropriations in film, see Shakespeare: *The Movie II: Popularizing the Plays on Film, TV, Video, and DVD*, ed. Richard Burt and Lynda Boose (New York: Routledge, 2003) and *New Wave Shakespeare on Screen*, by Thomas Cartelli and Katherine Roe (Malden, M.A.: Polity Press, 2007).

Index

actors 5; *see also* boys, boy actors; names of individual actors
Adelman, Janet 138, 143
Africa, Africans 1, 14, 91–3, 98, 148
Africanus, Leo 93, 96
age, aged 3, 4, 14, 15, 32, 88–9, 121, 130–6, 138–9; in early modern England 123–4
Agrippa, Cornelius 8, 74
allegory 25, 30, 96, 99, 139
Allen, William 20
All's Well that Ends Well 13
Altman, Joel 8, 98
Anger, Jane 74
antipuritan 12, 51
anti-Semitism 21–5, 29–31, 96; vs. anti-Judaism, 40
Antony and Cleopatra 15, 77, 82, 83, 135, 152, 153
aristocracy, aristocrats 10, 125, 127
As You Like It 7, 11, 12, 27, 57, 68, 80, 85, 94, 138, 140, 152, 154; disguise 73, 76–7, 82, 84
Auden, W. H. 151
Augustine 19

Balthasar (legendary black king) 93
Bandello, Matteo 111
Barber, C. L. 10, 40
bastard, bastardy 11, 15, 116, 121, 123, 124–30, 131
Bate, John 50
Battle of Alcazar 92
bear-baiting 5; compared to treatment of outsider 54
beauty, ideals of 94, 147
de Beauvoir, Simone 69
Bedlam (St. Mary's of Bethlehem) 136
Begg, Ian Maynard 179 n. 35
Bible 35–6, 50
Bilson, Bishop Thomas 21
Bishop, Thomas 27

blackness 87–8, 92–8, 103; *see also* colour (skin)
Blank, Paula 19
blindness 134, 137
Boccaccio, Giovanni 20, 21
Bodin, Jean 92
border-crossing 77, 153–5
Borris, Kenneth 40
Borromeo, St. Charles 18
boys, boy actors 77, 111
Bradley, A. C. 141
Branagh, Kenneth, director: *Twelfth Night* play 66, *Much Ado* film 79
Bray, Alan 40
Brook, Peter, director, *Lear* 141
Bullough, Geoffrey 24
Burckhardt, Sigurd 29
Burton, Jonathan 91
Burton, Robert, *Anatomy of Melancholy* 33

Callaghan, Dympna 160 n. 6
Calvin, John 20
Campion, Edmund 20
Carroll, William 124, 136
Cartelli, Thomas 8, 14
Castellio, Sebastian 20
Castiglione, Baldassare, *The Courtier* 74
Catholics 11, 18, 20, 26–7, 28, 30, 31
Cavendish, Margaret 2
Cecil, Thomas 20
Césaire, Aimé, *Tempest* 16, 150
Charles I, king 49, 66
Cheek by Jowl 60
children 4
Chojnacki, Stanley 40
Christians, Christianity 20, 22, 91
Cicero 19
Cid, El 113
Cinthio, Giraldi, *Gli Hecatommithi* 95–6, 140
class 10, 15, 88, 108–9, 126, 131, 132–5, 136–7, 144; of actors 5; clothing

restrictions 70; gentleman steward vs. aristocrat 48–9, 52, 53; merchant vs. aristocrat 32; mobility in hierarchy 2; nuances in dialogue 113; preoccupies Iago 113–14, 116; upperclass women more restricted about marriage choice 42, 74, 78; *see also* poverty, homelessness
Coffey, John 21
Coghill, Nevill 20
Cohen, Walter 28
Coleridge, Samuel Taylor 2
Collins, Patricia Hill 173 n. 5
colonialism 147
colour (skin): earlier plays 92–4; sonnets 94; Othello's 87–8, 91; revalued by Cleopatra 82
Comedy of Errors 10, 130
comedy, comic ending 12, 68, 80, 85; ambiguous 37, 60, 85; marriage 44, 48, 60, 63, 84
community: of bastards, rhetorical 127; of festivity 60, 62 67; of masterless men, disloyal servants 114; of men 98, 99; of order in household 60; relation to outsiders 9, 10; of outsiders, suffering 132–7; of women 71–2
Contarini, Gasparo, *Commonwealth and Government of Venice* 95
conversion: pressured 11, 4, 18; within Christianity 4, 11, 18, 26–9, 31; to Christianity 4, 11, 18, 24–5, 30, 40–1, 91; to goodness 129–30, 139; to Islam 25–6; language about 25–9; possibly regretted 41; sincerity of, from Islam or Judaism suspect 25, 30, 91, 160 n. 7
Coriolanus 15, 81, 84, 153
Covell, William 21
Cranmer, Thomas, Archbishop 10, 26–8, 31
Croxton Play of the Sacrament 24–5
cuckoldry 75–6, 99, 110
Cymbeline 8, 15, 75, 76, 129

Daborne, Robert, *A Christian Turn'd Turk* 25–6, 31, 40
Davidson, Nicholas 40
Davies, John 127

Davis, Natalie Zemon 178 n. 21
Declaration of Independence 19
devils: portrayed as black onstage 92; characters called or associated with 8, 23, 72, 87, 97, 99, 101, 107, 153
difference, marked 4, 33, 69, 90, 104, 153; otherness, theatre dependent on 5
disability, deformity 5, 116, 147–8, 157 n. 14; *see also* blindness
disguise, women as male 4, 7, 14, 25, 43–5, 62–3, 73, 76–7; man as female 81; male, cross-class 132, 136–8
Dollimore, Jonathan 127
Donne, John 19–20, 127
double standard 14, 70, 74–5, 110–11

Edgar, King of England 138
Egypt, Egyptians 15, 98
Elizabeth I, queen 18, 23, 28, 31, 61, 70
Elyot, Thomas, *The Governour* 138
Engle, Lars 128–9, 131
Erasmus 8, 20 n. 53, 134
ethnicity 3, 113; women in history plays 81; *see* Jews, Judaism
evil 96, 101, 153
exorcism 8, 10–11, 51
experimental psychology 15, 102, 103, 182 n. 75
Eyre, Richard, director, *Lear* film 83

family 15, 121, 140, 142, 145; *see also* household
Feinstein, Elaine, and Women's Theater Group, *Lear's Daughters* 141
Ficino, Marsilio 20, 59
Fiedler, Leslie, *Stranger in Shakespeare* 2, 32, 69–70
Findlay, Alison 125
Fiorentino, Giovanni, *Il Pecorone* 21–4, 28–9, 33, 36, 38
Fishburne, Lawrence, as Othello 103
Floyd-Wilson, Mary 92
Foakes, R. A. 139, 143
Folio/Quarto contrasts 96–7, 111, 135
Fonte, Moderata 74
Fool: free or excluded 66; shows everyone their folly 53, 66, 140; term for both old and young 134
Foxe, John 20, 21, 27, 28

Index 199

French, France 4, 81, in history plays 157 n. 10
Froide, Amy M. 175 n. 22
Frye, Northrop 68
Fryer, Peter 176 n. 2

gangsta rap 104
Gavelkind 127
Gay, Penny 107
generational conflicts 121, 123–4; opposition broken down 134, 138, 145
geography/humor theory of temperament 92, 96
Gildon, Charles 103
Girard, René 14, 17, 32, 46, 117
Globe Theatre 4
Greenblatt, Stephen 2
Greene, Robert, *Orlando* 89
Guépin, Jean-Pierre 9
Guess Who's Coming to Dinner 103

Haec Vir 75
Haigh, Christopher 51
Hall, Kim 103
Hamlet 14, 20, 83, 84, 130, 135, 154
Hammond, Paul 14, 33
Hazlitt, William 2
Heilbrun, Carolyn 175 n. 24
Helwys, Thomas 20
Henry IV 13, 81, 107, 128, 152
Henry V 4, 13, 81, 153
Henry VI, Part 3 5–6, 150; *Part 2* 70, 81
Henry VIII 28
heretics, heresy 20, 26, 28, 29, 31, 36, 45
Hic Mulier 114–15
history plays, women in 70, 76, 81; other outsiders in 5–7, 13
Hoensalaars, Ton 8
Holloway, John 14
homelessness 3, 15, 121–2, 132–3, 136–7
homoeroticism 56–60, 63
Hooker, Richard, Archbishop 19
household 4, 60–2, 71–2, 140
Howard, Jean 61
Hulme, Peter 187 n. 2
human equality, belief in 19
Hunter, G. K. 177 n. 19
Hutton, Matthew 20

identification, empathy 4, 9, 14, 68, 90, 99, 118
illegitimacy, *see* bastardy
Illyria 56
immigrant, alien 2, 6 , 18, 25, 55–6, 62, 81, 89–90, 100, 104, 113, 152
Indians, Native Americans 147–8
insider, apparent 140; confidence 88, 106–07; economic power 61, 70; geographic mobility 71–2; knowledge 113, 117, 148, 152; to play's value system 142; position aided by language 10, 151; in space of mutual love 15, 82–4, 135, 143; winning power struggle 44; women contrasting to ethnic outsiders 42, 69
intersectionality 70
Irish 13
Islam 1, 91

James I, king 20, 28, 34
jealousy 90, 93, 96, 98, 99, 109–110, 116
Jerome 36
Jesus Christ 20, 89
Jews, Judaism, attitudes toward in early modern culture 8, 19–24; in early modern England 19; in *Merchant of Venice* 7, 17–26, 28–31, 37–8, 40–1, 45–6, 86; in other texts 17–8, 20–21, 24–5; postHolocaust 67
Jim Crow 104
Johnson, Samuel 143
Jones, Ann Rosalind 180 n. 51
Jones, Emrys 89
Jones, Ernest 181 n. 69
Jordan, Constance 115
Julius Caesar 4, 14, 81, 135

Kaplan, Lindsay 18
Keats, John 2
Kemble, J. P. 59
Kinoshita, Sharon 95
King John 125, 126
King Lear 7, 15, 16, 31, 83, 101, 114, 121–45, 150, 154, 155
King Leir 122, 133, 136, 140, 141–2, 143
Kingsley, Ben, as Feste 66
Knapp, Jeffrey 27–8, 30, 55

Language: anti-Semitic 11, 22–3; exotic 98, 100; giving outsider appeal 10, 89; humanizing 11; racist associations 119
Lanyer, Aemilia 74–5
Laslett, Peter 183 n. 9
Lesser, Anton, as Feste 66
Liebler, Naomi Conn 14
London 2, 4, 6
Loomba, Ania 87, 103, 114
Lopez, Rodrigo 23
Lord Mayor's pageant 92–3
Love's Labour's Lost 10, 85, 94
Lupton, Julia Reinhard 91

Macbeth 7, 14, 82, 101
MacDonald, Anne-Marie 16
Machiavel 116
Machiavelli 19
Mack, Maynard 115, 139
McLuskie, Kate 122–3
McMillan, Scott 111
McPherson, David 95
madness 3, 52–4, 60, 83, 130, 133, 136
Malcolmson, Cristina 48
Manningham, John 49, 61
Mar, Raymond 182 n. 75
Marcus, Leah 96–7, 99
Marlowe, Christopher 14, 21, 24, 162 n. 28
Marriage 13; "compulsory heterosexuality" 84; early modern Italy 39; end of comedy 44, 48, 60, 63, 84; financial arrangement 44; heroic adventure, "impossible achievement" 119; system critiqued 13; vs. male friendship, same-sex love 34–9, 43–4, 46, 59–60, 67–8, 80, 151
Mary I, queen of England 26–7
Matar, Nabil 176 n. 2
Matthew, Tobie, Bishop 51
Mauretania 90
Maurice, St. 176 n. 5
Maus, Katherine 43
Measure for Measure 13, 27, 35, 84–5, 117, 138, 153–4
Mediterranean 147
melancholy 3, 11, 12, 43, 60, 116, 125; could be idealized in Renaissance 32; lover's 33

Melville, Herman 133
Merchant of Venice 3, 7, 8, 9, 11, 12, 17–47, 72, 76, 80, 84, 86, 94, 130, 144, 148–9, 153, 154–5; compared with *Twelfth Night* 47–8, 54–5, 56, 58–60
Merry Wives of Windsor 8, 10–11, 13, 75, 81
Merton, Robert 173 n. 5
Middleton, Thomas, *The Triumph of Truth* 177 n. 19
Midsummer Night's Dream 10, 57, 154
miscegenation 118
mirroring 5, 7, 16, 59, 63–7, 70, 139, 153–5
moneylending, usury 22, 24, 30; "spiritual usury" 46
"monster", monstrous 5, 18, 147, 148, 149
Montaigne, Michel de 8, 20
Montagu, Elizabeth 2
Montrose, Louis 185 n. 25
Moors 9, 88, 90–8, 104, 112–13, 115
moral outsider 3, 82–3, 88, 140–1, 153
Morality plays 92
Moran, Andrew 176 n. 5
More, Thomas 20
Much Ado about Nothing 7, 8, 13, 72, 75, 76, 80, 84, 116, 125, 129
Muslims 90–1, 102; *see also* Moors
Mystery cycle 89

Nashe, Thomas, *Unfortunate Traveller* 52
national identity 15
Neely, Carol Thomas 107, 169 n. 16
Neill, Michael 90–1, 96, 102, 111, 114
neoplatonism 33, 57, 59
New World 147, 148
Newman, Karen 44
Ng, Su Fang 56
Nicholas of Cusa 20
Nicodemism 30
Nunn, Trevor, director, TN film 53, 59–60, 66

O (film) 97, 99
Orgel, Stephen 5, 151
Othello 1, 8, 9, 15, 16, 23, 27, 72, 73, 83, 85, 87–120, 128, 130, 135, 144, 148–9, 154, 155
outsiders: admired 5, 6, 7, 14, 15, 17, 34, 43, 88–9; ambiguous 1, 11, 12, 13, 14,

16, 17, 32–4, 37, 40, 46, 48, 56, 59–60, 87–93, 95, 105, 137, 150, 152, 155; aristocrats by birth 144; barred from universities because of gender and religion 70; and class 32, 48, 69–70; common humanity 6, 7, 14, 17, 18, 19, 24, 53, 72, 74, 110, 134; compared to animals 7, 11, 23, 35–6, 54, 72, 89, 101, 102, 132, 141; compared to objects 7; comparisons among different kinds 3, 7–8, 11, 14, 16, 18, 45, 111–12, 114–16, 126, 148–51, 153–5; competition between 3, 4, 34–9, 43–5, 85, 126, 131; compromise vs. persistence 45–6; cultural 1, 43; defensiveness 8; dependent on money 46; and disability 3, 5; disinherited 125, 140, 142; ethnic 30, 113; exclusion 1, 4, 6, 7, 33, 125; freedom 59, 66, 152; friendly 149; fresh insight 70, 77, 151; group of similar outsiders 4, 6, 10; intense consciousness 14, 83; isolation 5, 37, 59, 66, 67, 83, 149; language 89, 98, 144, 149; laughed at in comedy 68; learn 150, 152; moral 3, 4, 5–6, 14, 16, 17, 82–3, 88, 98–9, 100–1, 140–41; moral centre of play 142; and music 149; naïve 105, 107, 151; overreaching 8, 9, 47, 52, 107–8, 149; power resented 47; punishment excessive 53; relative position 1, 3, 13, 16, 70, 79–80, 152; rejection of 13, 15; religious 3, 11, 17, 18; resourcefulness 8; revenge plans 149; rights limited 7; see social patterns 154; sense of loss 150; shifting position 1, 3, 4, 5, 6, 11, 15, 17, 18, 24, 28–9, 46, 47, 52, 64–5, 80, 88, 152, 155; silence 37, 151; situational 4, 10, 55–6; social 3, 17, 47, 56; solidarity among 9, 13, 85–6, 108, 112, 119–20, 134–6; speech headings for 29, 125, 179 n. 38, 184 nn. 19, 22; temperamental 142; threatening 13, 16, 24, 104; tragedy vs. comedy 9, 14; useful 148; verbal abuse of, rudeness to 1, 3, 4, 11, 22, 29, 72; welcomed, included 4, 10, 13, 16, 59–60; *see also* Africa, Africans; age; bastards; Catholics; class; homelessness; Indians; Jews; madness; melancholy; Moors; Muslims; pirate; poverty; prejudice; Protestants; puritan; scapegoat; sodomy; spoilsport; stereotype; sympathy; women

Painter, William, *Two Gentlewomen of Venice* 111
Parker, Oliver, director *Othello* film 103
Parker, Patricia 118
Parsons, Robert 20
Paul III, pope 22
Paul, Annie Murphy 182 n. 75
Payne, B. K. 179 n. 40
Pechter, Edward 115, 117
Pequigney, Joseph 58
pirate, piracy 3, 12, 25–6, 65; ambiguous identity 56, 58; and male bonding, sodomy 56
Plato, *Symposium* 59
polarized images: of aged 123; of bastards 124–5; of Moors, women 14, 104
polytheism 91
pornography 87, 118
Pory, John 93, 96
poverty 121–4, 131–3, 136–7, 144–5
prejudice 2, 9, 15; against Africans 91–2; against aged 123, 130; against bastards 124–5, 128; against blackness 88, 94, 96–7, 102–4; early modern critique 8; language and 11, 22–3; against Moors 88–94, 100, 102; parallels in attitudes toward Moors and women 114–16; against poor 132–3, 136, 144; against women 72, 74–5, 141; *see also* anti-Semitism; antipuritan; self-fulfilling prophecy; stereotype
primogeniture 127
projection 7, 116, 148
prostitution 5, 104, 108–9
Protestants 10, 18, 19, 20, 26–8, 31, 50, 55
psychoanalytic criticism 2; *see also* projection
puritan 1, 3, 12, 30, 49–52, 54–55, 66; puritan moneylenders 160 n. 6

race, concept 2; in process of consolidation 92, 98; becomes more important in late 17th century 102–3

racism, unconscious 103; see prejudice; stereotype; blackness
Radford, Michael 37
religion: conflict between puritans and state church in England 49–52; freedom, advocated in early modern world 8, 19–21; persecution in early modern England 18–22, 26–8, 31, 38; in Rome 22; toleration in early modern everyday life 19; *see also* antipuritans; Catholics; Christianity; conversion; Islam; Jews, Judaism; Muslims; polytheism; Protestants; puritans
revenge 63–4, 66, 98–9, 112, 115–16, 117
rhetoric of outsiders: code-switching 89; identity switching 7, 15, 72–3, 77; mirroring 7, 66, 153–5; modesty 43, 89; *see also* language
Richard II 27
Richard III 149–50
Robeson, Paul 16
Rocke, Michael 40
romances (late tragicomedies) 15–16, 149, 150
Rome; Roman plays 15
Romeo and Juliet 14, 57, 83, 124
Ruggerio, Guido 40
Rutter, Carol Chillington 180 n. 50
Ryan, Kiernan 46
Rymer, Thomas 103

Salih, Tayeb, *Season of Migration to the North* 89
same-sex love 3, 11, 32–9, 56–60, 63, 67–8, 70
Santiago Matamoros 112, 115, 116
Schalkwyk, David 168 n. 5
scapegoat 9, 13, 14, 15, 16, 17–18, 32, 35–6, 46, 60, 64, 65, 66–7, 117, 153
Sears, Djanet, *Harlem Duet* 107
self-fulfilling prophecy 8, 22–3, 97–8
servant, service 57, 64, 65, 136, 139–40; maidservants 71; *see also* steward
Setebos 147
sexual identity 67; ambiguity about early modern development of concept 12, 32, 38, 165 n. 55; compared to religion 37; *see also* homoeroticism, sodomy

sexuality, construction of 2, 12, 39
Shakespeare, John: links with Catholics 18, 27; money-lender 30
Shakespeare, William, as actor 5; as collaborator 6–7; money-lender 30–1; personal mythology 69, 129; religion difficult to categorize 30, 160 n. 6; and religious persecution 18, 30; writing associated with sympathy 2; *see also* individual plays
Shapiro, James 24
Shrew (newspaper) 16
"shrews" 77–8
Sinfield, Alan 34, 38, 59
single man 32, 47–8, 84
single women 79, 84, 85
Sir Thomas More 6–7, 154–5
Skura, Meredith 5, 53–4, 138
slave, slavery 91–2; slave trade makes race more salient 103, 104
Slights, Camille 52, 79
Smiley, Jane 16, 141
Smith, Bruce 34, 165 n. 55
Smith, Ian 89
sodomites, sodomy 12, 32; few prosecutions in England 39–40; English associate with Italians 33, 39; with pirates 56; punished in early modern Italy 39
Sokol, B. J. 100
Sollors, Werner 115
sonnets, Shakespeare's 34, 35, 38, 57, 94
Souernam, Esther 75
Southampton, Earl of 147
Spaniards 42; Inquisition 20, 113; opposition to Moors, alliance with Venice 113
spoilsport 1, 12, 48, 54
stereotype 6, 15; of bastards 18; of ethnic/religious outsiders 8, 42; relation of Othello to 96–9; structure of 114–16; of underclass 136; used for power though known to be false 116–17; of women 7–8, 105, 128; *see also* self-fulfilling prophecy
steward 1, 3, 48–9, 55
Strier, Richard 8, 144
Sullivan, Daniel, director, MV 37, 86
Swetnam, George 75

sympathy: for Goneril and Regan, only in recent reinterpretations 141–2; for outsiders 8, 9, 11, 24, 28, 31, 44, 53–4, 64–5, 68, 77–8, 85–6, 87, 88, 101, 126, 127, 128, 137–9, 143–5; from outsider characters 119–20, 132–40, 143–5; urged by female characters 64, 119; by male characters 6–7, 78, 143–4, 155; shifting 9, 31, 64, 65

Taming of the Shrew 124, 130; outsider becomes insider at end 3–4, 10, 77–8; receives verbal abuse 72; sympathy for 77–8
Tate, Nahum 143
Taunton, Nina 123–4
Tempest 16, 117, 129, 147–53, 155
Tertullian 21
Thirsk, Joan 184 n. 25
Thomas, Keith 170 n. 22, 183 n. 7
Thomas, William 178 n. 23
Tilney, Edmund, *Flower of Friendship* 74
Titus Andronicus 93–4, 116, 130, 154
tragedy, tragic hero 9, 14, 81–4, 98, 101–2, 119, 135
Traub, Valerie 58, 60, 173 n. 55
Troilus and Cressida 73, 84–5
Turkey, Turks 25–6, 91, 95
Twelfth Night 3, 4, 9, 12, 47–68, 71, 72, 81, 144, 148–9, 151, 155
Two Gentlemen of Verona 82

Vaughan, Virginia and Alden 150
Venice 1, 9; dependent on international trade 95; foreigners as generals 95; relative religious freedom 95
villain 5, 92, 100, 136, 141
Vitkus, Daniel 102
Vives, Juan Luis 71
Vogel, Paula, *Desdemona* 16, 107

Wales, Welsh 107
Walsham, Alexandra 19

Warren, Roger and Stanley Wells 59
Watson, Robert 89
Webster, John, *Duchess of Malfi* 34
Wesker, Arnold, *The Merchant* 16
whiteness, white privilege 107
widows 61
Wilson, Robert, *Three Ladies of London* 8
Winter's Tale 8, 129
women, ambiguous status 13, 40, 31, 42, 62, 59, 151; with class privilege 42, 70, 72; contrast between outcome in comedies and other genres 4, 76, 81, 84, 105; dominating household and other spaces 61, 71; emphasizing weakness 4, 70, 72; excluded from universities and learned professions 70, 72; literary attacks and defences of 8, 74–5; mistrust of refuted more than for other outsiders 8, 75–6; more easily accepted as Christian converts 40; officially losing power in marriage 42, 70; women speaking of women as a group 4; protesting 4, 13–14, 70, 72–5, 77–80, 108–12; singing a sign of outsider status 107; slanders of believed 13, 72, 75, 105; verbally abused 72, 104
Woodbridge, Linda 14, 22, 131, 132, 133, 136, 137, 144
Woodes, Nathaniel, *Conflict of Conscience* 31
Woolf, Virginia 185 n. 38
World Trade Center 104
Wright, Abraham 102

xenophobia 6, 42

younger brothers 127

Zagorin, Perez 22

The manufacturer's authorised representative in the EU for product
safety is Oxford University Press España S.A. of El Parque Empresarial
San Fernando de Henares, Avenida de Castilla, 2 - 28830 Madrid
(www.oup.es/en or product.safety@oup.com). OUP España S.A. also acts
as importer into Spain of products made by the manufacturer.
Printed and bound by CPI Group (UK) Ltd, Croydon, CR0 4YY

20/03/2026

02075172-0004